HAVE THEM BUILD
A TOWER TOGETHER

Jacques Hébert

Introduction by the
Right Honourable Roland Michener

HAVE THEM BUILD A TOWER TOGETHER

Translated by Sheila Fischman

ABOUT KATIMAVIK, A MEETING PLACE, ABOUT YOUTH, ABOUT HOPE.

McClelland and Stewart

Royalties from sales of this book
will be turned over to Katimavik

Copyright © 1979 by Jacques Hébert

ISBN: 0-7710-4057-1

McClelland and Stewart Limited
The Canadian Publishers
25 Hollinger Road
Toronto, Ontario
M4B 3G2

Printed and bound in Canada

CONTENTS

By the same author

To Bruno,
my son,
a bit of
a dreamer
too

Do you want men to learn to
love one another? Have them
build a tower together. Do you
want men to hate one another?
Throw them some grain.

Antoine de Saint-Exupéry

Introduction

I welcome the privilege of introducing this account of Katimavik, a very appealing and useful program for young Canadians, although I confess to being surprised to find myself doing so at this stage. When I left Government House in 1974 I thought that I had fully played my role as patron of almost every kind of national and voluntary good work; but not at all. A patron-general cannot shed his interests and his habits as quickly as he doffs his uniform. In any event, in early 1978, when I was approached personally by the Hon. Barnett J. Danson, then the Minister accountable for public support, and officially by Monsieur Jacques Hébert, co-Chairman of the governing body, with the beguiling suggestion that I should be honorary president of a new national program designed to interest young Canadians in doing something exciting and useful for their country, as well as for themselves, the sort of thing which I myself had been advocating, I could scarcely resist.

It appears that Mr. Danson had been searching for some years for a program for young Canadians that would blend volunteer service, discovery of country, friendship and team spirit, and offer a simple, natural, physically stimulating lifestyle. Around the same time, Monsieur Jacques Hébert, O.C., world traveller, prominent journalist, author and Montreal publisher, was actively sponsoring a project for a national youth program that was in many ways similar. His concern for civil liberties, social justice, and the right to development of Third World nations had made him well-known throughout the world.

He was also founder and President of Canada World Youth, which he has described in "The World is Round." Of this movement Michael Oliver said in his preface, "Canada World Youth would not be 'aid', would not be 'academic education', and certainly would not be

9

tourism... Through living and working together, and exchanging values and viewpoints, young people would become aware of the contrasting realities of the Third World and the developed world. To be really worthwhile the program would have to recruit young men and young women, both English-and French-speaking, from every province and region, from every income group, from farms and fishing-villages, city centres and suburbia, schools and factories."

At the end of 1976, Barnett Danson and Jacques Hébert met and discussed their respective projects and eventually decided to co-operate on a preliminary definition of what, a few months later, would be known as "Katimavik," the Inuit word for a meeting-place.

So it was that the Canadian Government and Parliament provided funds to put the program into operation, through a new private, non-profit corporation, with a national board of directors whose members would be representative of all the provinces, of various occupations, and different age groups.

It was an imaginative concept, well-designed to engage the interest and time of young Canadians, suspended uncertainly, for one reason or another, between high school and entry into a college or career. For some of them the reason was, and still is, unemployment, which at the present state of the economy falls most severely on those under 25 years of age. They comprise 52% of the 793,000 employable Canadians now without work. Many others are uncertain about how to live a useful life in a world whose many problems, such as over-population, exhaustion of resources and natural environment in the face of industrial technology and fearsome scientific changes, threaten the future of mankind itself.

After two years of experimental development, and the combined efforts of the Executive Committee, the Board of Directors, many other volunteers in the project area, and a substantial staff, located at the headquarters in Montreal and five regional offices, their program has been refined and stabilized in its third year to a point at which the story should be told in book form. It is fortunate that Mr. Hébert, who, more than any other, is the spiritual father of Katimavik, as well as the principal director and leader in its formative years, has undertaken the book. He writes it under the metaphorical title of "Have them Build a Tower Together"; and to be sure that it brings out the growing pains, as well as the successful achievement of the project as a whole, he has found the time to win the confidence and co-operation of 24 participants in one of the 30 groups which made up the first year of the program. Their tale begins with a brief account of their initial training, followed by three periods of service, each of three months, at (Larouche), Quebec, (Wilcox), Saskatchewan, (Grand River), Ontario.

It is an unusual story, told in an informal and conversational style, and with considerable feeling.

One has to remember that the book tells of a beginning. With a third year under way, the picture broadens substantially, as I can testify, having been able, since becoming the honorary president, to share the experiences of many of the young people, co-ordinators, group leaders, and active participants at work on projects in Ontario and the Yukon.

Roland Michener

1 Once upon a time there was a boy from Hong Kong

The other day I entertained seven young people from this country around my dinner table. Two years before, I didn't know them, they didn't know one another and – if it hadn't been for a sort of miracle called Katimavik – most likely none of us would ever have met.

Lap Wong from Burnaby, British Columbia, had barely arrived from Hong Kong with his family when he heard about Katimavik. A few months later, stumbling along in English and not knowing a word of French, he was with thirty or so other young people, from every part of Canada, in Larouche – a small village near Lac St. Jean in Quebec. That was where I met him, just after he'd arrived with his group. He'd already conquered the mayor – and his wife – in this village 9172 miles from Hong Kong!

But I'll tell you about that later. There's so much to tell about Lap and all the others, about the amazing adventure they all experienced together for ten months. I always want to tell everything all at once, with memories jostling, details piling up, everything spilling out at once – starting at the end, coming back ten times to the beginning, driving the reader crazy! I know, it's no way to behave ...

Anyway, that evening we'd all had a bite together: the Brie was exactly as it should be, the *foie gras* as velvety as a September evening, and the pâté de campagne – ah! Lap was there, and Cynthia and Lise and Mario and Yvan and Serge and Peter. I'll tell you about each of them in turn and

13

they'll tell you about themselves too, a little later. (Don't go looking right away!)

It's a wonderful thing, having a beautiful story to tell: you've won before you start. I don't deserve any credit for it, but I know this little book will make you happy, that you'll finish it with a feeling of joy: at last, you'll tell yourself, there's something in this world that isn't foolish or nasty, ugly or sad. There's hope. You'll be able to take a rest from pollution and Iran and national unity and McDonald's hamburgers! I know, it takes a lot of nerve to make such promises, on the very first page, to readers who don't even know Lap Wong yet and perhaps don't even know that Katimavik is an Inuit word meaning "meeting place," who feel a little uncomfortable as I get all excited over a meal of pâté and cheese (there was a very pleasant little red wine too) with seven young Canadians — including Lap Wong from Burnaby, formerly from Hong Kong.

I'll try to calm down a little, pretend to begin at the beginning — which for me requires an almost superhuman effort. The present moment, the cheese and all the rest, are so fascinating that what happened the night before seems prehistoric to me: yesterday there were dinosaurs — or, for the archeologists, CroMagnon man, if that's what entertains them!

Still, I'm going to make an honest effort. I won't say a word about the nicely sharp Roquefort we had that evening — but I will tell about why it was such a joy for all of us to be there sharing it.

Once upon a time there was a simple little idea, a tiny spark that set off a lovely blaze because the wood was dry and the wind a willing accomplice. An idea that appealed to the most generous and genuine qualities of today's young people — those same young people who are often targets of an older generation's mud-slinging. Those young people were told: "Katimavik will be a meeting place." Now, today's young people enjoy being with their counterparts elsewhere, they enjoy exchanging, communicating. Perfect timing! "Katimavik invites you to discover at least three different parts of this great country, to live and integrate yourselves in three small or medium-sized communities, to share family life with cowboys in the West, farmers in Quebec or Atlantic fishermen." Young people enjoy travel and discoveries too. "Katimavik will help you learn French or English." Because they want to communicate, exchange. "Katimavik offers the possibility of living in a group." Young people love the dynamics of a group of their peers, sharing, discussions, friendship, brotherhood... of which the communes of the '60s were an ephemeral and awkward illustration. "Katimavik offers a hard life, work that will often be difficult but that will be useful to some of the less favoured communities in our country." Young people don't shrink from challenges, they're generous. "Katimavik will sensitize you to environmental problems, ecology, to the "new" alternate technology that will one day replace the other kinds of hard technology that are so wasteful of energy." Now if there's one subject that causes young people anguish it's that one, a subject that ultimately leads to the single real problem of today: the tremendous misery of two-thirds of mankind and the tremendous responsibilities of the other third, of which we are part.

In a word, then, the wood was dry and the spark fell on it at just the right moment. A few months after Katimavik was founded, 1000 young participants were divided into groups of thirty (each group with three sub-group leaders and a co-ordinator), in as many worksites spread across the country from Whitehorse in the Yukon to Glovertown, Newfoundland.[1]

Spring, 1977. After several months of intense preparation, Katimavik was launched, thanks to a grant from the federal government. For a few months only, though. There were big risks. Many unknowns. Politicians, civil servants and the press had an eye on us. The slightest scandal would have been fatal for us that year. Of course there

1. A maximum of 10% of participants may choose the military option, i.e. spending one of the three-month sessions on a military base where they may learn about deep-sea diving, wilderness survival, physical education, map and compass reading, etc.

were a few hitches, we were sometimes off-target and — even worse than crimes, there were some acts of foolishness. As happens in the best families. And in a big family of 1000 young people between seventeen and twenty, such things must, of course, happen too. But in the end there were no real scandals, no dreadful catastrophes or significant acts of foolishness. If there had been, *they'd have been found out!*

The members of the board (now it can be told) were on pins and needles during that perilous first year. Each of us went to visit as many groups as possible, but you have to know what happens to those groups after only a few weeks: they become real families, with their share of family secrets and fraternal complicities. Oh, they welcomed us very warmly — but there was no danger that we'd find out very much in a few hours or even a few days! I probably had more trouble than my colleagues, as I don't have a gift for communicating with young people. They intimidate me, the rascals, without knowing it! I'm not the chief Scout type, I don't play the guitar, I get tonguetied: "Your name's Peter, eh? Where are you from? Ah, Edmonton ... yes, I've been there... Hmmm... And how are you finding the program?" You get the picture! Now, I'm very fond of our participants, but they intimidate me! It's silly, but that's the way it is. And I likely intimidate them too. Inevitably! I'm as old as their fathers, I'm co-chairman of the organization and all that. In a word, then, my visits to the groups of participants couldn't have been more frustrating. At the end of a day, when I'd finally stopped confusing Peter and Robert, when I'd tamed Lise and conquered Cynthia, it was time to go. Then with the next group, I had to start all over again. (Don't worry, I'm coming to the end of this psychoanalysis. I'm just about to get back to Lap Wong and the cheese ...)

I decided, then, to cut down on these rather disappointing experiences by making a major decision: I'd select a group at random and work unrelentingly at going to visit it as often as possible in the course of the year. As fate would have it, the group chosen was the one that included

Lap Wong, the boy from Burnaby who'd just arrived from Hong Kong. (You haven't forgotten already?) For the first three months of the program they were in Larouche, Quebec. The next three months, in the middle of winter, they would be in Wilcox, Saskatchewan, where it's always about -40°F., if I remember correctly, and finally, for the last three months, around Cambridge, Ontario.

I had my own little plan: to write a book or, even better have a book written by the group. It was risky. Year I of Katimavik might have some unpleasant surprises in store for us. All the elements of a disaster were there: a staff that was inexperienced — and with good reason, worksites chosen in haste — necessarily, without always taking into account all of Katimavik's objectives, improvised training camps, etc. I could have waited for Year II and my story would have been a better one, more reassuring for honest folks and more pleasant for the ears of the Treasury Board. But there's a certain charm to living dangerously, to betting on life, to putting your trust in mankind — capable of committing all sorts of foolishness but also gifted with infinite imagination.

So let the chips fall where they may! Let's show some courage! And some modesty as well ... (that's the hardest part!) I'm undertaking, then, to tell you everything I know about Lap Wong's group, chosen at random from thirty very similar groups. And Lap and the others in turn will tell you everything they've been kind enough to confide to me. Now, a little of the history of Year I of Katimavik. There's no need to add that Year II was a lot better from every point of view, that Year III is really going very well and that Year IV will be fantastic ... I'll do everything I can to keep from constantly repeating that *now* this or that has changed ... But I know myself well enough to be aware that I can't avoid slipping in, here and there: "*Now* the training camps are very serious ..." It would get on your nerves. I know. I'll restrain myself. As often as possible.

Now, back to the cheese. At last! The Camembert was really quite all right too. Just creamy enough, without being runny, creamy and mild and soft as a caress ...

What a good time we had that night! I was happy too. For the first time, perhaps, I felt I was part of the group. Not completely: that's impossible and I know it. I haven't lived through everything the participants lived through together, I'm still the same age as their fathers and I'm still co-chairman of Katimavik. Mario, always a little suspicious, told me, joking, "You must have something up your sleeve ... Inviting us here to your house like this, a year after the end of the program..." No, Mario, I didn't have anything up my sleeve. Only in my heart. I wanted to see the members of the group who were in Montreal, find out what was happening to them, find out from them what was happening to the others in the rest of the country, stir up a few memories of Larouche, of Wilcox, of Grand River — the few memories that I share with them. No, Mario, nothing up my sleeve. You'll find it hard to believe, but I didn't yet know that the story of our little supper of pâté and cheese on rue Prud'homme would become the first chapter of this book. The idea came to me two weeks later, when I was sitting and staring at a blank sheet of paper, wondering how to begin. That was when Lap's smile appeared, like a good starting point for telling about Katimavik; and your smile too, Mario, more mischievous when you're wondering just what people might have up their sleeves! I had nothing, I swear.

Mario is a tall fellow, bright and sensitive, with a black beard, nimble hands that are often holding a recorder which he played almost without interruption for ten months. In some families there's a canary that sings all day long. In the group, "my" group, there was Mario. The night of the cheese, he'd made a special trip in from Drummondville, Quebec, to see his friends. Drummondville, where he's been studying cabinet-making for a year, since Katimavik. But he's got an idea, several in fact, up his sleeve: cabinet-making is a technique he'll be directing toward music. He wants to make flutes and other ancient wind instruments of the kind used in baroque music groups. And he's got more than one string to his bow: next year he's going into a very different field: water purification. (Sounds like Katimavik!).

And then there was Lise from Montreal, tender and serious. Before Katimavik, she'd been thinking vaguely about business, she wanted to work in a bank, make money, buy dresses, spend, consume. "In Katimavik, I discovered simplicity." There was the influence of the group, but particularly the influence of Peter, the boy from Edmonton, also serious and tender. It must be my imagination, but when Lise talks to us about Social Sciences, which she's been studying since she left Katimavik, she looks at Peter with a smile as though she were thanking him ... (They'll want to kill me when they read that!)

And then there was Serge, born right here in Montreal, his parents of Italian origin. A live-wire, the clown of the group, joking from morning to night, making fun of everything and nothing, kidding serious people as though to hide the fact that he is the same, in his way. Words amuse him, he plays around with them so people can discover the crazy side of things. He was like that at Larouche, at Wilcox, at Luther ... At first sight you might think that Serge hadn't changed, but those who know him know he's changed a lot, more than many others. An only son, pampered by his mother, he had trouble adapting to group life. At the rare times when Serge talks seriously (but without ever taking himself seriously), he admits readily that he's changed a great deal, that he's learned a lot about himself and others and, most of all, that he's *learned to share*. Never again will he be an only son ...

And there was Yvan, from Ste. Thérèse, Quebec, the only one in the group who thought, right in the middle of the program, that Katimavik couldn't give him any more and that he himself had nothing more to give to the others. When he left Wilcox it was the first test for a group that was rightly proud of having never, until then, lost one of its members, something that was not the case in many other groups. But did he really go away? Because he was there with us that night, and the others in his group agreed, despite everything, with his decision, which he'd made after mature reflection. I ask the question, but I know the answer: Yvan is a full-fledged member of this fine family. I felt that throughout the year, even after Wilcox, from what the others said, from everybody's joy when Yvan phoned, when Yvan wrote or when Yvan came back to see the group. Oh, yes: right now he's studying Sociology at the University of Quebec.

And there was Cynthia, who'd come from Toronto especially for this dinner. A radiant girl, sensitive to the problems of the world, even more sensitive since Katimavik. She too learned a lot from Peter, to whom she barely spoke at the beginning of the program until one day she discovered by chance, during a walk in Larouche, that they had a lot in common and shared many ideas: she, the girl from Toronto-the-sophisticated and he, the discreet and modest boy from the other end of the Prairies. The night of the cheese, sitting close together, they understood one another almost without words, which is not surprising since they'd really talked together for ten months!

And there was Peter from Edmonton, who'd chosen to study law at McGill, in Montreal, rather than in his native province, because he wanted to keep in close contact with the Francophones of his country: he lives in a working-class neighbourhood in the east end of Montreal, where he continues to practise the French he started to learn in Larouche, thanks particularly to a family of farmers, the Tremblays, with whom he spent several weeks ... When I make the mistake of addressing him in English, I can tell that it irritates him. He answers in French.

Peter shares his apartment with Lap, from Burnaby, who also has come to Montreal to study, for exactly the same reasons. Lap likes French and he wants at all costs to be *trilingual*. His first teachers were farmers in Larouche as well, the Simards, and of course his Francophone fellow-participants. When the program was over, instead of going right back to be with his family, whom he'd left ten months earlier, he returned to Quebec where he enrolled in a French-immersion course at Trois Rivières. A six-week

20

course! Lap: from Hong Kong and Burnaby, British Columbia: He had to do it. And now for nearly a year he's been practising his French with his neighbours on Berri Street, in Montreal ...

Part of the evening was spent talking about all the wonderful things that were happening to the other members of the group, who were literally scattered from Vancouver to St. John's, Newfoundland, since they'd separated after ten months of living together. Claire from Pierrefonds, Quebec, is with Dorle in Burnaby; Roy from Kitchener, Ontario, is somewhere out West, a group leader for Katimavik Year II; Joyce from Newfoundland is working in Banff, Alberta; Kathy from Deep River, Ontario, and Cynthia from Don Mills, Ontario, are coming back from Vancouver where they went to see their friends Mark and Robert and Dorle; Michael from Brockville, Ontario, is working hard at an oil well in Alberta: he's saving to buy himself a farm in Ontario, his farmer's vocation having been confirmed at Katimavik; Michel, the co-ordinator of the worksite at Larouche, has gone to Mali, in the heart of Africa, where he's a co-ordinator for a group from Canada World Youth; Daniel from Drummondville, Quebec, is teaching French and studying at Memorial University in St. John's, Newfoundland, a province where he has lots of friends; Joyce and Gordon ...

I always get excited, jump up and down, when I talk about Katimavik. I admit it. But what else can you do when you see, even from the distance, what happened to some thirty young Canadians who, without Katimavik, most likely would never even have crossed paths on the street?

And finally that evening, there were cakes and good strong Mocha-Java coffee (half black beans, half brown). And a great deal of love in the air ...

2 You haven't been to Larouche in Lac St. Jean?

In August 1977, at the camp in Duchesnay in the middle of the woods near Quebec City, I'd had my first look at some of the participants in "my" group. A quick look ... because they got mixed up with the people in the two other groups who had come there for training camp: the ones going to Gatineau and Coaticook. With the training personnel, there were more than a hundred young Canadians of every sort. All delighted to be meeting one another in French, in English − or through gestures. Ah yes, it was something to see!

A month later, I paid my first visit to Larouche, Lac St. Jean, a pretty village in Quebec with 780 inhabitants whose existence, until then, I hadn't even been aware of. "He's travelled all around the world and he hasn't been to Larouche!"

September 8

The group has been here for just a few days. There's a press conference which will be attended by all the leading citizens of the village: Mayor Léo Lévesque, Father Isidore Taillon, the town councillors, the wife of federal M.P. Gilles Marceau and several friends of Katimavik. Claude Raîche, the Director-General for Quebec, and Mario Brunet, his assistant, have come from Montreal for the event.

A press conference can be stiff and ominous and deadly dull. Not at Saguenay, Lac St. Jean though. And certainly not in Larouche. The sun is dazzling, it's a glorious autumn day. It's decided that the event will take place under a tree, in front of the little restaurant that belongs to our friend Mr. Champigny (we'll have more to say about him later), three miles outside the village near the Katimavik house. All around, as far as the eye can see, is the forest. The participants, wearing their Sundaybest jeans, serve blueberry wine to the guests. A few short speeches, filled with emotion. And a few jokes! The ice is broken, Katimavik is part of the community now, for the next nine months. Or maybe longer ... you never know!

Larouche was really looking forward to Katimavik's arrival. Beginning with the first contacts, more than a month before the participants arrived, the mayor, the priest, everyone worked very hard so the marriage would take place. Projects were suggested that would be interesting for the participants and useful for the community: cross-country ski trails, billboards to sensitize the population to environmental problems, the decoration and distribution of garbage cans on the village streets, cleaning up the area around the municipal dump, putting up a stone wall around the Golden Age home, widening the road to the Aqueduct, participation in community social projects, etc. Work that wouldn't have been done without the volunteers from Katimavik. That's the golden rule: never to take a single job away from the community. What the authorities of Larouche invited us to do wouldn't have been done without us, as the municipality had no budget to devote to these works, necessary though they were.

The negotiations went easily then, all was for the best in the best of all possible worlds — when we realized there was no house in the village big enough to lodge our thirty participants and group leaders. Disaster! But, among the other leading citizens, the priest didn't want to lose Katimavik so easily. He went to see Mr. Champigny, a local contractor: "Champigny, do you think you could build a house for thirty young people? The absolute minimum: a dormitory for the boys, a dormitory for the girls, showers, a kitchen, a common room. *In thirty days!"* People from Saguenay-Lac St Jean are fond of challenges. Their entire history is a series of challenges, ever since the day in 1845 when the Curé Hébert came to the then-virgin forests with a few dozen settlers uprooted from the fertile fields of the county of Kamouraska, on the other side of the St. Lawrence.[1]

The day our participants arrived, the house was ready. Or nearly ... Well built, a nice little place — but no bigger than necessary. That was why the participants immediately decided to increase their living space by making three teepees, those attractive cone-shaped tents made by the Plains Indians.

During this first real visit I get to know some of the participants better. I joke with Michael from Brockville, Ontario, Bruce from Saskatoon, Saskatchewan, Joyce from Kilbridge, Newfoundland and — of course — with Lap, from Burnaby, British Columbia ... freshly arrived from Hong Kong, as everyone already knows! Must be sure to remember the names of these four, at least, when I come back ...

I leave Larouche with the mission of going to say hello to their friends at Gatineau and Coaticook. Even though they've spent only one month together, during the training camp at Duchesnay, strong ties have been formed in this group of a hundred young people. They write to one another, sometimes individually but particularly by means of a collective letter at least four feet long. It's pinned to the wall and each participant comes in turn to jot down a few friendly words, a joke, a poem. In a few days, when there isn't a single square inch left on the two big sheets of wrapping paper, they'll be sent off, one to the friends in Gatineau, the other to Coaticook — who'll be sure to

---

1. I wouldn't want to seem to be plugging my own family, but how could I resist the temptation to point out to the industrious population that the Curé Hébert in question was my great-grand uncle?

answer. And we hope it will go on that way when the three groups are in three other parts of the country, and so forth throughout a companionship that in many cases may go on forever.

More than a month later, October 24

Up at 5.00 a.m. No, it doesn't happen to me every day! Dorval, a plane to the closest airport to Larouche: Bagotville, where one of the group leaders — Matthew from Lethbridge, Alberta — meets me. He tells me — in French, of course, he's already getting along well — that Michel, the co-ordinator, is quite literally on his back. When he was moving an 800-pound woodstove into his cabin ("Save energy!" "Use renewable fuel!") he tore a ligament in his back. The doctor has ordered him to remain virtually immobile for two weeks, in bed. For a guy who's always on the move it's a real hardship. Over the years, I've seen him on the move at Canada World Youth, in Senegal, with his group of Filipinos or Gambians, always available, night and day, to discuss things, to laugh or sing or play the guitar or work hard ... to the full extent of his ligaments! Seeing him motionless in his bed is at the very least surrealistic.

While I'm here, then, I'll share Michel's cabin, which is just a step away from the participants' "big" house. There's an old sofa in the corner for me, with rather aggressive springs.

I light a fire in the splendid cast-iron stove and then pretend to be looking after Michel and his cabin — a superflous role because ever since the day of the accident the participants have been taking turns looking after him and entertaining him. For the moment I'm replacing Angela, an Anglophone from Nitro, Quebec, who's been watching over Michel as sweetly as an angel, as she embroiders a tablecloth.

We sum up the situation: what's happened since my last, too rapid visit, the reaction of the people in the village, the work that's been accomplished, the problems that inevitably arise in a group, etc.

This morning, the participants are expecting a visitor: Jacques Brassard, the local member of the Quebec National Assembly. He was invited to the press conference on September 8 but had to send his apologies, promising to come back later. Shortly after, he came for dinner with the group, along with the mayor of Larouche. At the café he had to apologize once again, as he had another meeting, though the participants had piles more questions to ask him. The Anglophones in particular wanted to hear the first Parti Québécois MNA they'd had a chance to see in flesh and blood. Jacques Brassard promised he'd come back again, and today he was keeping that promise. After a two-hour exchange with the group, he came to say hello to Michel and me. You get the impression he's quite pleased with the contact he's established with these thirty young people from every part of Canada. The Francophones asked more questions than the Anglophones, but the latter were quite obviously more interested. A girl from British Columbia told me Mr. Brassard had taught her a lot of things she hadn't even suspected about the Parti Québécois: "He didn't convince me, but his explanations will help me understand the independentists' point of view better, and help me make other people in British Columbia understand them too." An Anglophone participant from Quebec was more sceptical: "Pooh! politicians are all alike: they only give you their side of the story!"

Whatever the case may be, the visit of this Parti Québécois representative stirred up some interesting discussions in the group and — something that's always agreeable — dispassionate discussions.

Last Friday, the participants had another Québécois experience that might have an even more profound influence, for the language of poets is a universal one, that can touch people beyond the grasp of ideologies and perhaps despite linguistic barriers. Particularly if the poet is also a marvellous musician whose name is Gilles Vigneault. The group invested a large chunk of its tiny "cultural" budget to go to Jonquière, a few miles from here, to hear him. The twenty Anglophone participants were the only "Anglais" in the audience of some 500 people. "We were the only ones who didn't always laugh at the right time! Gilles Vigneault talks very fast and we missed bits of it. But he still had us, in spite of everything. His music's very beautiful, his poetry and his tenderness are very real, and his rhythm, his stage presence — we adored it all, even though we realized we were missing a lot." Bits of poems, scraps of songs and a few "tidelams" by Gilles Vigneault in Jonquière will continue to vibrate for a long time in the hearts of Gordon from St. John's, Newfoundland, and Dorle from Burnaby, British Columbia. And that's saying something.

In the afternoon, the participants show me what they've accomplished around the camp so far. The great object of their pride is the solar greenhouse they're building. It will eventually produce more lettuce, tomatoes, and cucumbers than the group can consume: they'll share their produce with the poor families in the village. In addition, the group knows very well that it won't see the first lettuce coming up. "We're working for the future," explains Daniel from Drummondville, Quebec, one of the enthusiasts of appropriate technology. "By the end of our stay in Larouche, in late November, the greenhouse will be finished. The group after us will do the planting and the third group, the one that'll come to Larouche in March, will get to sample the fresh vegetables!" He's glad it's working out that way: for Daniel and the other participants the greenhouse is a symbol. As they were building it ("Ah! who can forget the time we worked till midnight to finish the cement foundations — where everybody wrote their names for posterity!") they told themselves that the greenhouse wouldn't be producing just tomatoes; it would yield other fruits. More solar greenhouses would be built *because of this one.* Already, several people in the community are interested in this humble structure; they want to borrow the plans. Already several participants understand that their greenhouse is a sort of testimony, a challenge to the wasteful consumer society they're part of but which they want to contest — non-violently. Some of them — I know, they've told me! — can see even further: they realize that rich countries such as ours must not only stop consuming excessively while a large portion of mankind is dying of hunger, but that they must, without delay, radically change their ways of thinking, invent a new world economic order, find a fair balance between the rate of industrial growth and the potential of the ecosystem, prepare quickly to share in the full force of the word. To share the knowledge which the poor countries need most: large-scale technology, of course, but small-scale as well. Thousands of greenhouses like the one in Larouche might be built all across Canada and, even more importantly, in the Third World. And finally, sharing among all those who inhabit it, the limited resources of our battered old world. Equalization payments on the global level! A grand design that's appropriate for mobilizing the youth of today.

One of the phenomena of Katimavik, one that never ceases to amaze me, is the scope of the impact created by the activity of these 1170 young Canadians — a fairly small number, after all.[1] The impact in the forty-six Canadian communities where they work.[2] The impact on the hundreds of families who take in a participant for several weeks. The impact on the several thousand families of our participants and the training personnel, their friends, the schools they attended and with which they still maintain contact, and so forth. Thousands of letters are exchanged every week among all these people, letters describing each person's experiences, the greenhouse that's being built, the ecological path being marked out in the middle of the forest, the historical monument rebuilt from ruins, Gilles Vigneault's concert, the wilderness survival exercise, the evening organized for crippled children, the discovery of a

---

1. This figure includes participants and support staff from Year I, 1977-78; Year II, 1978-79 — 1485; Year III, 1979-80 — 1600.
2. There are only thirty groups, but several perform activities in two or three neighbouring communities.

new section of Canada, the friendship of a family of farmers — the Tremblays or the MacDonalds, the Simards or the Browns — the return to a simple life that respects nature, and so on. And in addition to the thousands of letters, the thousands of meetings, discussions, exchanges. Thousands of people, for all sorts of reasons, have visited our groups: neighbours bringing a cake or coming to consult the plans for a solar greenhouse or for explanations about how to produce hot water with an easily built device, neighbours who want a closer look at a young person from Vancouver or Saskatoon or Montreal or Newfoundland, mayors, priests, M.P.s in need of a dose of hope, other young people, finally, wanting to find out more about Katimavik — in case it's going to continue next year!

The day before yesterday Mme Lessard, a local woman, came to meet the group at Larouche for a very personal reason: her daughter is a Katimavik participant and her entire group is at present in Gravelbourg, Saskatchewan. She's delighted with what she's seen here: "If it's as good in Gravelbourg my daughter certainly won't be bored!" It's more common for parents to come and visit their sons or daughters: last week, for example, Claire's parents came from Pierrefonds, near Montreal. They ate with the group, then accepted an invitation from Claire's friends and found themselves a little corner in the crowded dormitories for their sleeping bags. Oh yes, Katimavik brings together a lot of people!

Michel, the co-ordinator, shows me a letter he's just received from a group leader in Luther, Ontario, the Grand River project, where the third and final phase of "my" group's program will take place. His participants have just found out that they'll be spending their second three-month phase at Larouche. And it seems that the news has been well received!

Luther Lake, Ontario
October 20, 1977

Salut la gang!

Yesterday, October 19, at 5.15 p.m. we got some memorable news that made my whole group jump for joy. As for me, I jumped right to the ceiling, I was so glad ... Ever since the beginning I've talked so much about wanting to go to Larouche that my group was just as happy as I was. We can't wait to see you, Michel; get ready, because my crazy bunch is on its way!

I can't really tell you what's going on in the other two groups (of ten) because we live separately: David's group is in Cambridge, Julie's is in Belwood, forty miles from there and mine's at Luther Lake (sixty miles from Cambridge and twenty from Belwood). My group's in great spirits, full of energy and get-up-and-go. Really far out!

We're working here for the Grand River Conservation Authority and I have to admit that sometimes there isn't enough work, but still there are interesting things to do: laying out forests, wildlife control, building fences, seed selection, etc.

The house we're living in is fantastic: an old farmhouse, in a fabulous setting.

We also work (one day a week) at an *FM* radio station, Radio-Waterloo, where we're working in groups of five at putting together a radio program of interest to the community.

So, see you soon, buddies. À bientôt!

Claude Vadeboncoeur, group leader

A few participants added a P.S. to their group leader's letter. Here's what Cynthia, from Calgary, Alberta, said: "I'm sure that, like all the participants, you've had your highs and lows as you tried to get Katimavik off the ground, but that's how we learn to live and to deal with the problems we run into. It's a little like being married: for richer, for poorer, for better, for worse!

"There's some drawbacks to living here in Luther, in the middle of the countryside and quite isolated, but I think we're happier than the other groups..."

The participants are involving me, too, in their plans to build three Indiant tents, teepees that will relieve the crowding in a house too small for thirty people who sometimes need a minimum of privacy.

Fifty-one pine trees have been cut down in the neighbouring forest. Each teepee requires seventeen. The branches have been stripped off, the bark removed and now they're been stored in a warm place — the attic of the house — to dry for two weeks. The heavy canvas covering has already been cut and sewn; all that's left is to erect the three teepees, whose "floors" will be beds of fir boughs. In the centre, there will be a fire, and an ingenious ventilation system will allow the smoke to escape, while keeping the temperature inside the teepee suitably warm. With these attractive tents, each of the three sub-groups of ten will have its own "meeting place" — its own Katimavik if you like! They can be used for meetings, for sleeping, even in wintertime — demonstrating that it's possible to live in a rudimentary dwelling, something the Amerindians taught us long ago.

One month later, November 24

I've promised to go and see the completed greenhouse, the first teepee put up ... In a few days the group will begin the second stage of its long trip: this is my last chance

Once again, Matthew from Lethbridge, Alberta, meets me at the little airport in Bagotville, as Michel is in Montreal at a meeting of co-ordinators. A few months ago Matthew barely spoke a word of French. Now he expresses himself quite adequately ... with just a hint of the Saguenay-Lac St. Jean accent! If I inadvertently ask him a question in English, he answers in French. In terms of language learning, one of Katimavik's countless objectives, this group has worked very well: there are no more unilingual Anglophones and some of them speak French remarkably well, particularly considering that at the beginning they couldn't put two words together. Christine from Ste. Foy Quebec, who is with Matthew, admits that she's neglected her English a little: "You know, we've been taking such pains to teach French to our 'Anglais' we haven't had time to learn their language! It isn't serious, though: we'll be spending the next six months in Anglophone communities. So like it or not, we'll all end up bilingual!"

I find all the participants in better shape than ever. You'd think they've known one another forever: brothers and sisters. I'm beginning to feel more comfortable with each of them and I hope the reverse is true as well. Still impossible to attach each of the thirty names to the right face, but I've stopped confusing Jo-Anne and Carol Ann, Yves and Yvan.

First, a visit to the greenhouse, where Peter from Edmonton, Alberta, Kathy from Deep River, Ontario and Lise from Laval, Quebec are putting in the final nails. The participants are more than a little proud of their work — a large solar greenhouse 40' X 20', designed by the Brace Institute and tested by Laval and McGill universities. In January, the next group will plant tomatoes and cucumbers ... which participants in the third group will be eating next May.

Then, Mario from Beloeil, Quebec, takes me over to the first teepee standing in the woods, in the middle of a clearing already covered with snow. It looks quite splendid, this teepee whose oval "door" is decorated with a motif — surely Indian! — dreamed up by Michel. Several people have already spent the night in it, with the temperature at -15°C. The participants are a little sorry they haven't had time to put up the other two teepees, for which the material is all ready. "Have to leave the next group a few things to do!"

At supper time I'm treated to an excellent seaweed soup, hot cornbread and oatmeal cookies, the work of Cynthia from Don Mills, Ontario, and Mark from Vancouver, who are on kitchen duty today. One eats frugally in Katimavik, but the food is always very nourishing, well prepared and made from natural, healthy ingredients. Although Katimavik issues few directives in this respect, most of the groups choose so-called "natural" cooking and, sometimes, vegetarian dishes. In discussions with the participants you realize that many are very sensitive to the problems caused by the excessive consumption of meat, the waste of protein, and the use of doctored food products filled with chemicals, which often have virtually no nutritional value.

Angela, our Anglophone Québécoise from Nitro, offers me some mint tea and we chat for a while. She speaks with astonishing emotion and enthusiasm about the month or more she's spent with a local family, the Lessards, who have seven children and run a dairy farm. The participants are generally delighted by the three or four weeks they spend with a family in each of the three regions. In Angela's case the experience was so intense the group almost lost her! "I was so happy with Papa and Mama Lessard I thought seriously about leaving Katimavik and extending my stay with that marvellous family I felt part of. But Katimavik has become a kind of family too, and it would have been hard to pull myself away from it ... We've already agreed that six months from now, at the end of the program, I'm coming back to Larouche, to the Lessards. And in the meantime we'll write."[1]

The group is leaving Larouche in three days and all the commotion of moving is already underway. The house is being cleaned from top to bottom: Daniel from Drummondville, Quebec, has practically taken the electric stove apart so he can scour every nook and cranny!

And the day before they leave, the group will make huge chocolate cakes to welcome the next group.

---

1. Based on the "statistics" of the Larouche group, some *quarter of a million* letters will be exchanged between all the Katimavik participants and other people during the ten-month program. Luckily our forests are a renewable resource!

This evening there's a party in the village: a farewell evening for the participants, organized for their friends in the community. In the parish hall are all those people who, when this bunch of thirty unknown young people first arrived, were a little bit concerned, and now are having trouble concealing their emotion as the group is about to leave: the Lessards, the Simards, the Tremblays, the Champignys, the Larouches and the others. And of course the mayor and the priest are there, as they were on the first day.

The participants are improvising a little show, not very professional I must admit, but warmly received because it speaks the language of the heart. Yves from Dorval, Quebec, acts as M.C., Roy from Kitchener, Ontario, does a few magic tricks in still-hesitant French, but very intelligible, Mario from Beloeil, Quebec — we might have known — plays the recorder, a group performs some folkdances; but most touching are the personal testimonials of several participants. Jo-Anne from Islington, Ontario, expressed the feelings of everyone: here is what she said to the village of Larouche, in French, a language in which she was almost incapable of expressing herself when she arrived here.

Three months ago we came here to Larouche, on September 2 to be exact. And now on November 27 we have to leave. A lot of us don't want to leave, but we must in order to complete the Katimavik program.

We're looking forward to the second project in Wilcox, Saskatchewan, and the third in Cambridge, Ontario. But Quebec is a different province! It has its own culture and a beautiful, beautiful language too — the French language. Most of us, Anglophones like me, have learned that language. In Duchesnay, we found it very difficult to speak French. Now, though, I think everybody's almost ready to be bilingual — and that's a good thing! The French can speak English and the Anglophones can speak French. A very advantageous cultural experiment for understanding the other side of the coin. For the other two projects, we'll be continuing in the other language.

One of the best experiences I had in Larouche was the farm. It was my first time on a farm and I learned a lot about that kind of life. I'd like to say thank you to all those people — the Simards, the Tremblays, Jean-Paul and France, and my new French family, the Lessards. And also to the Champigny family for their help and their hospitality. It was an invaluable experience for me.

The last thing I want to say is about the Katimavik group. I hope our group lived up to your expectations. It's too bad we didn't have enough time to become really integrated into the community. That's because we had a lot of work around our house — the greenhouse, the teepees and some building. But now we've finished our term here and the second and third Katimavik groups will take up where we've left off. So good luck, and thanks a lot, Larouche. We love you!

Oh, yes, Don't be surprised to see some of us back here in the future ... Thank you!

Then monsieur le Curé replied on behalf of the community, with a warmth and sincerity in keeping with the tone of this evening of friendship: "You, the participants in Katimavik, have all worked well and made every effort to become integrated into the life of our village. And you, the people of Larouche, have welcomed with open arms these young people from every part of Canada. That's why the Katimavik project has been a clear-cut success ... "

Then I carry on: "Yes, despite certain inevitable deficiencies, the Larouche project has been a remarkable success, which will contribute to guaranteeing the future of Katimavik. One day hundreds of thousands of young Canadians will live in hundreds of Larouches, and their experience will be as rich and stimulating as the one we've just shared here. One thing is obvious and certain: all of the participants will leave here with a little bit of Larouche in their hearts for the rest of their lives: Larouche, Michel, of course — but Larouche your beautiful village as well."

Really, the emotional level was beginning to climb! The party was threatening to turn maudlin ... But Michel Larouche, the co-ordinator who wasn't leaving, had the final word: "My dear friends, that's all very pretty, but next week we start again! With thirty new participants from God knows where! And we'll all be welcoming them together! Yes, we're starting again ... "

November 25

After lunch (whole wheat pancakes and fresh fruit) I gladly sign up for dishwashing duty. There are three of us and we eventually get to the end of the thirty plates, thirty cups, thirty saucers — not to mention saucepans and frying pans... My fellow-dishwashers, Cynthia from Don Mills, Ontario, and Yvan from Ste. Thérèse, Quebec, insist that I help them do the baking for tonight's farewell supper in honour of some of their friends from Larouche. Not all of them — the little dining room in the house couldn't possibly hold them all! Even thirty people are pretty crowded. So I boldly embark on making jellyrolls with Cynthia and hazelnut cookies, Yvan's speciality. I admit I'd have liked to chat with Yvan, who's grappling with a terrible problem: for personal reasons, he's decided to leave Katimavik immediately after Larouche, in a few days. In the end it's decided, but ever since yesterday he's been hesitating, thinking things over very hard, knitting his black eyebrows. The other participants respect his final decision in advance, but they're all very concerned. "He can't go!" Daniel from Drummondville says softly — as does Serge from Montreal and, of course, Cynthia.

In a program as long[1] and, let's admit it, as demanding as this one, it's quite normal for a certain number of participants to give up along the way,

---

[1] Ten months long the first year, the program was later reduced to nine months.

36

sometimes for perfectly valid reasons. It's always a very difficult experience for the participant who goes away and for his friends who stay behind, as is obvious in the case of Yvan. As the matter only concerns me from a distance, I don't discuss it openly with Yvan. But the temptation is great. I'm more and more attached to "my" group and if Yvan were to leave it he'd be the first to do so. Now according to all the others, Yvan's a great guy, an excellent participant from every point of view ... I don't say anything, but between two batches of cookies I can't resist making a discreet remark to him ... At least he'll know that I'd be as unhappy as the other participants if he were to leave. He smiles.

All is not lost ... Except for one of the jellyrolls, which is a little too thin and stayed in the oven a little too long, so it looks rather woebegone!

But despite all that, supper is a joyous meal. By candlelight. "Save electricity!" Michel, the co-ordinator, has gone to get his guitar and he sings songs in English, French and even in Tagalog. (He used to be a Canada World Youth Group leader in the Philippines and he still gets along well in Tagalog). But his greatest success was without question "Mon pays, c'est l'hiver," of which there's already sufficient evidence in snow-covered Larouche and which will be even more terrible in the northern village of Wilcox which is awaiting the group tomorrow.

The "big" house at Larouche, Quebec, where the group lived for three months.
(Photo by Serge Maddedu)

Lap, from Burnaby, B.C. (and Hong Kong!) sawing firewood along with Robert and Carol.
(Photo By Roger Côté)

The group completes the solar greenhouse.
(Photo by Serge Maddedu)

The first teepee rising against the sky of Lac Saint-Jean.
(Photo by Serge Maddedu)

3 At last, something up my sleeve ...

Now I must make a confession: I went only once to Wilcox, Saskatchewan, where the group lived for three months, and that was for just one day that I remember particularly because of the icy wind that took away any desire to be a tourist. Between gusts of wind, Russell Pocock, the co-ordinator, took me to each of the worksites in the village where our participants were hard at work.

One group was transforming an old building into a carpentry workshop to be used by the students at the Notre Dame College, a famous institution founded some fifty years ago by the remarkable Father Murray. As our participants were to realize, the presence of several hundred college students in such a small village (there were more students than residents of the village!) made Wilcox into a double community where everyone isn't always on the same wavelength. At first our participants, all the while maintaining good relationships with the college, had to explain to the rest of the community that they shouldn't be confused with the college students, that they wanted to serve the entire community and integrate into it as much as possible.

It took some patience, but when I saw Kathy from Deep River, Ontario and Carol from Scarborough, Ontario repainting the walls of the municipal curling rink with some old people from Wilcox, I realized that things were working out very well. "I like the people here very much," Kathy told me, "and I think they like us now too. Ever since they've found out what Katimavik is ... "

Another project was building a small café for the college students, right in the heart of Wilcox. The previous group had started the work and had completed the shell of the building; "my" group was responsible for finishing it. Before they left they would even have the pleasure of taking part in the party to celebrate the opening of the café, along with a group of Quebec musicians who just happened to be in the area. It was a party people will be talking about for a long time — in Wilcox and elsewhere in Canada!

The great novelty for the participants in Wilcox was to find themselves broken up into small groups of ten, in three different houses: two in Wilcox itself and a third in the village of Milestone, some twenty miles away. Unfortunately I didn't have time to visit Milestone, but later I heard very good things about it. There, too, the participants worked, among other things, at building a community café, this one intended for the older people in the village.

At least I visited the two houses in Wilcox, which weren't castles but where I feasted on carrot cakes, corn muffins with honey and I don't know what other delights of natural cooking. It goes without saying that the atmosphere in these small groups of ten was very different, far more relaxed, than in the large family of thirty in the famous house at Larouche: group life is more normal when there are ten members than when there are thirty, even though several participants missed the large group. Today, as a general rule, Katimavik participants live in groups of ten, with a group leader, not only in different houses but often in communities fairly far from one another.

This was the case in Grand River, Ontario, for example, where one small group was at Luther Lake, another at Fergus and the third in Cambridge — three communities I visited in the spring as arranged with "my" participants,

40

who were a little frustrated after my lightning visit to Wilcox!

This was called the Grand River project because the main sponsor was the Grand River Conservation Authority, which is responsible for the environment in this vast region of southern Ontario.

I saw the Luther Lake participants planting trees in the GRCA's huge nursery, the ones from Fergus germinating seeds in greenhouses, the ones from Cambridge making picnic tables for the parks in the region. But as I chatted with the participants I was amazed at the unbelievable number of varied and interesting experiences each of them had had during this last three-month stage, in Ontario. It would be tedious to draw up an inventory, because each participant will speak of them in turn, in the rest of this book. Each one will speak according to his or her temperament, sometimes with spirit and enthusiasm, sometimes with a critical attitude that is directed — and one can sense this — more at improving the Katimavik of tomorrow than complaining about the way it is today.

At the very end of the program each group of participants holds an evaluation session that lasts about four days. Together, they attempt honestly to get to the bottom of things, to evaluate the quality of the projects, the group's involvement, improvements to be made in the future. Have the goals set at the beginning been reached? To what extent has each participant become bilingual? Are the local sponsors satisfied with the work accomplished? Did the group really become integrated into the community? What new sensitivity does it have of environmental problems? To what extent has each one changed, matured, grown? And finally, they talk about going back to their own families, and communities, and of their new prospects in terms of study or work.

The group invited me to take part in these four days of evaluation at Collingwood, Ontario, in the mountains. With a splendid view of Lake Erie. This time, I arrived with something up my sleeve! Even worse: I had a tape-recorder and fifty blank cassettes, ninety minutes long.

Enough to record a lot of chitchat. The idea I had up my sleeve, though, was this: to interview each participant, taking as much time as necessary, leaving each one free to say everything, to speak as long as he or she wanted. (The most discreet took only forty-five minutes, while the more talkative participants went on for a full hour and a half!)

In order for the experiment to be worthwhile, I would ask more or less the same questions in each interview. A few questions would allow me to place the interviewee in his or her family, and educational, or cultural background and give us an indication of what the participant had been like *before* Katimavik; then, they would talk about Larouche, Wilcox, Grand River, and tell us, finally, what had happened to them at the end of this long road, how they had changed and what they intended to do with their lives after Katimavik.

I had agreed to send each participant the transcript of the interview, which I would have cut and corrected here and there, mainly to avoid needless repetition. Each participant, though, would be invited to restore sections they considered important, and to make any corrections they deemed necessary. I would then commit myself to considering this corrected text the final one.

Only one participant, Debbie from Stratford, Ontario, didn't want to be interviewed, for personal reasons. And I didn't interview Robert from Hampton, Nova Scotia, because at the very beginning of the program he was promoted to group leader in another group. The other participants remember him fondly and he made many friends among them, but as he lived through only a small part of their shared experience, I didn't consider his testimony to be essential.

Two other participants weren't in Collingwood when I conducted my interviews: Yvan from Ste. Thérèse, Quebec and Gordon from St. John's, Newfoundland.

We already know that Yvan finally left the program during the stay in Wilcox, but without really leaving the group, which was able to boast that there hadn't been one dropout in the ten months. In the course of the interviews, several participants spoke to me spontaneously about Yvan and his premature departure, and I decided it was essential to interview him as well, something that finally happened a year later. This was the case for Gordon, too, who I went to see in St. John's in the spring of 1979. As you will see, it was absolutely necessary to interview Gordon, whose hasty expulsion ten days before the end of the program was the greatest trial experienced by the group, a true tragedy of which several participants will speak with ill-contained emotion, even with a kind of rage in the case of Bruce from Saskatoon, who was a very close friend of Gordon. There's no need, for the moment, to try to explain this unfortunate story, which Gordon himself will speak about very frankly.

On the first day, then, there were twenty-six participants in "my" group, and I interviewed them all except Debbie and Robert ... who shouldn't be confused with Robert Yee from Vancouver.

When I told friends about my plan to make a book from these two dozen interviews describing roughly the same events, some were rather sceptical. Wouldn't it become monotonous by the time you got to the fifth or the tenth interview? Those who were confident, though, shared my conviction that there's nothing in the world more fascinating or varied than human beings. I am never bored when I hear someone telling about himself or herself with confidence, talking about the things that interest them, that preoccupy them or that they like. The rest is only literature ...

I reread each text several times, ten or fifteen times perhaps. Always with the same delight, listening to the young people of my country who, thanks to the experience of Katimavik, had just discovered *others* and — something that's equally important — had discovered *themselves*. And because I chose a group of participants at random, there's reason to think that I might have obtained similar testimonies from the 4097[1] young Canadians who lived or

1. The figure includes the participants, group leaders and co-ordinators from the first three years of Katimavik.

43

are now living, as I write these lines, the Katimavik program.

All the chatter you've read so far, the first three chapters of this book, had one purpose: to introduce you to the ones that follow. Listen then, listen to Lap and Lise, Cynthia and Peter, Yvan and Carol Ann and all the others.

The group cleaning the municipal dump at Larouche.
(Photo by Serge Maddedu)

The endless winter of Wilcox, Saskatchewan.
(Photo by Serge Maddedu)

Peter from Edmonton on mess duty for the group of thirty.
(Photo by Schuller)

Work session during the final evaluation at Collingwood, Ontario. From left to right: Joyce, Serge, Carol, Claire and Daniel.
(Photo by Schuller)

45

4 *Bruce Young,* Age 18,[1] Saskatoon, Saskatchewan

I was born in Saskatoon. Lived there all my life, fortunately or unfortunately, I don't know.

J.H.: Why do you say that? Don't you like Saskatoon?

Bruce: Oh, very much, but it narrowed my views quite a bit.

J.H.: You'd never left before you came to Katimavik?

Bruce: I never even got to go out of the province until about three years ago when I did a big trip to British Columbia. Even in the province itself, I've been to Regina but only with the class. I've been within about a hundred miles of home, so my views are pretty narrow.

J.H.: Are you from a big family?

Bruce: About average — three sisters. I lived for fifteen years or so in the slums of Saskatoon. Now it's all like upper middle-class, but then it was pretty bad. All the washrooms were outside. We were rich I guess, because we had a washroom inside.

J.H.: But you had a happy childhood?

Bruce: Yes, pretty happy. A lot of things I didn't understand seem so simple now.

---

1. The age given for each participant is his or her age at the time of application, in 1977.

J.H.: Before Katimavik, what were your views on the future? What did you want to do?

Bruce: Scared.

J.H.: You were scared?

Bruce: Because I didn't want to be a specialist like a welder or electrician or anything like that. I don't want to be a common everyday worker. If you are not a specialist, then you have to be a labourer. I couldn't see myself working all my life on a job I didn't like for little pay, for a pension, and just die after that. I knew I had to travel and get out of there.

J.H.: You knew what you didn't want to do, but you didn't know what you did want?

Bruce: Yes, I suppose that's right, so Katimavik was the perfect thing.

J.H.: How did you hear about it?

Bruce: My dad was reading about it in *The Canadian Magazine* and he knew I wanted to travel.

J.H.: But you were still in school?

Bruce: Oh no, I worked for the Saskatoon School Board for about eight weeks and was laid off. For the rest of the year I had been working part time at the Saskatoon arena and was going to night school. Being laid off kind of hurt me. I had started gaining the attitude that at every job I would be laid off and it would seem so pointless to get a job and I felt very insecure.

J.H.: You didn't care about studying anymore?

Bruce: I finished grade 12 and I didn't like school to begin with. I wasn't a guy who would skip school, but I just wanted to get my twelve years over with and that was it. I wasn't going to university. I really didn't have the grades because I didn't work that hard. Homework got to be a thing I hated the very most in my entire life. If I had done my homework, I probably would have got good grades, if I had been more interested. Some of the stuff I took, I could see myself never using unless I wanted to go on to special things like accounting and physics and I wasn't crazy about biology. They should make it so that if you're planning something in the future, then, okay, you can take these.

J.H.: But how can you plan when you are fifteen?

Bruce: It's true, but I didn't have anything planned where I'd need these at all.

J.H.: So, Katimavik came about. What struck you in that ad?

Bruce: Oh, to travel, to learn French which I very much wanted to do.

J.H.: Why did you want to learn French?

Bruce: I'm just a fanatic for languages. I studied Spanish through grades 7, 8, 9, I read books, and I'm real crazy about it; and German. I should have taken French all the way through. It seemed more logical than taking German. So I didn't know why I took German, I thought it was easier. But then I wanted to learn French very much.

J.H.: Then it was one of the appeals of Katimavik? What else?

Bruce: Meeting people. I really like people a lot and I thought to meet ninety more people would be just great, and from all over Canada. I realize the importance of having friends all over Canada, and to travel and to learn. I want very much to learn anything I can. I want to get every experience I can out of life.

J.H.: What was your reaction when you got to Duchesnay[1] with a hundred kids, all different?

Bruce: I loved it. As soon as I arrived and saw all those people, I hadn't even stepped out of the car and all these people were around me, shaking hands and saying, "Do you want something to eat?" and things like that. "Come over we're having a party," and "You're going to do stuff," and well, it's just great.

J.H.: There were a lot of French people. How did you relate to them?

Bruce: It was very strange because they were the first people I met who talked French and some of them couldn't talk any English at all. I said to myself, I have got to speak their language and I really wanted to. Unfortunately, I got

---

1. The regional training camp.

all the way as far as I could have. I motivated myself as much as possible but I have lagged, especially this month.

J.H.: But did you improve?

Bruce: Oh, yes very much. I believe I have. I didn't know hardly a word when I started because I didn't take it that seriously.

Larouche, Quebec

J.H.: So it was lucky that your first project was in Larouche, Quebec?

Bruce: Yes, that was good especially when I went billeting. I didn't know any French. It was very frustrating but I did learn an incredible amount in just three weeks.

J.H.: What family were you with?

Bruce: Jean-Paul and France. They weren't farmers.

J.H.: How did you like them?

Bruce: Very nice, but it is still very frustrating. I wish I could have stayed there for three months, then I would be very bilingual.

J.H.: What kind of people were they?

Bruce: Just everyday, just average, a very nice young family. Very good-looking couple. I'd say they were a little more fortunate because of the family ties.

J.H.: What type of work did you do mostly in Larouche?

Bruce: Not a heck of a lot. I was on crutches most of the time.

J.H.: That's right, what happened to you?

Bruce: One time, I fell off the stilts. The things I walked on fell down and I got my foot in a pot hole, bent my foot back and then I was on crutches for a couple of weeks. Then I went dancing about six weeks later at a Hallowe'en party and I was dancing too crazy, and I did it again and was on crutches for six more weeks, so this is about half the project.

J.H.: But with your crutches could you work outside?

Bruce: I could do it, but I'd get hassled all the time and I said well, I'm going to do it anyways. I helped with this house just across the lane, hammering, that wasn't too bad.

J.H.: So what were you doing all day?

Bruce: Well, I started sewing canvas for the teepees, reading, writing letters. Larouche wasn't all that great because there wasn't that much work for thirty people.

J.H.: How did you find the life in this house, all piled in together like that?

Bruce: Fantastic. It was a stunning experience. If it had been a better project, I would have liked it more, and it would have helped if more of the work had been away from the house. It's amazing how well we all stuck together ...

Wilcox, Saskatchewan

J.H.: Saskatchewan! It was your own province, you really couldn't find anything new in the scenery and living?

Bruce: Yes, exactly.

J.H.: I know, because some of the other participants were telling me they liked it there because it was so new and different, and the people and the scenery, the flat spaces, the sun in the morning, the sun at night.

Bruce: I loved to return, I missed the Prairies very much, but, like you say, there was no novelty.

J.H.: But there was a lot of work to do though?

Bruce: Oh, there was a bit but we didn't really agree with it. I had my best job there. The one where I did most was in the college cafeteria.

J.H.: What type of work did you do besides the cafeteria?

Bruce: Worked at general carpentry.

J.H.: Had you ever done that before?

Bruce: Oh, yes. I'd done all that ever since I was a little kid. I wasn't learning anything. It seemed I was just a labourer for the college.

J.H.: From what you have told me up to now, you sound very negative. You are always saying you didn't learn anything.

Bruce: There, I didn't. At the cafeteria I learned a lot, very much. Well, I did learn a little. I learned a fair bit from Ed, the man there, at the workshop, and at the start it was a lot of fun. The cafeteria I enjoyed a lot more because I did feel we were doing something, like we weren't doing it for the college. That was what the workshop was, all for the college, we weren't allowed to use it for anything.

J.H.: What was it like to find yourself in a group of ten people?

Bruce: It wasn't too bad. But, it was a little bit lonelier with just ten people.

J.H.: But didn't you get to know one another better?

Bruce: Yes, that was fun. Once we got here we were just starting to be a group. During the last part of Wilcox, everybody started to really like each other.

J.H.: Who are the people in your group?

Bruce: There is Debbie, Carol, Serge, Daniel, Christine, Joyce, Mark.

J.H.: That's a good group. Do you feel these people gave you a lot and that you gave them a lot?

Bruce: Yes, they gave me a lot of hell and vice versa! It's a good group because they care. If you do something wrong, if you do something silly, you know, you're given hell, "Smarten up, why are you doing that?" Sometimes, there are pretty bad arguments, not violent, or mean arguments and I know that some days it hurts, it's not fun. But if I'm told that I'm being stupid or foolish, I don't mind, because usually, they're right. If there is anything to be learned from Katimavik, it's being with all those people, just to learn from all the ideas, all the philosophies that people develop that might vastly contradict you. It is the most amazing thing that I have ever enjoyed. I have had a lot of my philosophies and ideas knocked down, really beaten out.

J.H.: Have you changed personally?

Bruce: Yes. At first, things are hard to see, like I look at myself and say I haven't changed very much, but then going home and seeing my friends and myself in relation to them, I realize I changed greatly. My parents saw it, my sister, relatives.

J.H.: Were they pleased with the change or worried?

Bruce: Pleased, for the most part, not worried, but wondering what happened to this kid. He goes out this nice clean-cut, naive kid, and comes back a know-it-all hippie! Maybe not a hippie, but a lot more carefree and less inhibited. You realize that a lot of things aren't worth arguing about; and just all the ideas people put in your mind about music, about your land. I'm not ignorant of Canada anymore.

J.H.: You know more about Canada?

Bruce: Very much so and I'm not ignorant about Quebec. What did I know about Quebec except politics and what I hear on TV? I go to the people. I went back home and one guy says as I walked in the room, this guy who is an ass hole, says, "What do you think about Canada or what do you think of the politics of Quebec, or what do you think of René Lévesque?" Well, I say, "It's not so bad. I understand where he's coming from, what he's trying to do, because..." He says, "Oh, he wants Canada, he wants..." He had all these false ideas about what Quebec really wanted, that Lévesque was a jerk, and everything else.

J.H.: So, you might have changed in a way about Quebec?

Bruce: Oh, yes. I never thought it was bad what they were trying to do. I was hurt that they wanted to leave Canada, because you could see a big chunk of Canada gone and you wondered how they could do it, but I see much more now. If they did separate, it wouldn't bother me now ... A little bit, not like it would have before.

J.H.: Those are your feelings about politics, but what about Quebecers themselves, about the people?

Bruce: Wonderful, very friendly. I realize that you hear a lot of silly things people say. Some of them are mean, but you go there and see they are just like everybody else.

J.H.: You mentioned before that your parents and friends thought that when you left that you were a naive, straight guy and when you came back you were a "hippie." It is funny, because we were just saying the opposite about another participant, Michael...

Bruce: He had long scraggly hair. He's had his hair cut, he's a little more serious, but I believe that is because of his group. It's very work-oriented, and he's adapted to that too, and so his mind about drugs and drinking has cooled down an awful lot. He used to be a real party-goer and now has changed considerably. This group that I'm with is passive, very passive which can be both good and bad, but I don't really mind. Well, if I want to wear army pants, army boots, my tie behind, I can. I wouldn't do it to go look for a job, but I really think that's not so bad and I let my hair grow long.

J.H.: If you met a friend in Saskatoon and he said, "I would like to join Katimavik," what would you tell him?

Bruce: I would tell him to do it for sure. I've already told a couple to try it if they want. I hope that Katimavik would be good for them. Just to get out and to learn and see that there is more to living. Some of them are very poor and their families can't take trips. Some of them have really big families and there is nothing else besides what they're doing. They can't do that all their lives, and coming into Katimavik shows me that now I can go anywhere in Canada.

J.H.: You have some friends everywhere ...

Bruce: I don't feel that it is so hard to go anywhere in the world. Before it seemed so impossible, like it would never happen. I can go to somebody in Toronto and say, "Hey, can I stay over for a little bit, get homecooked meals" and they'll have friends that I can meet, they can take me to parties and places they know where I can have a good time. I'd like to go to Newfoundland, take a little job up there to see Gordon. He's my best friend, he helped me a lot. There's Bob, in Nova Scotia. I'd go up and see him. He's also a very good friend. Bob's my best friend in Larouche and Gordon's my best friend here. So I'll see them. I've never seen the Atlantic Ocean. I've never been to the Atlantic Provinces. I've never been east of Quebec City.

J.H.: Do you have some people to see on the way there?

Bruce: Yes, I think I will see Daniel in Drummondville, then go up to St. John's, and drive back to Montreal to see a few people there, go to Toronto and see a few people and then go home. I have applied and hope to be accepted in Canada World Youth for next year.

J.H.: If you are accepted, what country were you thinking about?

Bruce: Indonesia, because I heard that it was a very poor country, one of the poorest in the Third World. I would very much like to see what it's like there. I got really aroused to hear how some people can be in hell that long and I would really like to try to see what I can do.

J.H.: Are you worried about the problems of the Third World and about the populations that are starving?

Bruce: Yes, I just wish there will be something I can do, but I must see it. I have to see it because I don't understand at all. I could read the books a lot but I want to see it too, to get a better understanding. Yes, I'm really concerned about that. What do you do when there are so many people and they have a hard time living and a lot of them don't have enough food to feed themselves and a lot of them have governments that are gypping them out of money all the time and they can't make it. I have been following the news about Nicaragua and how the peasants are starting an uprising against their government, and I really hope they do it. I don't know what I can do on a personal level, but I can find out as soon as I get there. I hope that I can get into other organizations in the Third World or in Canada that help poor people. At least it will be a good thing to start with and perhaps I can go into these again as group leader for Canada World Youth and try to get into the upper echelons of the organizations.

J.H.: So you are planning for the next couple of years. What after that?

Bruce: I have to see. I don't want to plan too far. I learned that in school. In grade 4, I used to worry what I was going to do after grade 12. I was a terrible worrier. It is a terrible thing to worry. I really don't have a big future. I'm liking what I'm doing and I like that kind of life. I realize that once I get to be fifty or sixty, I'll have nothing to do, and I may not have any major job with a big pension sitting there waiting for me. I think I could still get by. Maybe then I will start living like a hermit. But I couldn't do that, I like people too much.

J.H.: What good would it be to be a hermit?

Bruce: That's it exactly, you see I always used to have a complex about what good was I. How could I ever help anyone. Katimavik helped me with the rest. I liked them all. They were wonderful people. I was really closer with them than I was with my family. I don't know what I am going to do. I may not see some of these people for years.

J.H.: I prefer not to be there the day you all part.

Bruce: I prefer not to be there as well. It's going to be pretty sad. It's even hard to believe Gordon is gone. It's just like he died. I don't understand it at all. I was really hurt. I understood he broke a rule but to give up friendship for a rule and what he did wasn't so terrible. There could have been something else done, suspension, anything. If anybody helped out, it was him. Gordon is a very bright person. A lot of people went to him for advice.

J.H.: Then you feel that it was an injustice when he was sent home?

Bruce: Very much. I knew what he did was wrong but just to say "out" three weeks before the end and by people he thought were his friends, but they didn't seem to care. We asked for consideration from the co-ordinator and the group leader. The group leader was the mainstay behind it, but the co-ordinator as well said no and wouldn't listen to anything else. We thought we would change the decision to levy our own punishment which we thought would be just. We could not see the point in kicking the person out.

J.H.: Do you think it was the view of all the participants?

Bruce: Yes, unanimous.

J.H.: So you mean the participants were unanimous and on the other side you had the co-ordinator and the group leader. And of course, they have the authority and they put him out?

Bruce: Yes, I am very much opposed to this because we had the same situation with two people in Larouche. Their tickets were already bought to go home but the co-ordinator phoned Montreal and they said: "Okay, you guys handle it and then let us know the decision." We were given the power to decide and we levied a punishment on

55

them and things were okay. I don't know why growing plants that are completely harmless ... If the police had found them, they would just tell them to have them destroyed. They aren't even potent until about six months or so. How long could he have grown them? They might as well have been dandelions. It's because it was a drug. That's stupid.

J.H.: Why did he do it? He was a bright boy?

Bruce: I don't know why he planted them at all. They're not worth anything. He planted them on the site, but we were only going to be there two months. They're not potent at all. He had to leave and could not have taken them with him.

J.H.: Were there many of them?

Bruce: Not very many, four, I think.

J.H.: Four little plants? About two inches high, I heard?

Bruce: He is gone just because of that. It's not just. We asked for a compromise and the group leader said no, and she admitted later on that she closed her mind to this because she was afraid someone would have changed her mind. She was even going to kick one girl out because she just transplanted them, supposedly. With Gordon, that was all supposition as well. She had no actual proof that he planted them, only that someone said so. The whole thing was hearsay. If it ever had gone to court, the whole thing would have been thrown out. She had no actual proof that he had planted them.

J.H.: But apparently everybody thinks he did?

Bruce: Oh, of course, but a few other people could have planted them. Anybody could have planted them. It was all assumption. As soon as she walked in there she told Gordon, "I want those plants out." So he said okay and took them out. Then she went down to Cambridge and said she wanted Gordon and another participant out. He said okay, like he had to. She came back that night and said they were going. She never talked to them, just said "out!" That was it. It was so stupid and then she resigns.[1]

---

1. As a matter of fact, only Gordon was sent home.

J.H.: Because of that?

Bruce: That and the fact that some people hated her, though they had respect for her, I think. But that blew it completely sky high. Her good name ... like she could never have lived with them. She realized it would have been unbearable to live in. I'm glad she did what she thought was right, but to do it so hastily, it was very foolish.

J.H.: For the fun of it, let's imagine in your scenario that she would not have said anything about it. The police get a phone call about the marijuana from somewhere. The police come for a raid with photographers from the *Toronto Star* and then you have a front-page article about Katimavik growing marijuana with the taxpayers' money and there's a big scandal all across the country.

Bruce: But, she could have caused an equally big scandal. What if it were ever to get out? Gordon would have got angry and phoned the *Toronto Star*. I think that is a much more plausible thing because he would have been angry enough. Actually he thought of it, but realized it was stupid, that would have been another bad story about Katimavik.

J.H.: Yes, but what story would be told? I'm just making the comparison. I'm not taking sides. I just want to know your reaction. Suppose someone had gone to the paper and said there's a story. "I was kicked out or he was kicked out because he planted some marijuana." How would Katimavik be blamed for that? I don't say that they were right. I just say that officially, from the outside point of view of the newspapers and public, planting marijuana is against the law, it is a crime right now, so he was caught doing that and the group leader kicked him out. So what is wrong with that? I don't say she was right, but as far as the public is concerned they think she acted properly, that it was the thing to do.

Bruce: We had all thought of that. It could have been found out by someone else besides her. One of the guys outside might have recognized it and flipped out. She saw him and told him to get them out. She could have left it at that, just asked to have them destroyed.

J.H.: Were they destroyed?

Bruce: Yes, right away. He took them outside and they were destroyed. She could have left it at that and it would not have happened again. But no, she had to take it the whole way.

J.H.: It was a tragedy for the two of them and for all of you. What were the results after that? Have you heard from Gordon since?

Bruce: I believe he phoned Saturday and there was just a little conversation, nothing much.

J.H.: When you see Gordon, say hello to him for me and tell him I was sorry to hear about that.

Bruce: Yes, a very sorry mess ... It was rather hard to accept. It did seem like he died. He's not there anymore and I didn't understand. It's incomprehensible. For me friends are first.

J.H.: What is your final word about Katimavik?

Bruce: I don't know what to say. I'll be back, hopefully. I think I would like to give a hand at being group leader. Maybe I'm not the best, I'm not a workhorse, but I'm not lazy either. I would like to try it because I see some of the things some group leaders have done wrong, some did right, and I can see where I can improve upon them. It all depends upon the group you get, too. But I will come back.

J.H.: In spite of this terrible thing that happened, you seemed to be very happy?

Bruce: Oh, yes, I've always been like that because I have humour, a certain view of life that everything isn't quite so bad. People are the silliest things on earth. They have to be. Animals go by instinct, so they don't do very much wrong. People say and do things wrong all the time, including myself. I think it's quite humorous. Sometimes it gets me down, but most of the time I can look at things satirically. I joke around about all this. It was a little heavy for me when it was happening, but it's not the end of the world by far. There is a lot more ... for me it was an experience I could learn from but I hope I never see it again.

5 *Christine Blais,* Age 17, Sainte-Foy, Quebec

I was born in Quebec City and I've always lived there. Except for a year in Montreal when I was very young. I don't remember it. Before Katimavik I'd never been outside Quebec. The first time was when we went to Saskatchewan.

J.H.: What did you want to do with your life?

Christine: I'd finished a year of CEGEP and then I was going to go to university, in a field that interested me. I intended to go into history.

J.H.: You wanted to teach eventually?

Christine: No, I just found it interesting in itself. Teaching didn't attract me, but I knew that after a course in history that would be all I could do. So I thought, well, we'll see afterward.

J.H.: And how did Katimavik come about?

Christine: One of my friends was in Canada World Youth. I remember when she did it. I was too young to enrol. I'd seen the ad for Katimavik in the paper and I thought it sounded quite similar. It was perfect for me because I didn't know Canada at all. I sent in an application, and then I got an answer saying I should come for an interview. A week after the interview I was accepted. That's how it happened. I was happy and very very surprised too.

J.H.: What attracted you in particular? Living in a group? Physical work outdoors?

Christine: Yes, living in a group ... And we'd be going to places where people really needed us. You know, working hard but knowing it was useful. That's the way I imagined Canada World Youth too. That was what I said at Katimavik and that's what attracted me. But I didn't find it exactly ...

J.H.: Then one fine day there you were at the training camp in Duchesnay ...

Christine: Yes! Twenty miles from home!

J.H.: Yes, twenty miles from Quebec wasn't a great change of scene! But it must have been rather strange to suddenly find yourself with a hundred young people, more or less your age, from every corner of the country, and two-thirds of them Anglophones.

Christine: I hadn't had any contact with English people. When I saw an Anglophone I'd try to get by with "yes" and "no" ...

J.H.: You didn't know English?

Christine: No, no, no!

J.H.: And you didn't know any Anglophones?

Christine: No, I didn't.

J.H.: So you met almost a hundred people all at once? What sort of impression did that make on a quiet little Québécoise?

Christine: I felt a little lost. It's all right now, but for a long time I didn't really understand what was happening to me.

J.H.: It was a sort of shock?

Christine: Yes. But it's all right now.

Larouche, Quebec

J.H.: Then you were in a more manageably-sized group, at Larouche in Lac St. Jean. You didn't know the Lac St. Jean area?

Christine: No. I'm glad I started the program in Quebec. At first I told myself that Lac St. Jean isn't the other end of the world, but later I realized that it was good for me to proceed one step at a time. I stayed in Quebec, with

Anglophones, and then afterward when we went to Saskatchewan I felt comfortable.

J.H.: What was your impression of the famous house in Larouche?

Christine: It was fine for me. It was a little difficult because there were thirty of us all piled in there, but I got something out of it. There were lots of people so you didn't have a chance to think just of yourself and your problems. Things were always happening there and we were all good friends.

J.H.: A beehive!

Christine: Yes, I liked the beehive. I think I even liked it better when there were thirty of us than when we were just ten.

J.H.: It's strange, because most of the participants seemed to prefer the small groups that were on a more human scale.

Christine: That wasn't necessarily the case for me. At first I complained a little like everybody else but after I'd changed projects I realized that the house in Larouche wasn't all that bad.

J.H.: What work were you doing?

Christine: At Larouche I worked mostly on the teepees. The greenhouse. It's funny, but it seemed as if I didn't have the nerve to work on construction. I was timid.

J.H.: But work on the teepees was construction too?

Christine: Yes, but I mostly sewed the canvas. I studied the plans and helped put them up ... and then I slept in one to try it out! Then what did I do? ... It's so long ago now. Ah, yes! I helped clean up the municipal dump. That took us four days, with around fifteen participants, always the same group. Once a man came with his tractor to help us and we all cleaned up the road. I think we managed to sensitize the village as far as that was concerned. Before it was cleaned, it was really terrible!

J.H.: Did you have any contacts with the people in the community itself?

Christine: Yes, I spent three weeks on the Simards' farm. It was fantastic. I was with Lap, who didn't know a word of

French ... But it was a good experience for me, and for the Simards too. It was really painful when we had to leave ... they'd become so attached to us, you can't imagine ... I got along with them so well I was like their daughter. They don't have any children so it was really hard on them when we left. And they liked Lap — oh, they liked him so much, it was terrible!

J.H.: You have to admit, he has the gift of making himself liked.

Christine: Mr. Simard worked with Lap all the time. He didn't speak a word of English and Lap didn't speak a word of French at the time. But there was another kind of communication.

J.H.: What did you learn from the Simards?

Christine: I took part in the way they lived, I saw what they did and I liked it. For me it was a matter of establishing a relationship with a kind of people I didn't usually meet. And now I've got some idea of the way people live in the country.

J.H.: Do you correspond with them?

Christine: Yes. I still write and I'm going to see them this summer. I gave Mme Simard a plant and apparently it's really grown, it's unbelievable. They wrote Lap a while ago and said hello to me and they think of me when they look at the plant.

J.H.: Did you have any other contacts in the community?

Christine: It wasn't as hard for me as it was for the Anglophones. I talked with everybody at the parties. With Mme Champigny, who lived not far from us; I used to go and talk with her often. And I liked the village, even though we lived four miles away. I felt at home when I went there. Toward the end of the project we were starting to know the people better, but then it was time to go. Yes, I think that's the community where I had the most contacts. With the young people too. Sometimes we'd go to the bar on Friday nights with them. They liked us a lot.

J.H.: Had your English already started to improve then?

Christine: I understood a little more but I didn't speak very much, because we'd decided to speak French during the first project, because the Anglophones were in Quebec and they should take advantage of it to learn French. So we hardly spoke English at all.

Wilcox, Saskatchewan

J.H.: After three months in Larouche you woke up to that terrible cold in Wilcox ...

Christine: Yes, there was even a time when I thought of leaving! I felt absolutely disoriented. When the people from Wilcox came to our place and everybody was chatting I'd think, "What are they saying? What are they saying?"

J.H.: You understood practically nothing?

Christine: Nothing. The students at the college gave a party when we arrived: I was lost! I started learning when I worked at the day-care centre. Yes, that helped, because when I was there I didn't have a choice, I had to talk to them.

J.H.: What did your work consist of?

Christine: There were around three participants for every twelve children, and we planned the children's activities.

J.H.: For example?

Christine: All kinds of games, songs, stories, we showed animated films, we took them skating.

J.H.: Your English was still pretty hesitant, I imagine?

Christine: It still is. What happens in the group is that it's very easy for me to speak French because just about everybody's bilingual. But when I left the house in Wilcox I had to speak English. At one point I even changed the brand of cigarettes I smoked, because when I went to the store and asked for Du Maurier they'd say "What? What?" so I switched to Rothmans!

J.H.: What other contacts did you have outside the day-care centre?

Christine: I worked in the college cafeteria. We helped the cook. It was work, but we also had contacts with the students and with the cafeteria staff. I really liked that, because we were working with the students too. And I met people with different attitudes than mine.

J.H.: What did you think of the people in Saskatchewan?

Christine: They were fine, the ones I talked with or had contacts with. In fact I'd expected them to hold back a little, because I was a Francophone, from Quebec. Separatism, all that ... But it was just the opposite ... They didn't even take it into account.

J.H.: Were they hospitable people?

Christine: Yes, but you had to make the first move; they wouldn't come and see you if you didn't go and see them. I really liked the Prairies because of the landscape. You feel very different from the way you do where I come from, when you look around you ... I wish I'd been there in the summer, with the wheatfields!

J.H.: Were your contacts with the Anglophones made harder by the fact that you didn't become bilingual until the middle or even the last part of the program?

Christine: Yes, they were. It's very important for me to have a friend I can talk with and that was something I missed in Katimavik; there was Jacqueline, the group leader, who I'd have liked to get to know better, but she left. There was Lise, but we weren't in the same group. I felt closer to Lise than to the other girls, who were Anglophones. I don't know why, it just happened that way ... It's not that there were any misunderstandings or anything like that. It was always very friendly, but no more than that. I never really communicated with any of the Anglophone girls in the group.

J.H.: But in Wilcox you were in smaller groups. Didn't that give you a chance to communicate more easily with the people in your group?

Christine: Oh, for sure, but maybe it was easier with the Anglophone boys than the girls. I don't know why... There's Bruce, who I didn't know, and I adore him, he's fantastic. Unbelievable! And Mark Forrest, I adore him too ... It isn't hard to communicate with him. And there's Daniel Dupuis and Serge — I get along really well with them too.

Grand River, Ontario

J.H.: And now you're in Ontario. What do you think of the people here?

Christine: The people I've worked with are very nice to me. I'm really happy. I've had a lot of contacts with the students because I gave French lessons, helping the teacher at the school.

J.H.: What sort of physical work did you do?

Christine: I worked a lot in the woods, cutting trees. After the first day I told myself I'd never come back because I'm not all that strong and a chainsaw's pretty heavy. I remember, I was working with Serge and I was really discouraged. I was crying, I had trouble holding it to cut a tree. But it's all right now. I'm used to it.

J.H.: How long did you do that?

Christine: Almost every day when the weather was nice. Of course I had days of kitchen duty too, like everybody else.

J.H.: Do you feel that you've changed a lot in the past ten months?

Christine: Of course, yes, a lot. But to tell you how ... The worst thing is that I've changed a lot positively, but also really a lot negatively. Because I remember what I was like when I arrived, I was always smiling, always positive. At Larouche everything was fine for me. I was happy; I mean there were more good times than bad, I thought everything was perfect. But at a certain point, I don't know why, I felt more nervous, less secure. At first, of course, everything's new and lovely, you find out how to get to know people, and then at a certain point, I don't know what happened.

J.H.: But you could have left ...

Christine: No, I didn't leave because even though I had bad moments I always pulled out of it.

J.H.: By yourself, or did someone help you?

Christine: Of course I had help. But I was able to take care of myself too. Besides, I was a little that way before. I've always wanted to get along by myself. I was still that way in Katimavik, but less.

J.H.: What do you think of the people in your group?

Christine: There are two children in our family. When I was with our group, at the good times, I'd think, "My Lord, this is something you've always dreamed about, having a lot of brothers and sisters around the table." That was something I missed a lot before. Terribly.

J.H.: Do you think it will last a long time?

Christine: Yes, I'm sure. For instance we all told each other: "If you're in my part of the country you'll have to come and see me!" We all exchanged addresses. You can see that the group is strong and that it's united when there are problems, like for instance what happened to Gordon. At times like that you see how attached you are to the people you're with. For example, when you see someone leave, when we saw Yvan leave ...

J.H.: Tell me about Yvan.

Christine: We were good friends. I spent quite a lot of time with him at Larouche. I don't know why he left. He thought he didn't belong. He decided to leave once before, then he changed his mind. I had the impression it was other people's feelings that made him change his mind. Everybody told him, "Come on, Yvan, stay!" After that he realized he should have left the first time, that he didn't belong. He was looking for something else, that's it. But he came back to see us and he wrote to us. We write to him. He's supposed to come back the last weekend. He said, "I miss you, it's terrible!" He called Lise once, around two weeks ago, and he told her: "I'm calling you because I'm thinking about all of you this week, it's terrible!"

J.H.: In a way he didn't really leave you.

Christine: Yes, I feel as though he's still here. And I feel as though it's going to be like that for everybody when we leave.

J.H.: Do you ever think about the day when you'll be leaving?

Christine: Oh, my Lord, I'd rather not! I just saw Gordon leave and everybody was ... Oh! I just can't imagine it, I don't dare to.

J.H.: What are you going to do afterward?

Christine: This summer I'm going to try to get a job, travel a little, but I'm staying in Quebec. Next year I've been accepted as a language monitor in Prince Edward Island.

J.H.: A little like Daniel, who's doing the same thing in Newfoundland?

Christine: Exactly like Daniel. We went for our interviews together in Saskatoon and we were both accepted.

J.H.: What attracts you to Prince Edward Island?

Christine: I've always dreamed of going to Prince Edward Island. The Maritimes, the ocean ... And it's very small.

J.H.: I can understand, I like Prince Edward Island very much. I spent two years there at St. Dunstan's College, when I was sixteen or seventeen. I have wonderful memories of it. But how did you get the idea of going to Prince Edward Island?

Christine: During the stay in Saskatchewan we met a girl from Regina who was doing that, the monitor program. She gave us the address of the regional co-ordinator. I went for an interview with some other participants and then I said: "It's Prince Edward Island." I had that in my mind. I expect it's a small university. I don't want to go to some big concrete thing, I couldn't take that. I wanted Prince Edward Island ...

J.H.: It isn't so cold in the winter ...

6 *Mark Forrest,* Age 21, Vancouver, British Columbia

I was born in Montreal and stayed there for about the first four years of my life. Then I moved to Toronto for one year and then moved to the north shore of Quebec, to Baie Comeau and stayed there one year. And then five years ago I was living in Waterloo, Ontario, and I moved to Vancouver and that is where I am living right now. I finished my high school and continued university there and I plan to stay there for quite a while. I enjoy living in Vancouver. I seem to have become a western person, if there is any such thing. I say that because coming back to the East, I have noticed the different attitudes in people. And I am a bit more casual about things than Easterners seem to be. And I am comfortable in a western environment.

J.H.: So, you had already a good view of the country before coming to Katimavik?

Mark: Yes, but the move to Vancouver did shake me up a bit, education wise. I lost a bit of the scholastic edge that I had. My marks began to flounder a bit just because of the change in school systems. And because of the difference in curricula, I had a lot of problems in finishing high school.

J.H.: Are you from a large family?

Mark: I have two younger sisters, one is thirteen and the other one is twenty.

J.H.: Before Katimavik, what were your plans for the future?

Mark: I was in university, I had finished my third year before I came to Katimavik.

J.H.: Studying what?

Mark: Studying linguistics. I had chosen linguistics as my major because my interest in languages was so great. And learning other languages is something I really like to do.

J.H.: Have you learned some French?

Mark: I have been learning French since public school and there was a moderate exposure to French in the house. That is what got my interest in language started. When I go back to university, my plans right now are to switch my major from Linguistics to French. And possibly pursue a teaching career at the primary level in French.

J.H.: How did you hear about Katimavik in the first place?

Mark: I saw the article in the *Weekend Magazine*. My parents pointed the article out to me and said this might be something I would be interested in. I looked at it again and said, "Yes, it is something I would like to do." The possibilities that it offered seemed quite inviting.

J.H.: You applied, you were accepted and one day you arrived in Duchesnay, Quebec. What was you first impression there?

Mark: My first impression in Duchesnay was a lot of optimism. The environment that Duchesnay presented to me was quite a desirable one. I said to myself, this should be a good learning environment. As the days went by, the planning of it was not there. There didn't seem to be any kind of structured learning experience. I felt that the stress should have been transferred to learning although in thinking back, there were probably some things I learned in Duchesnay I will be using in the future.

Larouche, Quebec

J.H.: Let's move to the first project, Larouche. The group was down to thirty young people, that was a little bit easier, but at the same time, these thirty people were stuck inside four walls. How was it?

Mark: Very easy. It could have been quite unbearable.

69

Surprisingly, I found no problems. I didn't have any qualms about living in a group house. The size, of course, of the house was a bit of a shock at the beginning. I tend to adapt to things very quickly and rather than react actively to any problems I tend to be a bit more passive about things. I am not one, I hadn't been one at least, to look for things and try to search out solutions. I will just look at the situation and deal with it.

J.H.: What kind of situations did you have to deal with in Larouche?

Mark: Everything from cooking for large groups to just planning work schedules. I don't know if it was acting under pressure but there was a pressure to get things done, to make sure that the group worked well, at least for me. I wasn't discouraged during Larouche. The work that I was doing, mainly working out in the woods, clearing the cross-country ski trails, was something that I wanted to do. One of my thoughts at the beginning had been to get in physical shape, I wanted to get a bit more aware of what I could do physically.

J.H.: Had you done anything like that before?

Mark: No, all my work before had been mainly in the restaurant field, mainly doing cooking, so when it came to cooking, I felt really comfortable because I like to cook very much and I even like to cook for large groups. As far as the group was concerned, there were stumbling blocks. I think we found that there were gaps in thought. People had different opinions on things. There has to be that period of adjustment, of just getting to know people. So, it was a hard time as a group.

J.H.: You know, they were very different people, people that you probably never could have talked to.

Mark: That's true. You choose friends that tend to be like yourself. You have to deal with them. That was good. You have a broader vision of the way Canadians think. It is quite revealing.

J.H.: What did it reveal to you for example?

Mark: That young people aren't as free thinking as people think they are. They're fairly much following the ideas of their parents, they're just in the process of forming their own opinions about things.

J.H.: Was there a language problem in the group?

Mark: In Larouche we made it a problem for some reason. There was this desire for both sides to be "placated." It didn't have to be that way. For the whole three months, there would certainly be an initial period of finding out where people's confidence was in regard to each language. There was too much time spent on finding who could understand what in what language. What should have been done was to deal with it on a personal level. We made it a group thing, a group controversy, it didn't have to be that at all.

J.H.: But did it turn out well finally, this confrontation or whatever it was?

Mark: The language problem, after all, is thunder and lightning; it seemed to just become more calm as we discovered each other as individuals. And as we were leaving Larouche, things were looking better. We saw that we were going to Wilcox. It was just going to a different place, living in a different lifestyle, the groups of ten.

J.H.: In Larouche, you lived with a family for some time.

Mark: La famille Simard. I had a bit of a problem dealing with them because I made some false assumptions. I thought they would be a bit more open than they were. I just assumed that they would be directing my activities. I got a bit of the feeling about a French family, certainly not everything but there was a bit of an insight. I can say I enjoyed my time there. Besides being a time away from the group, it was a time to get to use my French. There was a pressure of a very gentle nature. There was no stress of any sort. It was just you have to react to family life, the way that the situation dictates. So that was good. I felt more comfortable with my French at that time.

Wilcox, Saskatchewan

J.H.: And then, you went west. Was it your first contact with the Prairies?

Mark: I had travelled to the Prairies on holidays with my

71

parents before. Passing through, you just get the usual impression that people get. It's flat, that is about all you can think of. People still have that stereotypical opinion of the Prairies and there was an opportunity for me to straighten out my views, so I was looking forward to getting out there. And living in a smaller group.

J.H.: That was a big change.

Mark: It wouldn't have bothered me that much if we had continued living in a group of thirty because there would not have been any great transition involved. I just took it very naturally. I didn't have to make any great changes. I got a chance to get a bit more in touch with the community. We were living right in a community, a small one, one hundred and fifty people.

J.H.: What do you think of these people?

Mark: Prairie farmers, the town of Wilcox is made up of that mainly. The other people in Wilcox who aren't farmers are employees or teachers at Notre Dame College. The farmers there are quite well off. They work quite large sections of land and they reap the profits from that land and to a certain extent it shows. They are as down to earth as you could imagine. Friendly, they have definite opinions about things. I don't know if they are any more conservative with a small *c* than anyone else but their opinions are the way they are. I enjoyed the people in Wilcox very much.

J.H.: What did you do as far as work is concerned and what did you learn?

Mark: Well, I learned a bit of carpentry, something that I was never really good at before.

J.H.: Are you good now?

Mark: I am better now. I have some basic knowledge of how to put things together and a bit more confidence in a lot of things. I found that out. I had a chance to do a bit of construction in the renovation of the workshop. My main job there was painting the workshop. That wasn't the most exciting thing to do but I enjoyed it. I didn't grumble all the way through. I found that when you paint, you just don't have to paint the wall white. You can think about

72

how a room looks. We had this dark hallway that we were supposed to paint dark green. We did that, it made it look like an entrance to a wax museum or something. And we had to do something to brighten it up. So, I had to think of a way and with some help there, a solution was reached. We put bold stripes on the side of the hall, in white and yellow and along the ceiling on the other side. And the way the stripes were done, they were quite wide in diagonal, starting at the top of the ceiling and moving down the wall. So the combination of the brighter colours and the motion of the diagonal stripes lightens up the hallway enough to make it look a bit more bearable. Besides being a concrete solution to the problem, it was fun to do. Besides doing all the painting I did, I got back into doing some cooking for an even larger number of people in the college cafeteria and I enjoyed that very much.

J.H.: How many were they?

Mark: In the college, there are about 250 students. They eat a lot so you have to cook a lot and, the only negative aspect of that experience was that we weren't cooking the best food, nutrition wise, for them. It is hard to change people's opinion about what food is good for them and what food is bad. There was a bit of change, getting more fruits in their diet, more vegetables, a bit less of the standard hot dogs and french fries and things like that, a bit more home-made things. The change was small but there was a change.

J.H.: So you were living with a group of ten, that was quite a change?

Mark: Not as much as I would have thought. The only change was that there were less individual lifestyles to deal with. Instead of keeping in mind thirty people, you only had to deal with ten people. I didn't have any problems dealing with the group myself, although a lot of the people in the group, or some, felt that Wilcox wasn't really a valid work project.

J.H.: And it was not your opinion!

Mark: No, it was not my opinion. I was learning things and as long as I was learning things it was valid for me.

Some people's minds were wandering. Should we be doing work that people in that community could be doing themselves, was there a necessity for us to be there, given the apparent wealth of the citizens there. I didn't have that question. I still thought the experience profitable.

J.H.: So, you were happy in Wilcox?

Mark: I was, although there was a time in Wilcox when I had a small personal dilemma as far as my usefulness in a group context was concerned. I put a question to myself, "Is there any reason why another person in any part of Canada should be here besides myself?" I thought, "Is it really fair for me not to give someone else an opportunity to enjoy this experience?" People said I was sacrificing too much, they said, "Well, it is good for you, you can stay, there is no problem with that." There was still that question in my mind, there are lots of other people who could be profiting from this experience. I thought that maybe it was time for me to leave.

J.H.: But I don't understand that exactly, because if you had left, you would not have been replaced by another participant, you would not have given your place to someone else.

Mark: That didn't cross my mind at the time. I didn't think about that. I didn't know that possibility or that fact was present. I just went under the impression that somebody could profit from the experience after I left.

Grand River, Ontario

J.H.: So, after Wilcox, you moved to Ontario, very near your former home. Maybe you weren't very excited about that?

Mark: No. There was a definite discouragement there. I wasn't really looking forward to going back to that area.

J.H.: Did you think of quitting at that time?

Mark: No. I just was a bit discouraged. So there was an initial rebellion against the whole idea ...

J.H.: Of going to Ontario?

Mark: Of going to Ontario, given the fact that a good

number of people from our group are from Ontario. And we had even gone so far as to propose a change in rotation. We had the impression that this would be a project where outdoor work would be the focus. We thought that would be a good end, a strong end to the program. And getting involved with the environment, we thought one of the areas of concern with Katimavik would be focused upon in Cambridge. That encouraged me to continue for the last three months. As it turned out, we found that we were dealing with an organization which was certainly too big for us to change. They have a certain way of proceeding, they have their schedule and we found our place was just to fit into it. There didn't seem to be any room for experimentation.

J.H.: But did you learn something nevertheless?

Mark: I learned a little. I did have an opportunity to work with the chainsaw for a period of time and a major part of our work in Notre Dame was the maintenance of a wood lot. Due to the bad weather, we could not do a lot of that work, but that couldn't be avoided. So the Luther experience was not a profitable one for me, as far as doing the physical work I thought I was going to do. I did a bit of work with the community of Arthur, which was the nearest large community there. I did a bit of work in the high school.

J.H.: What kind of work?

Mark: Teaching French classes there. That was something I wanted to do, that was quite a good experience, given my desire to do some teaching. It gave me an idea of how I work with kids.

J.H.: Did you work well?

Mark: Fairly well. There was obviously a bit of nervousness at the beginning, but just giving the information made me feel good. If I know something, I like to tell a lot of people about it and that was enjoyable. I am in the process of documenting that now, getting it into the form of a report of some kind.

J.H.: As a whole, would you say that the project in Ontario was positive for you?

Mark: I have mixed feelings about that, having talked about it and seen the stumbling blocks that came before us. The problem is with the sponsors in this project, the lack of clarity of purpose.

J.H.: Maybe there was a lack of clarity on the part of the Katimavik people who dealt with them at the first place. Because, you know, we were starting. Now, we are at the end of the project, the end of Katimavik. Do you feel that you have changed a lot? So many people told me they have. What about you?

Mark: I don't know if I changed a lot, but I feel a lot more confident about myself. I know a bit, a lot more about where I stand in relation to other people. My opinions, although they might have changed, are a bit more firmly rooted than they were before. I can deal with people on is-sues with a bit more certainty. You can put it down to self-confidence. I have gained a few skills along the way, a lot of knowledge about all sorts of things.

J.H.: What about Canada? Do you feel that you learned something about your country?

Mark: I can't say because, given different opinions that different areas might have, I haven't been able, as yet, to correlate them and see how they changed my whole perspective of the country. Although my opinions of dif-ferent areas have changed.

J.H.: Not only through the project itself but through living with people coming from all across the country. Did it help you understand it better? Talking to people from New-foundland, from Quebec, from ...

Mark: Yes, now that I think of it, you get a very clear idea from the centre of what happens in a province, for example Newfoundland. I had really no perception of what hap-pens there, I had no opinion on the way the province works or anything like that, but having talked with Gordon and Joyce, you get a view, you get a kind of idea of what a Newfoundland person is like.

J.H.: Most of the participants I have interviewed told me that the group was like a family for them, that you were like brothers and sisters. Is that your view?

Mark: It is very much like a family in many ways, in that there are some restrictions, and a lot of freedom as well, definitely more freedom than restrictions.

J.H.: But the links that you formed with the other participants, do you think they will last?

Mark: I think a lot of them will last. I'll definitely be writing to a lot of them, just because they are close friends. I'll try to see as many as I can, as opportunities present themselves. I am now not one to miss opportunities. That's one thing you do learn in Katimavik, not to miss your opportunities. So, if I am travelling, I won't be missing people along the way. People will be coming out and seeing me.

J.H.: So, you are expecting a lot of visitors in the near future?

Mark: Quite a few. I will be seeing people during the summer.

J.H.: What are your plans for the day after Katimavik?

Mark: The day after Katimavik, I will be travelling and visiting in Deep River, and then I will be spending a bit of time in Ottawa, visiting some relatives. That will take a couple of weeks and then I'll be heading home and settling down. That's a priority, I want to apply some of the things that the Katimavik lifestyle has taught me. That has been the learning experience for me. I have decided what kind of life I want to live and I want to start living it as soon as possible. I will be going back to Vancouver, that's where I have chosen to live the way I want to live. I could do it anywhere else, but Vancouver is definitely my first choice. I don't want to go back to school immediately, just because I want to establish myself, establish a home for myself. I have been living with my parents all the way along before Katimavik and they want me to move along. I want to move along. There is no reason why I can't. I'll be doing that. As far as the kind of work I'll be doing, there is no orientation in a certain direction, although my past interest in broadcasting will make me look for a job in that field. Probably, I'll be looking for a job in a restaurant field as well, because I find it interesting and enjoy it there.

Katimavik in Year II. And if I am accepted, I'll do it because I have got the taste of the lifestyle and I want to keep living it.

J.H.: And after that, you plan to go back to university?

Mark: After a year of working, at whatever job I get, I'll be going back to university and completing my education. Beyond that, I don't know ...

J.H.: Teaching French some day?

Mark: I would like to do that, not just because French is our second official language, but because people don't realize how much the learning of a language can expand your mind. Language learning involves more different brain processes than other kinds of activities. And French is a good language, a good second language to learn.

7 *Serge Maddedu,*
Age 17,
Montreal, Quebec

I was born in Montreal, right downtown. As far as family goes, there's my mother and me. My father went away. They're separated. I was fairly young when it happened. Aside from that, my childhood was pretty weird, lots of things happened, because since my mother was all alone with me she had to work and leave me somewhere. So I moved around a lot. School? Same thing: it wasn't too fantastic either. I was good but I didn't like it.

J.H.: That's rare! Usually, when someone does well ...

Serge: I don't know. Lots of people don't understand that. I didn't work but when exam time came it went all right.

J.H.: That's a way of saying that you were pretty bright?

Serge: Maybe. Some people say so but when I looked at the exams I didn't think I was all that bright. I left school pretty young — I was fifteen. I was wondering what I was doing there. I told myself, "I've got a lot more to learn outside of school ..."

J.H.: Did your mother agree?

Serge: More or less. She told me, "You want to leave school? Get yourself a job." It shocked her a lot but she had to go along with it. So that was what I did: I worked.

J.H.: What did you do exactly?

Serge: Lots of different things. I worked in shipping, and in a hotel, for a little over a year.

J.H.: In a hotel?

Serge: I did just about everything. I was a busboy, a bellboy, a banquet waiter, a room service clerk. In hotels, you keep going up. And then Katimavik happened.

J.H.: How did you hear about Katimavik?

Serge: I was reading *Perspectives* and there were ads for Katimavik with about two or three lines of explanation. I don't even know why I read it, or why it interested me so much. Let's say it sounded like an adventure. So I said, "OK, that's just the thing for me, it'll take me out of my routine."

J.H.: If I remember correctly, it said in the ad that the Katimavik program would be very demanding, that there'd be a lot of physical labour ...

Serge: That was what sounded like an adventure to me. Go away, do all that and try to discover myself, learn new things. When you do a routine job every day there's nothing left to discover. It's as though you're stuck there.

J.H.: Have you done any travelling before Katimavik?

Serge: Oh yes! I'd gone camping. I'd travelled a little in Ontario, for the tobacco harvest one year, and a few times to Maine. Never any longer than that.

J.H.: You didn't know a lot about Canada ...

Serge: No idea! Except from geography books. It seemed nice, but nothing special. I had a very vague idea about Canada.

Larouche, Quebec

J.H.: So your first "adventure" at Katimavik was the training camp at Duchesnay, in the middle of the woods, with a hundred other young people from every part of the country, from every social class, half boys and half girls, one-third Francophones, two-thirds Anglophones ... When you got there what was your first impression?

Serge: I was lost! The first two or three days I was absolutely lost! I kept wondering what was going on around me. I was lost but still it was fun, because I was meeting all those people, all new people. Before Katimavik I had friends, I was used to them. But it was pretty well always the same friends. Then all of a sudden I'm with a whole pile of new people! Ah! You really had to ... I'd force myself to go and see somebody, talk to him. Meet one person or another ... I spoke a little English, I forced myself.

J.H.: You spoke a little English?

Serge: Yes. I had to learn it when I worked in the hotel. I had, let's say, a little base. I practised a little. It was fun. But I'd never had to share a bedroom with anybody and that was something I found a little hard. In fact that was really what I wasn't used to. I'd always had a room of my own. I was lost, but it was fun! After a while I started to get into it, the parties we had and all that. It was really great for getting into the place.

Larouche, Quebec

J.H.: So then one day you were broken up into groups of thirty participants. In fact there were three groups of ten, but at the first site, in Larouche, you lived in the same house. It was hard for you to share a room with two other people — what was it like in that house that was quite obviously too small for thirty?

Serge: The first day, I didn't realize it I was there ... And that whole pile of people ... There were so many people I couldn't believe it! I was sort of unconscious so I couldn't really see what was going on. After a while it got harder. But then we sorted things out. Some of us went to live with families. Everybody organized their own little corner in the two dormitories. I did mine. So it was all right.

J.H.: Aside from the lack of privacy, what was the hardest thing about living in a group? The fact that there were unilingual Anglophones and unilingual Francophones?

Serge: Yes, a little. Most of the Francophones already knew some English, which made it easier for them to communicate. But it didn't help the Anglophones, because they could come up to a Francophone and speak English to him. Even if the Francophone couldn't speak English all that well, he'd understand and he could make himself understood. So that slowed down their learning French a little. At a certain

81

point we realized not much French was being spoken in the house. And Larouche was supposed to be a French worksite! But some of the Anglophones finally woke up and they really started to push their learning French. Not everybody. It was too easy for them to speak English. It was too bad.

J.H.: At the time, yes; but now I'd say that most of the Anglophones get along pretty well in French.

Serge: Now, yes. It's very very rare to find one who can't get by in French. Most of them can make themselves understood and some of them even speak both languages very well. Same thing for the Francophones: they all learned English.

J.H.: While you were at Larouche what kind of work did you do?

Serge: I helped a little drawing up plans for the greenhouse. I did a lot of manual labour when we built the greenhouse and then there was the cross-country ski trail we laid out. That was really fun!

J.H.: A ski trail for the people in the village?

Serge: Yes, that's right. Between the village and our house. It was about five miles long. But we didn't finish the five miles, we didn't have time. We did about three miles.

J.H.: The group that came to Larouche after you must have finished it?

Serge: Yes, I think they did. Then there were the teepees we built. I helped set them up at the end. And we started laying out paths in the forest for the next group. We had a lot of work to do besides on the house, because when we got there it wasn't finished. We had to arrange storage space, re-organize the beds a little better, make the kitchen more convenient.

J.H.: You worked on a farm as well. How long?

Serge: Three weeks. On a dairy farm in Larouche. That was quite an experience!

J.H.: With what family?

Serge: The Lessards. A family with seven boys. A husband, a wife and seven boys. No girls. My Lord, that was quite a scene!

J.H.: In what way?

Serge: Every way. First of all, you had to get up at 6.00 a.m. to go and milk the cows. And let's say I wasn't very familiar with stables ... I was more used to the pollution in Montreal than the smell of stables! Starting the first morning we had to clean them out. By hand! They didn't have an electric cleaner so we had to do it by hand. I shovelled ... and I thought ... "I'm going to die here!" But I got used to it after a few days. The real scene was the family life of the Lessards.

J.H.: Tell me about it.

Serge: Well, seven boys and just one woman in the house, it made for a whole different way of looking at things. Angie and Claire, the two other participants who were with me, those poor girls were almost always doing the dishes and things like that. At the Lessards a guy doesn't wash dishes, a guy doesn't cook. When I helped Angie and Claire with the dishes everybody'd look at me, "What's going on? What's he doing?" Yvan had been at the Lessards before me and he used to cook often, he liked that. The whole family thought he was queer, things like that, just because he liked to cook. I learned a lot about them, about the way they looked at things, but I didn't always agree with them. The mother was nice. She didn't talk but she was very very nice, I don't know why. She had a gift, a power. She had to, to stay there. The father was funny. He was a good guy. The kids were always fighting! They didn't have time to think about a lot of other things.

J.H.: You mentioned Yvan just now. He's the only participant who left the group on his own. Were you friends?

Serge: Yes. Especially in Wilcox, more there than in Larouche. In Larouche we didn't get much chance to know each other as individuals. We got to know everybody superficially. But Yvan and I got to know each other and we had lots of fun together. He didn't keep things inside, no frustration, he didn't keep things bottled up. As soon as something was wrong he'd say so, everybody had to know about it, be aware of it. I thought he was funny because of that.

J.H.: How did it affect you when he left?

Serge: It really bothered me. He'd decided the first time at Larouche. He'd said, "I'm going." But the rest of us told him, "Come on Yvan, try and hang in there, that's what everybody else is doing, you can do it too." But he said, "No, no, no, I'm going." But then finally he said, "I'm going to stay, I can't leave, I can't go away from all of you ..." We got a little closer in Wilcox, a lot closer even. So when he left it was hard on a lot of people. Really hard.

J.H.: I'll tell you quite frankly, it was hard on me too, even though I didn't really know him well. He seemed to be a good participant.

Serge: Oh, yes! He was really great. He got along with everybody. He'd make jokes about "*les maudits Anglais*" but he didn't think like that, it was just for a laugh. Things like that ...

J.H.: Why did he leave?

Serge: First of all, he didn't really get along with his group leader. Second thing, the project didn't interest him. He wasn't crazy about the physical work. There were some things he liked, like the day-care centre and all that. He was interested in that kind of activity. But to go and work in the workshop every day, he didn't like that at all. He's a very emotional guy. I think that contributed to his leaving too.

J.H.: He left but he still has ties with the rest of you; he's even come back to see you.

Serge: Oh yes! He came here to see us once, he wrote to just about everybody. Last time he came to see us he told us he missed us. Not that he was sorry he'd quit the program. What he missed most was the participants. There were a few, like Lise, Christine, Jo-Anne, he got along very well with. A few of the guys too. So they really miss him a lot.

Wilcox, Saskatchewan

J.H.: Then after Larouche you went to live in Wilcox, Saskatchewan.

Serge: After two, three, four days on the train, something like that, we got to Wilcox. I'd heard that Saskatchewan was flat but in my own head I couldn't really imagine what that would be like. So we get off at the station, a little CN station in Saskatchewan. We get off, I get off the train, I look around me. I said, "I can't believe it! It's impossible! There isn't a tree for a hundred miles!" We could see everywhere, all around us. Next morning, I got up very early. You can see the sun rise over the prairies, as far as the eye can see ... It's unbelievable! I couldn't get over it! The sky's always blue, there's never any clouds.

J.H.: You found that a little disorienting?

Serge: At first. Then, very very beautiful. But it isn't a place I'd like to go and live forever. But it's lots of fun to see.

J.H.: What were the people you met in the community like?

Serge: They were a little hard to get close to, I don't know why. They've got a lot of prejudices against French-Canadians in Saskatchewan. If you talk to them about the French it doesn't go so well. But it isn't serious, some of them were all right, like the students at the University in Wilcox. They were very nice. If the people were hard to get close to it's because there was a college in the village, a college that puts 300 students into a little village with a population of 165. So for the village, the thirty young people in Katimavik were just some more students, that's all. They didn't really know who we were. After a while some of them started to understand what we were doing there. Some of the participants set up a day-care centre, others joined some of the clubs in the village, little things like that. That's how we established the most contacts. And then, finally, we had the curling tournament with the community. It was the first time in my life I'd ever curled. It was pretty funny.

J.H.: But even though you didn't know them too well, what kind of impression did the people in Saskatchewan make on you?

Serge: Very, very conservative. They may have some new

ideas but their traditions, the way they live, it's slower, a lot slower than in other places. I come from a big city, Montreal; things are happening there, always happening, it never stops. But in Wilcox it's quiet. What doesn't get done today will get done another day. And as far as new ideas are concerned, they're afraid of them. Some of them are very hospitable. But also, it's a small village. You go into practically any house, you hardly even have to knock at the door. You just give a tap and walk in, you say hello and right away they'll say, "Sit down. Do you want a coffee or something?" They're very hospitable.

J.H.: Did you work hard in Wilcox?

Serge: Yes, quite hard. There was lots of construction. There was an old Legion Hall they were turning into a workshop for the students. The college wanted to set up a carpentry class. Then they'd have everything they needed for the college right there. So we did a lot of construction, especially carpentry. It was pretty hard.

J.H.: Did you learn anything?

Serge: About carpentry, yes, a lot. I learned how to make door frames, things like that. We worked with a guy named Ed, the carpenter.

J.H.: Big Ed.

Serge: Yes. I'd even called him fat Ed. He was a really good carpenter and he liked to teach us. If you had a question about anything at all he'd take the time and show you properly. His moods would change, but he was basically a good guy. And we also worked on the café across the street. I did a lot there. The group from Katimavik that was there before us started the work. We had to put on the gyprock, make the cement, seal the joints. Daniel, Yves and I worked on it for most of a month, mixing cement every day, trying to make everything nice and even. It was hard. Not hard physically exactly, but it took a long time.

J.H.: Now you know how to seal a joint?

Serge: Yes, that's something I learned how to do properly. Mainly thanks to Ed. Ah! he's too much of a perfectionist for my taste! He'd come and look at our joints. "That isn't right, you're going to do another one." And I'd say, "Oh, no!" And he'd say: "Yes! it has to be done right." And I'd say, "No," and he'd say: "Yes!" Sometimes, in the beginning, we'd start over three or four times.

J.H.: It's a café that's used by the students now?

Serge: Yes. The Katimavik group that was there before us started it. We finished it and we were able to use it a little. It was very well finished, very nice. Just by chance there was a group of Quebec musicians going through Saskatchewan just then, so we invited them to put on a show. The first show in the brand new café! The students from the college came, and it was probably the first time in their lives they'd seen a group of Francophone musicians. And the musicians thought the place was fantastic. They'd never given a show in a small village before. They were very surprised to find ten Francophones there. They wondered what we were doing in Wilcox, so we explained to them about Katimavik.

Grand River, Ontario

J.H.: So after three months in Wilcox you moved to Grand River, to a more familiar setting.

Serge: Yes, a lot more. Beautiful countryside with big farms, beautiful land. Very, very beautiful.

J.H.: And there, as in Wilcox, you lived in small groups, each one with its own house, each house in a different community. Tell me what your weekly activity was like.

Serge: It was the first time we'd been really isolated in groups of ten in three distinct communities fairly far apart. On Monday morning, most of the time, when it was nice, we'd work on the reforestation project of the Grand River Conservation Authority, our sponsor. We planted trees, in rows. In fifteen years when the trees are bigger, some of them will be cut so the others can grow better. After we'd really learned how to handle the chainsaw and all that, we'd go into the woods and cut down trees. When it wasn't nice out we'd go to the workshop and build wooden "sidewalks" that were put along the path in the forest, for the tourists to walk on. The forest was very, very swampy. On Wednesday, there was Radio Waterloo, the University of Waterloo community radio station. Every participant had the chance to put together a program on the subject of his choice. I did one on the community services you could find in Waterloo. It isn't finished yet, but it will be before we leave. Other people did programs on music, like Quebec music for instance. They haven't got a lot of Quebec music in Ontario, not even in the record stores. It isn't very well known. We tried to do something about that, to see if it'd catch on. And then I started to make an Indian sauna. You know, when you cut down trees you leave them on the ground, let them rot. In five years they say it turns into earth; you can't sell that wood, it isn't big enough. You can't even use it for firewood. So we tried to find a use for it. We made an Indian sauna. It's nearly finished, it's coming along slowly.

J.H.: What's an Indian sauna?

Serge: It's a little log cabin with a stove inside, and stones on top of the stove, with bricks all around it. You cover it with stones and heat the stove very very hot. When the stones are hot, you pour water on them, the water evaporates and it becomes very hot. That's an Indian sauna.

J.H.: So now we're at Thursday ...

Serge: Oh, I don't know — it all depended on the weather. If it was really nice we'd cut trees. If it wasn't so nice we'd make sidewalks. When it was nice but we weren't cutting wood, we'd work on the sauna and then on Wednesday we'd always be at the radio station.

J.H.: There was also one day, wasn't there, when you were on kitchen duty?

Serge: Yes, we all took turns. In Luther every team of two would have its day for cooking, dishes, housework. Cooking didn't bother me, I like that ... but dishes and housework! It takes so long! Dishes for ten people ... When you're used to doing the dishes for two and then there you are doing it for ten or, like in Larouche, for thirty, it takes time to get used to that.

J.H.: Did you do any work in the community?

Serge: The group that was in Cambridge did a lot more than we did. In Luther we were too isolated from the community. But we gave French lessons at the public school. In Ontario not many of the French teachers in public school really speak French. It's a big problem. So we'd go to the school and help them teach French. I looked after the kids aged ten to twelve. I was quite a lot of fun. We showed them old Quebec folkdances. We'd try to teach them the dances in French. *"Un, deux, trois, quatre, tournez en rond!"* So they'd just look at you: "What does that mean? *"tournez en rond!"* So then you'd go in a circle and they'd understand and they'd do it too.

J.H.: Overall, what's your impression of people in Ontario?

Serge: Very very sharp. They've got a lot of prejudices, but it's just words. For instance, Russell, the guy we worked with most of the time, when he talks about Italians they're "wops," when he talks about the French they're "frogs," when he talks about the Polish they're "polacks." They're all like that, but it's just for show. Basically, when you talk with them they're really interested in you, to know where you're from and what it's like there.

J.H.: Did you learn anything in Luther?

Serge: Oh, yes, quite a lot. I learned a little about forestry, not all that much because when you'd ask a workman, "Why are you cutting down that tree?" he'd answer, "I don't know, my boss told me to cut a tree." You'd have to go and see the boss to find out why it was that tree, but in the end you'd know. I learned about some other things, like trapping, I learned quite a lot about that. A little about fishing.

J.H.: What will you do afterward?

Serge: That's the big question. I've never really planned my life. I've thought about maybe going back to school, enrol in adult education courses. I don't know yet, but it's possible. I'd like to finish CEGEP. Oh yes, there's something I forgot to mention: in Wilcox, we took photography lessons. I really got into that because of the guy who gave the lessons! I'd like to do that if I had the chance. But first I'd have to finish CEGEP so I could go on in photography.

J.H.: Did you learn things from the other participants?

Serge: Yes, a lot. Especially about different ways of looking at things, how they see things here, how they see them somewhere else. I learned a lot about the different regions of the country. For instance Joyce, who's in our group, she talks about Newfoundland all day long. She's always saying it's the most beautiful part of Canada, that it's the most beautiful place on earth. She talks a lot about it. Anyway, I'd like to go and visit Newfoundland, especially because we didn't have a project there.

J.H.: You might go there some day?

Serge: Oh yes, probably.

J.H.: There'll be people there expecting you ...

Serge: The participants who live there, yes. This summer, for instance, I think I'm going to travel till I go back to school. I'm going to the west coast. I haven't had a chance to go there and I know two or three participants in Vancouver who'll put me up for nothing. That helps a lot. It costs a lot less. And it's fun to go and see them. If I went next summer, not this summer but next year, a year later, see what had happened to them in a year ... A lot of things can change ... Lap, Robert ... I'll be seeing Lap in Montreal because he's going there to study.

J.H.: You all seem very close.

Serge: It depends. When nothing special happens you say: "They're people ... " But when something happens or there's a party or something rotten happens to somebody, then you realize you all get along really well, better than at the beginning. When people are sometimes a little sad you see the whole group is sad, sharing their sadness. It's really funny the way you get attached after all those months you've spent together. For instance what happened to Gordon a while ago ... Everybody came together, tried to help him. It didn't work but that doesn't matter, we tried. That's when I saw how the group could stick together.

J.H.: Do you think those friendships will last a long time?

Serge: No idea. I don't know. Well, I'm very close with one person in particular. We'll certainly see each other. And there's lots of others I'd like to see again. But I won't push those friendships any farther than I should. I met the people in the program and once the program's finished I think I have to be on my way, do other things, meet other people.

J.H.: Do you feel as though you've changed a lot?

Serge: Yes, tremendously. I know myself a lot better than I did at the start. I discovered sides of myself I'd never suspected before. Learning with people, learning how to live with people, to share with people. That's something I'd never done before. At first it was hard, I had to make a lot of concessions. If I hadn't made those concessions I wouldn't be here, that's for sure. Over all, I've learned a lot. Especially about myself and about the others too. Katimavik helped me find myself. Before, I'd go from one job to another, I was going around in circles ... The same park, the same restaurant, the same bar, always the same place. But thanks to Katimavik I've learned a lot. Just now I've got about fifty ideas in my head. I don't know which one I'll choose. But I know it's a good start.

J.H.: You're full of plans?

Serge: Oh yes, really full! For the moment I only have to pick one. I've got a few plans in mind for later. For instance, I was never interested in photography before. But then along came the photography lessons in Wilcox. And then Daniel, in my group, takes pictures. I took some with him and I did a lot during the course. Now I'm really very interested in it. But sometimes you feel homesick. You say, "Ah, I'd really like to be back home!" Once I even thought about going. But I thought about it again and I told myself, "I'm going home ... Okay, the first days it'll be fine, lots of fun, I'll see everybody again, but it'll be the same old story." I said: "Oh no, it's too much fun here, I'm staying!" I think pretty well everybody's thought about going at some point. But you weigh the pros and cons and you decide there's more on the pro side ... And you stay! I have to admit, we helped each other. We'd say, "Come on, think about it, what'll you do if you go away? You'll miss us!" And the guy would say, "Yes, that's true ... "

8 *Carol Graham,*
Age 18,
Scarborough, Ontario

I was born in North York, a borough of Toronto. I have
one brother and one sister. We moved to Scarborough
when I was about two or three and I've lived there since
then, so I went to school in Scarborough.

J.H.: Did you like it?

Carol: Oh, yes. I finished grade 13.

J.H.: What were your plans then? Before Katimavik?

Carol: To go to university and study forestry. So I am going to do that now anyway. I just took a year off.

J.H.: You always had that in mind? Why forestry?

Carol: Because I always wanted to live up north and work
outside.

J.H.: What did you know then about Canada? Have you
travelled?

Carol: A bit, yes, East. When I was really young, we would
go to Nova Scotia, New Brunswick, and to Quebec City,
Montreal. Sometimes with my family, sometimes with my
friends. I really enjoyed that, especially Quebec City. I
liked travelling.

J.H.: How did you happen to learn about Katimavik?

Carol: It was from the *Canadian Magazine.*

J.H.: What struck you in the ad?

Carol: You could learn all about technology, you could
learn about the Third World. There was just a lot in it that
I wanted to learn.

92

J.H.: What do you mean when you say that the Third World interests you?

Carol: It's not that it really interests me. It really bugs me that people are starving and that we're partly responsible. I think it's a subject worth studying to see what our response can be.

J.H.: You applied and finally they said yes, and you packed your things and arrived in Duchesnay.

Carol: Yes. When I first got there it was half French and half English so it was a real challenge to speak the two languages.

J.H.: Did you speak any French?

Carol: Yes. I took an immersion course just before Katimavik. It was only five weeks, but I could manage a bit. Picked up a lot in training camp. Learned a lot of French there.

Larouche, Quebec

J.H.: You had your first project in Larouche. What kind of impression did you have when you got into that house? It couldn't have been easy, was it?

Carol: In a lot of ways, no. It was a real challenge to live there with thirty people. We tried to make up rules but they didn't work out a lot of times because they wouldn't obey after a while. We had quite a few problems. For the first two weeks there was no real work, which is a problem because everyone was walking around or writing letters. I wanted to do something, I didn't want to sit and write letters. After that we came up with a project. Daniel was the one who got the plans for the greenhouse.

J.H.: Everybody seems to be very proud of the greenhouse.

Carol: There was a group of us who sort of worked on it and the others who didn't now wish they had because we learned so much, like how to lay a foundation, how to finish off things, the outside of the greenhouse. It was a real learning experience, especially if you have never been on construction before, as it was in my case.

J.H.: Do you think you could build one on your own?

Carol: I don't know, but I'd like to give it a try.

J.H.: Did you live on a farm while you were in Larouche?

Carol: Yes, the Tremblay farm.

J.H.: Tell me about it.

Carol: That was probably the only thing that kept me sane after seeing the house. I went out the first three weeks. There were four of us out there, four English, who did farming. It was a lot of fun because we got a chance to talk to the Tremblays. They were a big family, with ten kids, mostly older than us. They were very quiet a lot of the time. They were really friendly, but they never had so many visitors before. We learned a lot about farming when we were out there, dairy farming.

J.H.: What would you say you learned during the three months in Larouche besides building a greenhouse and farming?

Carol: Well, in terms of personal relations around the house, we learned not to worry about everybody else. They are going to do what they want to do and it's they who are going to get the benefit or not. It was really discouraging getting up in the morning working on the greenhouse, and going to bed late at night because people were making noises. But I had to get up anyway because I was getting a lot from working on the greenhouse. If other people weren't working on the greenhouse it was their own fault that they were not getting anything out of it. It was a great opportunity. If you want something from Katimavik you must go out and get it for yourself. If you want to learn about the Third World, for example. We did a bit, we had one speaker I think, but that was all we did and if we really wanted to do something, it would have been nice to have to do it. I learned that.

J.H.: Do you think Katimavik should have provided you with more information and more resources on the Third World?

Carol: I don't know. Maybe just to get us started, they could have put out something and said, here are the possibilities, now go do it yourself.

J.H.: Yes, but sometimes people wait and wait and wait

and finally they start doing things after having wasted many months.

Carol: Yes, that's true, but in terms of what people learn by that experience, maybe they learn more than they would have if they'd had things given to them.

Wilcox, Saskatchewan

J.H.: After three months in Larouche, the whole group goes to Wilcox. Here you were divided into smaller groups. What about this new life in the group of ten?

Carol: It was a lot better than thirty because you got to know everybody a lot better. You could speak to each other a lot more openly.

J.H.: Most of the people told me that but I was amazed to see that some participants thought that it was better with a big group. They felt lonesome.

Carol: I sure wasn't lonesome, no, because you could see the other people if you really wanted to. For meals you didn't have to line up anymore, it was on the table. It was nicer to eat with just nine other people rather than twenty-nine.

J.H.: Did you get along well with the group?

Carol: Yes, at the beginning we all had a lot of problems getting adjusted, but in the last month at Wilcox and in the time spent here, it has been pretty good.

J.H.: What did you do in Wilcox?

Carol: We worked on the curling rink. They were putting a roof on it and I was interested mainly because we were working with the people of Wilcox, with a lot of the farmers from the area. We got to meet a lot of Saskatchewan people.

J.H.: Did you curl?

Carol: Yes. I don't know if I'd do it again but it was an experience, that's for sure.

J.H.: So, besides working on that, what did you do?

Carol: Worked in the Legion Hall workshop.

J.H.: Did you learn something there?

Carol: A bit, yes, not as much as I could have, but enough; mainly about using power tools. There was a lot of equipment around so that it was possible to learn from that. I also worked in the college cafeteria for a week or two. That was okay. It was an experience watching the other students eat, preparing meals.

J.H.: How did you like the people in Saskatchewan?

Carol: The ones I met, I really liked. There is a difference in Wilcox between the townspeople and the students. The students were really separate and the townspeople were really, really, nice. Compared to Quebec, they're really reserved, but it was really interesting learning about their way of life and what they were doing there.

J.H.: Do you like their way of life?

Carol: It wasn't too bad, you know. They were mostly farmers, which is a way of life I really like. But the type of farming they were doing, I don't know — they had great big huge farms, 5000 acres, lots of machinery.

J.H.: What about the physical aspect of Saskatchewan?

Carol: At the beginning it was really amazing to go out at night and see Regina, thirty miles away. After a while we got used to it. It was so flat, no trees, no anything.

J.H.: After these three months you had certainly a new idea about what the West was all about?

Carol: Yes, I suppose I did. I really knew what it was all about. There were new things I learned.

Grand River, Ontario

J.H.: Then you moved to Ontario, near your own home. Did that bother you? Would you have preferred to go to B.C.?

Carol: Not really, because as it worked out I'll be at home after Katimavik for about a week and then I'll be leaving again.

J.H.: About the project in Grand River, where were you exactly?

Carol: Luther. We had a really nice house, very comfortable, lots of room, three bedrooms, nicely fixed up. What we were doing there was, like, we were cutting down trees

96

for the whole two and half months, with chainsaws. After a while it was not all that thrilling.

J.H.: So now you know how to cut trees with a chainsaw?

Carol: Definitely.

J.H.: Which I don't. Isn't that thing heavy for a young girl?

Carol: Not really, they weigh about twenty pounds. After you've worked with it for your first eight-hour day, it doesn't seem heavy the next day. You get used to it. We really worked hard on it for about a month and a half and then we started doing bits for the last month and a half.

J.H.: Did you go to the Waterloo Radio Station?

Carol: Yes, a couple of programs came out of our house. I did one on multi-nationals.

J.H.: Did you learn something about broadcasting?

Carol: If you had been really interested in broadcasting it would have been a great place to learn, but I wasn't really too interested. I learned quite a bit because I had to do my own program.

J.H.: On the whole what did you learn during your stay? Can you summarize your third project?

Carol: I went to work on a farm and learned a lot about dairy farming, which was in Ontario. The possibilities of having a farm, and stuff like that. I learned a lot about group life here because group life really improved a lot. We did a lot of things together as a group and learned a lot about each other.

J.H.: Would you describe your group to me?

Carol: There's Christine, she's quiet, stays in the background, stays calm a lot.

J.H.: Doesn't make trouble?

Carol: That's right. There's Serge who doesn't stay in the background, he does what he want and is very open about the way he lives. There's Joyce who is from Newfoundland, she was my roommate for most of the time, so we got along really well and had a lot of good times. Daniel is a little more serious. Debbie is very involved in nutrition and alternate technology and different styles of living. Bruce was really funny and a lot of fun to have around the house.

He's changed a lot since the beginning, since Larouche. He had a lot of problems there and he was always by himself. Now he's really come out and it's a joy to have him. There's Mark who is sort of quiet and writes a lot, serious.

J.H.: So that's the group and you all survived together?

Carol: We had a lot of problems earlier on, but it's okay now.

J.H.: How did you feel about each other?

Carol: Sometimes like brother and sister. Lately we kid each other and joke around a lot. I suppose we'll see each other after Katimavik. If we're in one another's city, we'll call, and some of them will be travelling together right after Katimavik for a couple of weeks.

J.H.: You mentioned that Bruce changed a lot. Did you change at all?

Carol: Well, I'm not all that sure yet. I'm not sure whether it was good or bad but for the most part it would have to be good, I hope. I learned a lot about going out and getting what you want, which I wouldn't have been able to do before. I learned a lot of skills that way. I have, maybe a different view of people, probably I'm a little bit more accepting of other people. I'm more relaxed and able to take things as they come, because you have to do that around here or go crazy. I am more able to express myself with another person if I have a problem, go up to a person and say I have a problem.

J.H.: What do you plan to do right after Katimavik?

Carol: Go to Europe for ten weeks. We'll be landing in London and then going around the Continent, just visiting. Travel very lightly.

J.H.: And after these ten weeks in Europe?

Carol: I'll go to university and study forestry.

J.H.: Going into forestry with a greater motivation than before?

Carol: Well, I suppose I've had a little more certainty about it in the year that I have been thinking about it, so I am pretty sure that it's what I want to do. This last project has been a help, because we have been working as conservationists and I really enjoyed that. I like the type of things that they do, so in forestry it will be a help too.

J.H.: Do you think Katimavik was positive for you?

Carol: Yes, but it's been rough a lot of times, mainly group problems and group living, but I suppose overall it's been okay. It wasn't such a bad experience.

J.H.: But as a whole you were rather happy about your experience?

Carol: I'm not too sure whether I am happy with it or not.

J.H.: Well, you stayed until now. If it had been bad you would have left?

Carol: I considered leaving, for sure.

J.H.: Everybody did, I guess. Everybody told me they considered leaving at one point or another.

Carol: But the reasons for staying might not have been that good. The only reason I stayed in Larouche was because I was on a farm. After that it was sort of late in October and we had the greenhouse to do or something. If it hadn't been for the farm, I would have gone. And besides that, wherever I was, like in Saskatchewan, I met a lot of people from the town, so I got an opportunity to go out and visit with them, I suppose that's part of Katimavik, meeting people.

9 *Daniel Dupuis,* Age 20, Drummondville, Quebec

I think Daniel Dupuis, is a fairly calm guy who has some long-range objectives and who tries to follow a certain logic in his life, to know as many people as he can. Maybe not all that many, but as well as possible. As deeply as possible. What counts for me isn't so much the length of the contacts, but most of all how deep they are.

J.H.: Where were you born?

Daniel: In Drummondville, where I went to school.

J.H.: A big family?

Daniel: Seven children — six boys, one girl.

J.H.: So group life wasn't new to you?

Daniel: No. Especially when I was younger, five of us boys shared the same bedroom. We learned how to live in not much space.

J.H.: It wasn't so much a shock as for Serge, for instance, who's always had his own room. What kind of background do you come from? What does your father do, for example?

Daniel: My father runs a decoration centre. It started out very small, then it became, let's say, fairly big.

J.H.: Did he build it up himself?

Daniel: Yes. He built it but all the children were involved in one way or another. We often worked on weekends. I think that was very useful, in the sense that we learned when we were still very young how to work with our hands. And it was also important for us all to contribute to supporting the family.

J.H.: You weren't spoiled children who just took life as it came ...

Daniel: We were never rich, we lived simply. And the relations between all the members of the family were good, because everybody had to work.

J.H.: In a big family like yours, you must have had a happy childhood.

Daniel: Yes. I don't think the bad times lasted long because there was always someone to pull you out of it. That's very important.

J.H.: So you went to school in Drummondville?

Daniel: Yes, to high school and then CEGEP. I stopped for a year to work. During the summer I travelled to the west coast, then I finished my second year of CEGEP. When I came back from the west coast I thought of going to Europe the year after. I'd saved all my money during the year I worked in preparation for that trip. It was very important for me to see other people, to see what happened in a different world.

J.H.: Did you go to Europe?

Daniel: Yes. To France, Spain; mostly in the poorer countries, Spain and Portugal, where I spent most of my time, because the people were so warm.

J.H.: Did you know a fair bit about Canada?

Daniel: I don't know the east coast at all. I know the west coast, the Rockies, British Columbia. I know Quebec very well too, because when I was in high school I worked for a junior hockey team, as a statistician, which took me around Quebec: Chicoutimi, Hull, Sherbrooke.

J.H.: What made you decide to come to Katimavik?

Daniel: When I came back from my trip I said to myself, "All right, I've travelled, I've met people, but what have I done with those people?" Katimavik offered me something more than travelling; it offered the possibility of meeting new people, but most of all to do something constructive with them. I could have new experiences, with new people.

J.H.: What was it in the publicity for Katimavik that you saw that particularly attracted you?

Daniel: It spoke about things most people really don't know a lot about: like solar energy, the oil problem and all that. Questions on which we should spend more and more time because we have to save energy for the future. Our future and other people's as well. Katimavik offered the chance to live in groups, in small groups of ten or thirty, which makes it easier to get to know people. Twenty-four hours a day, finding activities in common, being as productive as possible, using all your available time, trying to bring something to one another. It wasn't clearly spelled out in the ads, but I had a sense that this new organization was really something: it seemed dynamic, and I was interested in contributing to it.

J.H.: So one fine morning there you were in the middle of the woods, in Duchesnay, with a hundred other young people from every corner of Canada!

Daniel: I think my first impression was, "I'm going to have a lot of work to do if I want to get to know all these people! I'd better start right away." You had to start right away, to start building something together. From the very first day I was very, very positive. I always tried to find the positive side of situations, which could improve the balance of things.

J.H.: Did you have the impression that you'd be an ideal participant for Katimavik?

Daniel: I don't think I'm the ideal participant! I just try to do my share. I don't think the ideal participant exists. There are some people who adapt better than others to certain situations. Most likely because of my earlier experiences I was fairly well prepared to meet an assortment of people, to deal with the problems of group life.

Larouche, Quebec

J.H.: You weren't prepared, for example, to find yourself in Larouche, in a house with thirty people all piled in on top of each other?

Daniel: Perhaps not. I'd never experienced anything like it, but perhaps I was mentally prepared; I'd agreed in advance to live through difficult situations. Basically my first idea about Katimavik, what I wanted, was for it to be really hard. That I be forced to measure up to difficult situations, force myself to face them. Yes, the house in Larouche was small, but that had advantages; it was easy to find someone to talk to, it was easy to start something spontaneously, to have fun together. Those are the good points. Larouche was an experience and you had to try to live through it ...

J.H.: To survive ...

Daniel: To survive with everybody's habits.

J.H.: In the beginning when there weren't many Anglophones who spoke French and there were still some Francophones who didn't speak English, there must have been a serious problem in communication.

Daniel: Yes. It was difficult, especially because the project was supposed to encourage bilingualism. It was even harder for the Francophones. When you're always in the minority you always have to fight.

J.H.: You must have enjoyed the challenge.

Daniel: Yes. I wasn't inclined to withdraw into myself. I knew that respecting the Anglophones was a first step on the path that would lead them to respect us as well. If you don't respect others you can't expect them to respect you. I think language is something that touches human beings deeply. It's something important and you must look after it. You must learn the other person's means of communication in order to try to know that person better. There are always other ways, visual or other, that you can use, but language is one of the best ways to make yourself understood.

J.H.: You were quite involved in the work at Larouche?

Daniel: In Larouche it was difficult at first, because we had no projects.

J.H.: When you're a pioneer . . .

Daniel: We had to invent a project, like the greenhouse. That was an experience I enjoyed. Because it was a sizeable challenge. In the absence of any other work project, the greenhouse became a project that could use a good many people and that met the objectives of the program.

J.H.: In what way?

Daniel: Solar energy ... It wasn't a matter of simply building it, we had to look at the symbolic side of it too. In fact a number of people, families who lived nearby, asked for copies of our plans to see how to build a greenhouse, what its productivity was, etc. I found that very positive. And then there was the challenge — we had very little material available, few resource people. In the end it was better that way because instead of counting on other people we had to count on ourselves. Start from scratch and follow through to the end of the project. At first it began with two or three participants. Then there was the famous evening when we made the cement and we didn't have enough. When you pour a cement foundation you have to do it in one shot. I made a few calls and at the ninth one we found someone who was prepared to sell us the bags of cement we were missing. We took the truck to get them. It was really a strange sensation to see the other participants, even the ones who were already sleeping, come and help us pour the foundation. It wasn't work, it was more like a work of art we were all sharing ...

J.H.: Suddenly there was a sort of euphoria around the greenhouse ...

Daniel: Yes, that's really what it was. It was euphoric, and we sang as we worked.

J.H.: Until late at night, I think?

Daniel: Yes, we finished around half-past midnight. Afterward we had something to eat. It's a good memory, one of the ones that struck me most. When we left Larouche we left the greenhouse to the second group and we were proud. We were proud we'd reached our goal, finished it. It was one of my best memories. That wasn't the end of the greenhouse. I've kept the plans, we made photocopies. I think I'll be using it, and other people will too. Those plans won't just sit in a drawer.

J.H.: Does that aspect of Katimavik interest you in particular – everything that has to do with ecology, with appropriate technology?

Daniel: Yes. Because you have to aim at self-sufficiency. If I'm capable of being self-sufficient, that's one less person for the rest of the world to feed. So that allows people in the Third World to have a bigger share. And then if we could export that knowledge, we'd be on the way.

J.H.: How long did you spend on a farm?

Daniel: Three weeks. It seemed short.

J.H.: With which family?

Daniel: The Tremblays. It wasn't a terribly big farm but there was lots of work to do. I lived the life of a farmer. That's why I found it interesting. Let's say it comes close to self-sufficiency. It's not just taking someone else's farm and not producing, the way a lot of people do just to live in the country. What's important is to make your bit of land as productive as possible, as naturally as possible too.

J.H.: What was your impression of the Tremblay family?

Daniel: I liked their attitude very much. As soon as you walked into the house you were a member of the family. You weren't a guest, you were part of the family, and that helped a lot. We washed the dishes, and did the housework as well as the farm work. They were really very nice people. There were no barriers, you could talk about anything. It was a human exchange, not just an exchange in terms of work.

J.H.: Have you kept in touch with them?

Daniel: No, but Yves still writes to Diane Tremblay. I'm planning to go and see them one of these days though. It's interesting, Diane learned a lot too because she was interested in our main project. I think we brought something to the Tremblays and they gave us something too. It was an exchange.

Wilcox, Saskatchewan

J.H.: After three months at Larouche and I don't know how many days on the train, your group arrived in Saskatchewan ...

105

Daniel: Yes, in Wilcox. That was something else. I found Wilcox harder than Larouche, maybe because we were on the Prairies, maybe because it was winter. In winter you spend more time inside the house. So you're not exactly forced but there's a greater likelihood that you'll enter into relationships with other members of the group. It was harder to go outside and see other people and come back with your little stock of new acquaintances, bring them to the group and exchange them.

J.H.: But there was another difference too: you were no longer a group of thirty but three groups of ten, in different houses.

Daniel: Yes, that was a big change in our lives because the contacts were even more direct. Even though they were direct at Larouche, when something wasn't going well with someone you could always go and see someone else. That's much harder when there are only ten of you. If there's a problem you have to deal with it, settle it; you can't spend a whole month with the same problem with the same person. So you tend to solve your problems more quickly, I think, otherwise life with the group very quickly becomes intolerable.

J.H.: You had a lot of work to do in Wilcox, though, much more than in Larouche.

Daniel: In Wilcox the main project was manual labour, but it didn't stop there. For example, we took courses in photography. That was a very good exchange.

J.H.: The courses were given at the college?

Daniel: No, there was a farmer who was a professional photographer. A very interesting man. He gave us lessons in exchange for two or three days' work on his farm. They were really excellent courses, especially for beginners like us. The time and material were free.

J.H.: How many participants were interested in these courses?

Daniel: Six, mostly from our house; that developed another common interest.

J.H.: So you traded photography lessons for a few days' work on a farm?

Daniel: Yes.

J.H.: Was that when Serge discovered his taste for photography?

Daniel: Yes, and it was something Serge had never suspected, nor did anybody else. That was very interesting. Some of the participants weren't all that attracted to photography at the start, but they took the lessons because they wanted an exchange with other people. But in the end they knew a little more about photography and they'd had a very close relationship with a family from the region.

J.H.: And your group also worked on building the student café?

Daniel: Yes. That was nothing new for me, because I'd had experience at building in the past. But I was glad to be building something and showing the others what I knew. We didn't think we'd have time to finish the café but we ended up putting a lot of energy into it, working the last two weekends of the project, and we managed to finish it and be there the night it was inaugurated. That's something I'm proud of having participated in, I'm proud of having found the necessary energy in other people so we were able to carry something out together. The café was an interesting project and I hope it will bring a lot to the students at the college because they don't have any well-defined activities aside from sports. They didn't have a place for cultural activities, and no budget either, or organization. I think the Katimavik group that came after us looked after organizing the operation of the café.

J.H.: You didn't know Saskatchewan at all before you went to Wilcox. Obviously Wilcox doesn't represent all of Saskatchewan — it's a very special little village. But in spite of everything does Saskatchewan mean something to you now?

Daniel: Yes, it represents a great deal. The Prairies are another part of the geography of this country that I didn't know at all. In Saskatchewan there's an enormous amount of space and I think that influences people's nature, their attitudes.

J.H.: What did you think of the people?

Daniel: I think they're different from people in Quebec, from any other people. They're rather reserved the first time you meet them, but as you get to know them better you become closer to them.

J.H.: Isn't it a little like that everywhere?

Daniel: Maybe. In Saskatchewan, the attitudes are Anglo-Saxon. People are reserved at first, but if the first contact is a good one everything afterward goes well. For instance, we went curling, a sport I'd never played before. That helped us make contacts with people — something that was made harder by the winter and because there were fewer people than in Larouche. So it was a good opportunity and it was offered by the community itself. There were two tournaments with Katimavik. There were two participants from Katimavik on every team, and two people from the community. We ended up knowing our teammates very well.

Grand River, Ontario

J.H.: After Wilcox, you came here, to Grand River. Another contrast ...

Daniel: Yes, but not as strong as the contrast out west. Ontario's close to Quebec and it's not just the landscape that's similar. I think the attitudes are similar too. It's more industrial than agricultural.

J.H.: Your group was in Luther. What did you do there?

Daniel: We cut trees for the GRCA. We learned a lot from the people we worked with, Russell and Larry. We learned a lot about animals too. A lot, because those people were trappers, hunters, who know a lot about the migration of birds and about hunting seasons too, about the periods when beaver bear their young. That was something I liked a lot: learning about the lives of the animals in the area. Then our work was mostly in the woods; cutting trees was the main project.

J.H.: Was there some community work too?

Daniel: Ah, yes! At the day-care centre.

J.H.: Do you like working with children?

Daniel: Yes I love it, I adore it. I've always dreamed of

working with children. That's the direction my university studies are taking. My first experience was in Wilcox, with fairly young children, finding things for them to do in the day-care centre. Here, I taught French to students who came voluntarily during their lunch hour. Which was very different from their obligatory courses. The reaction was fantastic. I worked with Joyce. One day we made a "French" meal with the students. Christine came to help us too. They all helped with the cooking and they learned the French terms for the cooking utensils, the ingredients used in the various dishes. They enjoyed that a lot. Other times, we played games in French and danced Quebec folkdances. We had a discussion about Quebec and the French language in the world and within Canada. And the importance of knowing not just French but two or three other languages. Perhaps the students didn't learn a lot of French, but at least they learned a little more about Francophones and their culture. The experience taught me a great deal and I'll be putting it to use soon. I've just received a bursary from the Newfoundland Department of Education which will allow me to give French lessons to young people there while I continue my own education at Memorial University.

J.H.: Ah! You're going to teach French in Newfoundland?

Daniel: Yes. The experience I acquired here will be very helpful. I'll be helping a French teacher. I think I acquired some experience from that point of view in Katimavik. I'll be more productive.

J.H.: You know English quite well now?

Daniel: My English isn't bad, but I want to improve it till I'm completely bilingual. I think it's necessary. And when I learn something I like to learn it thoroughly. University will be another way to perfect my English.

J.H.: You've talked about the things you learned in Katimavik through your work, but did you learn from the other participants too?

Daniel: I learned a lot about people. When you live with people you come to know them in a very different way, more in depth. I learned how to reconcile my differences with other people without hurting them — helping them, I hope. The relationships between the participants in Katimavik were warm. Things aren't always perfect, of course, but it's through conflicts that you learn. You learn how to calm down and discover what's positive about every human being.

J.H.: Several people have told me they think of the group as a real family ...

Daniel: Yes, I think it is like a family, with all the members at the same level, which is different from the usual family.

J.H.: There are no little brothers or big sisters ...

Daniel: I think that's an important point. No one's more important than anyone else. Sometimes one person is more of a leader, but that person will be able to reassure someone else who's not so strong. And perhaps that other person will give the first one something in return, cheerfulness, say. It's what you might call a constant exchange between equals who have different qualities.

J.H.: Do you have the impression that the friendships that have developed among the participants during the year will last?

Daniel: Yes, even if we don't see one another for a year or two. I don't think time is a factor that destroys friendship.

J.H.: Some people are afraid of that.

Daniel: It doesn't frighten me. I spent a period of my life with those thirty participants. I gave them something, they gave me something. We're leaving one another, but you don't really leave because a part of me is going to remain with them and a part of them will stay with me too. I think we really love one another. Perhaps everyone doesn't realize it, except in exceptional circumstances. Perhaps we should say that we love each other more often ... Of course there are some members of the group I don't know as well as others, there isn't the same degree of friendship with everyone, but still there's something that will remain and that something is already a great deal.

J.H.: Do you feel that you've changed in the last ten months?

Daniel: Yes, I think I've changed a lot. Before Katimavik I was very very positive and perhaps not realistic enough. I was stable, I didn't change my mind very often. I like to make a choice and then follow it through. It would be a final choice unless something exceptional happened. I'd tell myself, "Why get involved in three or four things, reduce the amount of energy I devote to each one, not take each one far enough?" This summer I don't plan to take any holidays. I'm leaving Katimavik full of energy. I have enough to get involved right away in something else, and to go on using what Katimavik has given me. Help other people take advantage of it. I know that next year I've got something interesting to do. And I don't think that stops, I don't think I'll reach the point when I'll say, "I know enough, I can sit back now." As soon as a person does that he stops growing.

J.H.: I'm not too worried about you, Daniel!

Daniel: Thank you.

10 *Joyce Aylward,* Age 17, Kilbridge, Newfoundland

I'm Joyce Aylward from Kilbridge, Newfoundland. I was born in Newfoundland and lived there all my life until Katimavik. I come from a big family, seven children and Mom and Dad. Five girls and two boys. We have a small store and we used to kind of fool around in it before Katimavik.

J.H.: What kind of childhood did you have in a big family like that?

Joyce: It was group life because the way it is in Newfoundland, quite often, like all the family lives around. Both my grandparents, the Murphy's and Aylward's, had neighbourhood farms and so all the Murphy and Aylward children lived in the same neighbourhood together. There are about a hundred Murphy's now living around and we're all related to somebody on either side of my family. So, everyone growing up there is either a cousin, aunt or uncle, like a clan.

J.H.: Did you travel much before Katimavik?

Joyce: Well, I lived in Miquelon for two months, St. Pierre and Miquelon, to learn French.

J.H.: Did you?

Joyce: Not very well. When I came to Katimavik I realized how little I'd learned. I also went down for a two-week holiday to London and I've been around the province a few times and around the Maritimes, and I lived in Montreal for a month before Katimavik.

J.H.: What was Canada for you in those days?

Joyce: A beautiful country, the best in the world. I'm very proud to be a Canadian. I always wanted to travel but I always thought I'd come back to Newfoundland and settle because I was a Canadian. Kind of naive. Like the Canadian government was all bright and beautiful and nothing at all like the United States, nothing "under the table" with the Canadian government. It was always straight-forward and honest and a hard-working country.

J.H.: All of a sudden Katimavik came into your life. How did that happen?

Joyce: I was in the university, and because of the way I grew up with everyone around, the relatives, I felt kind of smothered. All my friends were getting married. Most of the aunts and uncles and their children, when they reached eighteen or nineteen, they got married, settled down and had children. Mom brought us up wanting all the girls and the guys to be very independent. Mostly all my sisters moved away as soon as they hit eighteen.

J.H.: To do what?

Joyce: Three of them moved to Montreal.

J.H.: What were you planning to learn at university?

Joyce: I was going to go in for Psychology, but I didn't really like it.

J.H.: How did that happen then?

Joyce: Because of three other girls. My three older sisters had not gone to university. Mom really wanted a daughter with a university education and so it fell on me.

J.H.: Fell on you!

Joyce: Yes, Mom didn't say anything. It was Frankie, Kathy and Dale who said Mom would be very happy if I was to go to university. They thought I should have a university education. So I said yes, okay. I went and I really didn't like it. I didn't like the classes; it's very different from high school. I decided I wanted to leave and I couldn't think of how to do it, so I was going to join the army. I applied and was going to go in for photography. It

113

was all ready and I didn't think of asking Mom and Dad because I was sure they would say yes. Everyone said I should ask my parents. Mom had some old-fashioned ideas about the army, so did Dad. I was only seventeen and they had to sign and they absolutely refused to. Mom could tell I was really restless, and she was the one who heard about Katimavik. There was very little advertising in Newfoundland. She heard it on CBC Radio and she told me about it and said, "You know, you should really get into it instead of going into the army."

J.H.: She told you what she'd heard about Katimavik on the radio. What did she tell you to make you say yes, finally?

Joyce: She said that I would travel around the country, and seeing the country is one of the reasons I wanted to join the army. And that I would live in groups with young people, and work and learn different lifestyles, live in the woods and things like that. So I applied and got accepted.

J.H.: And one fine morning you arrived in a training camp in Duchesnay. What was your first impression of all that?

Joyce: Panic. I was nervous because I was a week late.

J.H.: You were? Newfoundland is not that far.

Joyce: No, no, it was the air strike. I was nervous about coming anyways because I find it hard to meet people and talk to someone when I don't know who they are.

J.H.: Are you shy?

Joyce: Yes, I never had to meet new people. There was always enough relatives around so I never had to meet new people in Newfoundland. So I really felt uncomfortable meeting new people. I figured if I went the first day, everyone would be new. But then I came a week later, and by then you know there will be friendships arising the first day, so then I knew there would be friendships already and I feared that. Luckily on the plane I met Gordon. Did you meet Gordon?

J.H.: Oh yes.

Joyce: He was on the plane with me, and we had something in common because we're Newfoundlanders. The first day we got there, there was a corn roast and I met some other people who were from Newfoundland. It wasn't as hard as I thought it would be. It was interesting.

J.H.: Could you manage a little bit in French through your stay in St. Pierre and Miquelon?

Joyce: No, the French that I knew there, it was Parisien, not even Parisien, it's the French of France three hundred years ago. When I left Miquelon, four years ago, I could understand what they spoke and they could understand me, but for four years I had no French at all. Then I came here and I thought I knew French, but when the Québécois started speaking French, I didn't have any idea what they were talking about. It sounded like a completely different language from what I had heard before.

Larouche, Quebec

J.H.: So after a month you were down to thirty in Larouche, Quebec. What was your impression there?

Joyce: When I first got there I really hated it because the people that I hung around with in Duchesnay, none of them came to Larouche.

J.H.: Well, there was Gordon.

Joyce: In Duchesnay I stopped hanging around with Gordon. He was hanging around with the guys and I was hanging around with the people who were quieter. I knew Gordon but I hadn't talked to him in a few weeks. I didn't feel that I knew him. So when I went to Larouche I felt really odd. I was really quiet and felt really out of it for a long time.

J.H.: Well, you were really near everybody in that house, almost tied up.

Joyce: That was always the problem because we were so close. I felt I was getting really homesick.

J.H.: Did you think of going home?

Joyce: Yes, but I had promised myself that I would finish it. When I started I was definitely going to finish Katimavik. In Larouche there was no work to do for half of the project. We were always bumping into each other and there were all these meetings and I was so close to all these people I didn't know, I felt really uncomfortable for

115

a long time. The only two people I felt comfortable with was Serge and Daniel, because they were always joking and I was teasing them. That was really strange because I had never made friends with guys before, never as a friend. I really found that nice.

J.H.: Two French-Canadian boys.

Joyce: Yes, that was interesting too; and a few girls.

J.H.: Were you approached to go on a farm or anything like that in Larouche?

Joyce: I went for a month. You met Jean-Paul? He wasn't a farmer. He was Jean-Paul Vignon. It wasn't a farm at all, it was a beautiful house and there was no work there to do. The only thing I did was maybe watch the baby and it didn't need that very much because we were on shift watch, and he was always with his parents.

J.H.: Did you learn something through that?

Joyce: Oh I learned a lot of French.

J.H.: Did you learn something about what a French-Canadian family was like?

Joyce: Oh, yes. It was very different from my family.

J.H.: What did you like about that family especially?

Joyce: The week before I left the house I was in utter confusion, it was really all ganging up on me and I was getting claustrophobia and everything. I just couldn't stand all the noise and all the people and no privacy at all; so when I went to that house they were really nice. I felt close to them, they were like in my brother-in-law's and sister's house, that's what the situation seemed because they have one child too and the situation seemed like I wasn't living with a strange family, I was living in a friend's house.

J.H.: Do you write to them at all?

Joyce: Yes, I'm going to visit them just as soon as I go back. I'm going to Daniel's house after and we're going to visit Jean-Paul.

Wilcox, Saskatchewan

J.H.: Then finally you moved to Wilcox and there you were. Again, you were starting with a new kind of family. How many were you in your group?

Joyce: There were ten of us when we got there.

J.H.: How long did it take you to get to know the people ... to feel at ease with them?

Joyce: Good question. Well, I sat with Carol, we had a room to ourselves. I got to know her best really quick. I didn't know her at all in Larouche. The same with Christine, I got to know her. I really didn't get to know Debbie until the very end and Daniel and Serge, I got to know them a lot better.

J.H.: The laughing friends?

Joyce: Yes. I got to know them more than just laughing, like I know them personal, what they thought. Mark Forrest, it took me a very long time to know him. I just got to know Bob and he was gone, which was really bad because I could see that Robert was a steadying force. In Larouche we thought we had the best group, there were ten of us and it was mostly because of Bob. We felt closer than the other groups. Then Bob left.

J.H.: He became a group leader?

Joyce: Yes, he left to become a group leader, and then our group leader left and for a week or two we were out of a group leader. During that time we got to know each other a lot more because we had to do all the work, like we had to get each other up and arrange the schedules.

J.H.: There are some strong people in that group; there was no real problem there?

Joyce: No, that was one of the reasons we thought our group was really good. None of us was so quiet that we would let someone else tell us to do things, and no one else was strong enough to tell us.

J.H.: What was your first impression when you got to see the Prairies, stepping out of the train and seeing nothing but flatness?

Joyce: The day we got there it was − 80°F. with the wind, it was in the middle of a storm and it was really, really strange. It was flat, very flat and open, like an awful lot of sky. I didn't really see it until after the last month, nor did anyone, because we'd leave our house and walk very quickly to the workshop and very quickly back, because it was too cold and we couldn't walk around. In the last month we started going outside, started going places. It was really, really different from what I knew.

J.H.: What did you do as far as work is concerned?

Joyce: I worked mostly on the café with a group leader and Daniel.

J.H.: What kind of work did you do there? Carpentry?

Joyce: The café was just about the whole project, it was carpentry.

J.H.: Did you know anything about carpentry before?

Joyce: No. I learned a lot. We did the whole thing; it was gutted and we had to do the roof and the walls and the floor. Daniel and the group leader knew what they were doing and they were really patient.

J.H.: With you?

Joyce: Yes, very patient and they were really good. I also worked in the college. They needed a telephone operator for a week, so I enjoyed it. It was really fun. I got to know people at the college and I was also getting to know the students. Another week I worked in the head office at the university.

J.H.: What do you think of the people in Wilcox?

Joyce: The townspeople were very friendly, except they associated us with the college and they don't particularly like the college people so they didn't particularly like us. Well, they didn't right away but they did go curling with us and everyone at the curling was really really nice.

J.H.: Could you live there?

Joyce: No. I guess if I had been there in the summer, it might be different. It's just that I don't like cold weather. I like small towns.

J.H.: But there's no place like Newfoundland, is there?

Joyce: No, no place like Newfoundland.

J.H.: Why? What's so nice about it?

Joyce: The people. They seem a lot more friendlier than other people I've met. And I just love the sea and the whole countryside. It seems a lot quieter and a lot slower than anywhere else in Canada. We don't hear so much about when to get the work done, they get it done eventually. It may take a week to do what some Montrealer can do in a day and it doesn't really bother them. It's slow. The whole land is beautiful; where I live it's all barns with little trees and it's all mossy and all rocky and lots of beautiful beaches. It's just cliffs.

J.H.: You like that?

Joyce: Oh yes. Things are a lot more free, a lot more nature, that's the way it is.

Grand River, Ontario

J.H.: So after three months in Wilcox, in cold Saskatchewan, you moved to southern Ontario, Grand River. Was that another shock, the difference?

Joyce: No. I expected it. I was told that southern Ontario was really warm.

J.H.: Where were you exactly?

Joyce: In the Luther house. There's more trees but it was still all white and we were still pretty isolated.

J.H.: But you were a lot more comfortable with your group by then?

Joyce: Yes, we were, but I think one of the main reasons we were so together at the time was because we were against our group leader which wasn't very good. It really drew us together but it's not a very good way to be drawn together.

J.H.: What work did you do?

Joyce: Chainsawing in the woods.

J.H.: What was it like with the chainsaw?

Joyce: Pretty good. I'm pretty good at it. They're not hard. The people we were working with are super nice. They don't rush and they like to talk, they like to joke and they get their work done. They don't say, "Do this," and you would have to do it. They'd say, "Well, now I guess we'll cut this tree here today, and we'll cut that one tomorrow." Also, we had the French classes and French clubs set up.

J.H.: What was that?

Joyce: Two people go every Tuesday for two and a half hours to teach French to grades 9 and 11.

J.H.: Were you teaching French by then?

Joyce: I went there one day. There were kids who had just started French in grades 6 and 7 and we went and tried to get them interested in something French.

J.H.: Your French must have improved quite a lot?

Joyce: Oh yes, we spoke a little bit of French in the house. I think everyone in the house now can understand French, maybe not speak it properly or maybe not even understand it, but they're an awful lot better than they were. Do you know Bruce?

J.H.: Yes, of course.

Joyce: Did you try to talk French to him in Larouche?

J.H.: He couldn't speak a word.

Joyce: You should try speaking to him now. He's really improved.

J.H.: I'll do that.

Joyce: Debbie really couldn't do French at all and now she's taking courses and reading French books, writing French stories. And Carol took a course before she came here and Mark was bilingual. Our group is pretty good in French. For the most part, nine-tenths is in English but there is a little bit of French spoken.

J.H.: So, as a whole the experience in Ontario was good?

Joyce: Ontario for me was ... like not only the people I was working with, but all the people in Damascus, I really got to know them, I think this is the best project so far.

J.H.: Have you changed in any way through Katimavik?

Joyce: Oh yes. I feel a lot more confident now. I remember going to Wilcox and there was the Katimavik group, I didn't talk with them because I didn't know what to say. Coming back I talked with them, I didn't know how to talk and I'm lousy at small talk. Now, I'm also standing up for my rights. In Larouche if they said something and I didn't really agree with it, I'd put up with it and just let it pass because I didn't want to say anything out loud in front of people. But now if I don't believe something, I'll say so. I don't know if it's just because the group is more like my family now and I don't know if that will stay when I get back to Newfoundland and meet new people. But I feel I've changed a lot. Some for the better and some for the worse. I feel I bitch a lot more than I ever did, and like gossip.

J.H.: Do you really feel your group is like a family?

Joyce: Yes, it may even be more.

J.H.: More than a family?

Joyce: Yes, because like my little sister, she was my little sister, she wasn't a person, she's just my little sister. I didn't really know her, she'd bug me and I never thought of sitting down with her and asking, "Now why did you say that?" With the group I can discuss anything I want. Certain topics we don't even discuss at home, I'm more open with the Katimavik members. For nine months I've been away in Katimavik and I've wanted to go home. I liked it but I couldn't wait to go home, but now I don't see what I'm going to do when I go home.

J.H.: Let's talk about that. What will you be doing then?

Joyce: That's a pretty good question. Possibly other people have something they're going to do, like university or French program or things like that. I've no idea.

J.H.: None at all?

Joyce: Maybe back to the university. I'm getting some "trades college" information sent to me by mail to take a course.

J.H.: Are you going to join the army?

Joyce: No.

J.H.: You've given up on that?

Joyce: Yes, I don't want to do that anymore. I can travel now by myself, I don't need the army to do it.

J.H.: Do you think these links that you have with a lot of people now, will last long?

Joyce: I think so now more than I did before. When I was in Miquelon for two months I lived with five people. When I came back, the ties died and I figured with Katimavik, like when we left Duchesnay I told myself the ties were going to die because it's the way they really do. But I seriously doubt that I'll forget them. Debbie is half planning to come and stay with us for Christmas and Carol is leaving university for a week in winter and planning to come up. Daniel's coming to Newfoundland for all winter.

J.H.: For all winter?

Joyce: He's going to university. And Serge ... I didn't think I would bother visiting people but I figured once it's over, it's over and forget about it, but I think if I was in Quebec, I'd visit Serge ...

11 *Yves Landry*, Age 18, Dorval, Quebec

There's a lot to tell ... I was born in Dorval, then I moved to Lachine, I don't know exactly when. I'm not very clear about my baptism either. And I don't know what hospital I was born in either! All those things got kind of mixed up in '67, when my parents got divorced.

J.H.: How old were you?

Yves: When it happened I was eight or nine. My sister's fourteen now and my brother's twelve. I'm the oldest.

J.H.: How did your parents' divorce change your life?

Yves: I was young and it didn't really affect me that much right away. What did influence me was being alone with my father. All the problems he had and the way he reacted. He had to change jobs often, which meant moving. I went to live in Campbellton, New Brunswick, for almost a year. Then to Moncton. After a while I lived with my uncles, in Evangeline. My father was working so he couldn't take care of me and my brother and sister at the same time. There were diapers to change. So he left my brother with his sister — that's a way of saying he gave him out to be adopted, that he had new parents, but he's still in the family. My sister stayed with my father and me because she was a little older and easier to look after than my little brother. I remember I cried a lot because I was really close to my father, I didn't want him ever to go away ... He was always going away for a week or two; sometimes he'd come back in a month. That's because he had to travel on account of his work: he was a sales representative. So I was pretty well alone, with my relatives. When I was little I felt as though I had a father, but he was far away. So in practice, my uncle was more like my father and my aunt was my mother. I've never really known what it was like to have a mother. Recently, though, I've been seeing a little more of my mother ... Three times a year, during the holidays, at Christmas, New Year's ...

J.H.: Do you think that your particular circumstances had some influence on your nature?

Yves: It showed me another side of life. Serge, for instance, tells me I'm like an old man — I hang on to the old traditions. But maybe that's because when I was young I didn't know the traditional values ... Except maybe a little in New Brunswick because they hung on to their customs and also, they're more religious than in Montreal, let's say. So in that sense Serge is right and sometimes I think it's a defect. But it doesn't bother me! I didn't feel like an unhappy child. No, but sometimes I'd need my father when he wasn't there. When you're a child you always find the time to have fun, to discover things, and run and laugh ... And I live in the country. I used to play a lot in the woods behind my uncle's place. That was really something! I'd go there all by myself, I remember ... We'd build little houses in the woods ... My aunt had a store and I'd go there and buy bubble gum for a penny and sell it for two cents. That was in 1967 or so. I remember during Expo we used to play guitars that had strings that didn't even vibrate; there was a record playing in the back, with a cord that went all the way into the house. People down there were really impressed by that.

J.H.: For you who have lived in two parts of the country — Quebec and New Brunswick — what did Canada mean to you?

Yves: For me, nothing. When I was young all I knew was Montreal, the west end of Montreal. New Brunswick meant my relatives, fishing ...

J.H.: Your family's Acadian?

Yves: My father is. When I lived with him I was often in New Brunswick where I felt that he had deep roots. Of course that had an influence on me.

J.H.: How about you, where are your roots?

Yves: That's hard to say. As far as politics go, I'm independentist. But it makes me feel kind of bad. In the sense that I've got roots in New Brunswick and if anything happens to Canada I'm going to feel badly because something's going to be broken ... A tie ... Maybe it won't happen. When I identify myself I identify myself as a Québécois first of all, because I went to high school here, with other people from here. It influenced me too. But most of my experiences have been in New Brunswick: my contacts with nature. Those contacts influenced me a lot. Fishing, the Acadian festival where I worked one summer for nothing ...

J.H.: How did Katimavik come into your life?

Yves: It was strange. I was living on unemployment insurance benefits for six months, till the end of July. My friends would say, "Ah! you're living off our parents' taxes," and all that. But I didn't want to be on unemployment insurance, I just took it to support myself during the time when I wasn't working. And the longer it went on the worse I felt where other people were concerned, just because I was on unemployment.

J.H.: There was nothing else you could do?

Yves: No. I knew my father needed his money to pay his debts, because he had debts; he'd been paying them off for ten years and I told myself, "I'm going to contribute something to the family. But since I'm not working the only way was through unemployment insurance. To pay for my clothes and all that." In June I started hearing about Katimavik. There was a song on the radio, Edith Butler sang it. She didn't pronounce it too well so it sounded like "Cadi ma vie." I thought she was saying; "L'Acadie, c'était ma vie — Acadia was life to me." Afterward, she'd say; "Come and have a look, it'll be interesting, a good experience!" and all that. I didn't really understand that part of the ad, maybe because she was saying it too fast. Then finally I woke up one Saturday morning, I was listening to some FM programs on the radio. They played that song at the beginning, then two people came to talk about Katimavik. I was interested in what they had to say. I turned up the radio, I'd just wakened up and I was still a little bit in the clouds when I listened to them ... They explained the program and then there was a sort of pause and they played the Edith Butler song again. That time I understood right away: I'd thought she was saying, "Cadi ma vie," but it was "Katimavik" that she was singing!

J.H.: So one day you came to the training camp at Duchesnay with about thirty other young people from every part of the country. What was your first impression?

Yves: I don't know if this was normal or not, but the first thing I did was look for the other Francophones. I was distant with the Anglophones. I've always been distant with Anglophones, maybe because of school: there was a Francophone side and an Anglophone side and we never mixed. Maybe that was why at Duchesnay I didn't feel I had to mix with the Anglophones right away; I knew it would come later on, during the projects.

Larouche, Quebec

J.H.: The first project was at Larouche, in Lac St. Jean ...

Yves: We took a bus there. We realized right away that the house wasn't finished. The first thing everybody said was, "My Lord, are we going to live in that shack?" Thirty of us — it would be kind of like hell ... From the outside it looked big but inside it was pretty small. There was the kitchen, two big bedrooms and two small bathrooms. But we moved in, and there were suitcases all over the place. Then we started to realize it was a little crowded! After that we went to the City Hall, for the official reception. Everybody was tired, nobody was really in the mood to listen to speeches and all that. For the Anglophones, arriving in Larouche was a bit of a shock. They really felt far from home. I didn't really feel that: the way people talked in Lac St. Jean reminded me of the people in New Brunswick. I didn't feel like a stranger at all. I think it was pretty much the same for a lot of the Québécois.

J.H.: So then all thirty of you moved into the house ...

Yves: In the beginning, yes, it was all right, but everybody had a different nature, a different way of living. I never left things out on my bed but the participant who had the bed above mine didn't take care of his things and there was always crumpled clothes on his bed. When he went to bed at night it would spill over and the clothes would fall on the floor. That was hard to put up with because I'm used to having everything neat and tidy. It was hard for me. I wasn't the only one, but some of the others didn't talk about it openly. But I talked about it at the meetings.

J.H.: What were the meetings like, with the unilingual Anglophones and unilingual Francophones?

Yves: We always had to be translating, and that made the discussions drag on. Some people understood the other language fairly well because at Duchesnay they'd made the effort to learn. For some of the others you had to repeat things at least two or three times before they understood, in French. I remember one meeting that lasted all night. For me, I think it was at Larouche that everything was decided — whether I'd stay in the project or not. Because at our meetings we really gave each other hell. Sometimes there'd be somebody with enough sense of humour to sort things out, but it was a real test for everybody at Larouche. The group leaders had lots of problems. In fact, they left. But it really was a test for everybody. The biggest headache was probably the house, because there were thirty of us and we had to arrange everything for thirty people. So everything was in order and clean — because thirty people, after all! The same dishes for everybody, the same toilet, the same two bedrooms. When somebody got the flu, it spread practically right away. The hardest thing was to organize the groups. We talked about being three separate groups but then there was always the thirty of us in the house. We were a big group. Sometimes we'd pick on the Anglophones; we'd say, "The Anglophones are this or that," but that didn't last long. Afterward, when we really were in groups of ten, we started getting to know each other better.

J.H.: However, you didn't spend three months in the group, because there were the individual stays at the neighbouring farms ...

Yves: Yes, I spent three weeks at the Tremblays.

J.H.: Was that an interesting experience for you?

Yves: Yes, because I really like farms. You take any animal, a cow or anything else, it's something you can look at, watch it live. The day I arrived there, I remember I got up the next day at 5.00 a.m. I didn't need an alarm clock or anything. I woke up at the same time as the grandmother, who was making her breakfast. In the big house I got in the habit of waking up at 7.00, but there, the first morning, there was a sort of "click" in my head. I got up at 5.00. I knew there were cows to be milked. They'd shown us the farm so we'd get an idea of how it worked. In a family like that all the conversation is about the farm. There wasn't too much personal conversation. I felt comfortable, I didn't feel as though I had to talk, I was fine ... I tried to understand their life on the farm, what they got out of it.

J.H.: Did you have any contacts with other people in the community, with people from the village?

Yves: Yes. For instance, at the social evenings they organized. There were three altogether. The first was put on by the community if I'm not mistaken. The second was at Hallowe'en, and I organized that with Serge. I remember, it was a Saturday and we went tearing all over the place, handing out announcements. We went from door to door and we went to see the curé too so he'd announce it at mass on Saturday night. Just by going from door to door you find out what kind of people live there, the work they do. There were lots of people who worked at Alcan.

J.H.: Have you kept in touch with anyone in Larouche?

Yves: Yes, with the farmers, the Tremblays. I wrote to them just a while ago. They told me about their farm, about the changes. They have hardly any cows to milk;

they kept a couple for their personal needs. They're going to raise pigs now.

J.H.: Do you think you'll go back and see them some day?

Yves: In the last letter I got they said there was lots of work to do this summer, since they've turned the stable into a pigsty. I think there's going to be another building. Mme Tremblay told me, "You'll be very welcome here and if there are any others who want to come they'll be welcome too." That's hospitality!

J.H.: Are you tempted to go?

Yves: Yes. This summer, yes. I'll see what's changed on the farm since I left.

J.H.: What were your other jobs at Larouche, aside from the shared projects?

Yves: I did a lot of secretarial work and I looked after the meetings. I should point out that Michel, our co-ordinator, was sick. I felt — maybe I'm patting myself on the back! — but anyway, I felt I was qualified enough to help him in those areas.

J.H.: In a way you became the secretary of the group?

Yves: In a way, yes. Because nobody else took the initiative to do it. At one point everybody was feeling a little bored and I tried to pull them out of it, keep up morale. So when people were down I'd try to stimulate them, tell them, "For Christ's sake, listen, there's things to do!" I got involved. I made a plan for a henhouse. I don't know if it was built or what, if they accepted the budget in Montreal. Last I heard, they had, on condition we didn't go over the budget for the greenhouse. Maybe the group that came to Larouche after us started to build it.

Wilcox, Saskatchewan

J.H.: After three months in Larouche you moved to Wilcox, Saskatchewan, thousands of miles from Lac St. Jean. It was the Francophones' turn to have a shock?

Yves: I'll say it was a shock! It was really a change. It was flat and there weren't any trees. But there was snow and that reminded me a little of the ocean, which was sort of comforting. There wasn't any water but it reminded me of the ocean, in wintertime.

J.H.: What was your main work in Wilcox?

Yves: I got involved in construction mostly. There was a very good resource person. I didn't always like the way he thought, let's say, he was a little bit old-fashioned, in the sense that it was hard for him to accept women hammering nails.

J.H.: A bit of an "old man"?

Yves: No, not an old man, but a little chauvinist maybe ...He really didn't like to see girls driving in nails. He didn't think it was the kind of work they should be doing. In other words he'd give them a paintbrush instead of a hammer, "Go paint the walls!" The boys had built door frames and window frames, and we'd fixed the floors. We were fixing up a wood-working shop for the students at Notre Dame College, an old building they'd bought for $1000. or $2000., anyway not very much.

J.H.: Did you spend a lot of time at the college?

Yves: Yes, but there was some pettiness involved. The people in the community didn't like the college, especially since Father Murray left. They don't really like the college because of the young students, who might get into some mischief in the community. So the community and the college were like cat and dog. They should have stuck together, but no, there was nothing you could do. But on the other hand, without the college there might not have been a community. Because a lot of people from the community worked in the college, which has twice the population of the village itself. And of the 150 people in the village, three-quarters are retired or old people.

J.H.: Did you learn something about carpentry?

Yves: I learned a lot, not as much as in a course, but enough to feel independent, in the sense that I could help somebody else make a door frame, or repair a house or whatever. We worked a lot, really a lot. When our group left Wilcox all the painting was done, the offices were nearly ready, they just had to put in the furniture and the lamps and turn on the electricity. There were a lot of other things to do in the main hall but most of it, the partitions, was already done.

J.H.: So you really helped out at Notre Dame College?

Yves: Yes, I did. And toward the end I also did some work on the café that was built for the students. We worked on the curling rink too, we rebuilt the whole inside of the arena. That was the first time I'd seen curling, or done it myself. It was something really typical of the area. That was the thing that impressed me the most.

J.H.: Curling, really?

Yves: In the villages all around, everybody curls. You hear about tournaments all over Saskatchewan! It's their national sport. Another thing that impressed me was the big grain elevators. They are impressive and beautiful. When I looked at them I tried to imagine them in the summer, what it would be like with the different coloured fields, in September, October ... But getting back to curling, it was through that game that I had more direct contacts with the people in Wilcox, with my "skip" for instance, which is what you call the captain of the team in curling. A guy around sixty ... He'd been curling for at least forty years. On our team we were really proud of winning the first matches. But we lost all the others ... And that made me unhappy. Still, though, I played really well for someone who'd never played before. And that's my skip's opinion, not mine!

Grand River, Ontario

J.H.: So after three months the whole group went to Grand River, to a place where once again you were separated into three small groups. Where was yours, exactly?

Yves: In Cambridge, in a stone house ... With a fireplace ...

J.H.: The old historic house?

Yves: Yes. And they want to demolish it!

J.H.: I know. You might be the last people to have lived in that house ... And what work did you do there?

Yves: For me, it was a chance to work in forestry, an area I'm very interested in. But I was disappointed at the Grand River Conservation Authority's idea of conservation. For them, it mostly had to do with waterways. I think forestry only accounts for 3 per cent of their organization. The work they gave us at the beginning was splitting wood for fireplaces. At first we told ourselves, "Fine, it has to be done, it's cold ... The wood's frozen so it's easier to split." We did at least 150 cords, if not more; we cut it, split it and classified it. It wasn't for the parks, it was for private individuals who bought it from the GRCA. We weren't very happy about that, but we did it. With the two people who were working with us we must have cut and split around 200 cords. That's one hell of a lot of wood!

J.H.: What else did you do for the GRCA?

Yves: Robert had a position in a laboratory. He collected bugs in the lakes and rivers, samples of larvae, insects. From the kinds of larvae you could calculate the degree of pollution in the water, because there are some insects that are less resistant than others. As for me, after those cords of wood I made picnic tables. Everybody made picnic tables. We had 200 to make and we sent 100 to the group at Belwood. Our group made 100. I remember, Michael and Peter made thirty in one day, while at Belwood they made eight per day. Since the group before us had messed up realtions with the GRCA a little, we tried to win back the confidence of our "silent partner." We did a lot of work, and fast. It was pretty hard on us.

J.H.: But you had to rebuild the reputation of Katimavik?

Yves: Yes. And get more interesting work from the GRCA, which happened later. Besides the physical work there was social work, in the community. It was mainly in the day-care centres. At the YMCA they had courses for old people. We helped the old people swim. At Christopher House we worked with children. And in addition to all that, once a week we went to work at the community radio station in Waterloo. For me, Radio-Waterloo was a chance to teach the people in Waterloo and around it something about Quebec music. They played a lot of American music. I'd like that to change a little. I took a kind of inventory of the records they had, the records that came from Quebec and other French-speaking regions.

J.H.: Have you done your radio program?

Yves: Yes I've done, I did it quite quickly, actually.

J.H.: A one-hour program?

Yves: In the end it went on for nearly two hours!

J.H.: Now that it's nearly over, do you feel that Katimavik changed you a little?

Yves: I think I'll realize later, when I go back home. For the moment I'm beginning to think that yes, it changed me a little, or it oriented me. Let's say I'm still oriented toward forestry but I'm looking into self-sufficiency even more. At one point, in Wilcox, I really felt lost. Luckily there was one person in the group in particular who helped me a lot. By the way, the rule about co-habitation at Katimavik is really hard. Drugs, you can understand, it's illegal, you've got no business! But co-habiting, that's something else. When you live in a group how can the guys not have contacts with the girls, or the girls with the guys? It's hard. At a certain point you feel you have to communicate with one person in particular, whether it's a guy or a girl. In my case it happened that it was a girl.

J.H.: It's quite normal for that to happen. But we know that "lovers are all alone in the world." They end up keeping to themselves to the point where they're no longer part of the group. And that's what causes problems in a program like Katimavik.

Yves: Yes. It happened to me. It happened in Larouche. In my case, I went and worked my four days a week with the group and at night we had our meetings. Fine. When I had any spare time, though, I'd go and see the person, I'd talk with her.

J.H.: There's no rule against that, as far as I know!

Yves: Over the ten months several couples formed, but nobody went beyond the limits ... "Lovers are all alone in the world." You see what I mean? We know we have to live in the group, that we can't just stop at the little world formed by the two of us. Just now, because we're coming to the end of Katimavik, it's a little different. Let's say we're a little more inclined to be dreamy. Some people are wondering, for instance, if they might not live together.

But as far as the group's concerned, nothing's changed, we stick together. If something goes wrong everybody's there, no more couples, but everybody together.

J.H.: Do you think you'll keep up your ties with the group, later?

Yves: Yes. It's normal that I'll have more contact with the participants who live in Quebec than with the others. As for the Anglophones, there's a few who want to come and study in Quebec. I'll probably see them fairly often. For the moment I don't think I'll keep in touch with the people in my group once a week or anything like that. Except, of course, with the ones in Montreal.

J.H.: In my life, there are some people I see very seldom but to whom I feel very close. We might write rarely, see each other three times a year, but when we're together I feel as though we'd seen each other the day before. Do you think that will happen in your group?

Yves: Yes, because we're like brothers and sisters. I don't think we could ever separate completely. We'll go our own ways, like in a family, some will get married and so forth... For me, that's the best way to explain the phenomenon: we'll be like a family.

J.H.: Can you really say that you have brothers and sisters in all ten provinces?

Yves: Yes, in a certain way. Maybe not exactly brothers and sisters, but more than friends. Just on the border ...

J.H.: Now that it's over, do you think it was worth all the effort?

Yves: Yes. I learned a lot about work and all that, and about human relations, with the community and in the group. And about responsibility to other people. I learned something about morale too — not in the sense that it got me down, but in the sense that you always have to be there; if somebody else is down you have to pull them up. Everybody has to stick together. I've seen a lot of different parts of the country. I don't think there's a lot for me to do around here, it's pretty far advanced technically. People live pretty well, I don't need to try to do anything for them. I think there's more for me to do where it's underdeveloped, like in New Brunswick for instance. I've made a lot of friends. With thirty people. But I know that I've already started to plan my life with one other person from my group ... Maybe we'll be heading in the same direction. In other words, look toward the future. I believe in it, even though the situation in my family was never good. But maybe that's why I believe in it.

12 *Michael Match,* Age 17, Brockville, Ontario

I was born in Kingston, Ontario, and moved with my parents to Brockville. I went to school there, but I haven't finished grade 12 yet.

J.H.: Are you from a big family?

Michael: There are five kids and the parents and everyone is older. I'm the baby of the family, I guess.

J.H.: The spoiled baby?

Michael: I guess my mother was supposed to have spoiled me ... My father doesn't, that's for sure! A different type of family than most people, a very European type of family.

J.H.: Did your family come from Europe recently?

Michael: Yes, my father is Austrian-German and my mother is from England.

J.H.: You were not born here?

Michael: Yes, my brother just before me and I were born here. The three others were born in England.

J.H.: Well, in any case you are Canadian.

Michael: Yes, first generation Canadian. My father is a school teacher and my mother works as a secretary in an out-patient office at the hospital. They're very "town" people, like Brockville's the kind of town people look all their lives to find.

J.H.: Before you joined Katimavik, what were your dreams for the future, what were you planning to do?

136

Michael: To farm, basically. All my brothers are farmers and I farmed a few summers.

J.H.: How did Katimavik come into your life?

Michael: I was reading a newspaper and one day in the *Weekend Magazine* there was an ad for Katimavik. I didn't want to go back to school, I didn't know if I could find a job.

J.H.: Why didn't you want to go back to school?

Michael: I didn't like school. It was dragging me down. I find it easy to get high marks but then I gave up getting high marks just as sort of a protest, so my marks were going down and I was just hating it and fighting it all the time.

J.H.: How did your parents react to your leaving school?

Michael: They didn't like the idea. My father was going to let me quit school if I had a job. I was committed to doing that. He was going to withdraw his support and that was the way I was brought up. I would make it by myself as soon as I left school. Then when Katimavik came along, they were very much for it.

J.H.: Were you running away from anything or getting into something?

Michael: I was running away.

J.H.: From school?

Michael: From Brockville. Brockville is a very upper-middle class town. Everybody knows everybody, sort of thing. I just felt it was time to change, but I was running away though.

J.H.: So it was a real change when you got into a training camp in Duchesnay.

Michael: It was a change, an environmental change, but there was no change within myself. Before I came to Katimavik I was spending all my nights in bars and like I was dealing dope and things like this and I was making a lot of money. I had a lot of money to spend and everything I wanted and then I came to Katimavik. I kept on drinking a lot, having a great time of it for the first two months or three months or something. But the funny thing was that, when I got to the training camp, the one thing I really went out to do was to learn French.

J.H.: You didn't know much French then?

Michael: No, I didn't know very much at all. I had some in school. I just chased after learning French all of a sudden. I saw it as an opportunity.

Larouche, Quebec

J.H.: And so after that month you arrived in a small town called Larouche in a house where you had to live with thirty others like you, all squeezed in ...

Michael: Yes, that was pretty bad. Good and bad.

J.H.: In what sense was it good?

Michael: It was good that in the beginning we got to know everybody. There was a lot of aggression, a lot of pressure from those people. Like if you did something wrong, then everybody was there watching, whereas in our house now, with ten people, it is easier. Basically we were like sardines, it was pretty bad, and it was something that I wasn't used to really.

J.H.: None of the participants were used to it, I don't think.

Michael: It was good though, I guess. It was helpful at that stage in the program.

J.H.: What did you do as far as work was concerned?

Michael: I didn't do any work really at all.

J.H.: Some of you did a lot.

Michael: Some of them did.

J.H.: What about you?

Michael: I spent most of my two months in bed, the first two months. I really did. Like we had three group leaders who were totally lazy and apathetic, busy telling me that I was cool, sort of thing, that everything was all right. I never did any work because I never had to. I remember writing home that this was a great program, that it was going to be a ten-month vacation, that I was having a great time, just lying there in bed all day reading. I read a lot of good books.

J.H.: You were not a little bit ill at ease, having it so good while the others were working hard?

Michael: Well, at that point, I didn't really care too much, I never thought about other people too much. Like right now I wouldn't be able to do that. I came to Larouche and after the first week everyone was sitting around and we were told to settle in for a week or so and then we would start working and I asked if we could get started as I was sort of enthusiastic and I wanted to get working. "Oh, come on, just settle down, we'll get going, don't worry about it, here, play a game," and so on for about a week and a half. I said great, if they want me to read books and be by myself then I would just do that.

J.H.: There was no pressure coming from the other kids?

Michael: No, the pressure couldn't be focused on one person. Peter and Kathy, they're hard workers and I'm sure they were quite upset and everything but they didn't know who to blame, like who to put the blame on. It all came from the group leaders. If you have lazy group leaders and there are lazy people, then they're going to be lazy. So I was a lazy person. I really didn't do anything, I can say that quite honestly. At the end I was starting to do things because I had all the pressures and the hassles.

J.H.: Were you on a farm?

Michael: Yes, I was on a farm for three weeks.

J.H.: Well, you must have worked there.

Michael: That was another thing because, like I told you, I'm used to farming. We got to the farm and it was a hobby farm. I don't know if you know what that means. The lady who was supposed to be billeting us was on unemployment, she'd been on unemployment for a year. It was just ... this is what Katimavik was putting us on, this kind of farm. I knew something about farming and I knew about good farming and bad farming. They were very bad farmers, very, very bad and they let us sleep in, in the morning and things like this.

J.H.: What about the family itself? Did you have any personal contact with them, did you talk with them?

Michael: Yes, we talked with them. I sort of understood

French and I could talk a bit; so we went to bars and stuff together and it was interesting doing that. That was the complete contact with the family.

J.H.: Were they nice people?

Michael: Oh yes, they were nice people. I would have been suited on a farm down the road where they needed someone. I don't know, for the first few months of this program I needed a kick in the pants which no one was giving me. I don't know if you know about the problem about the farm out there. We came back from the farm and there was a whole co-habitation thing with me and Carol Ann. I guess I put the blame on the group leaders; I should have known that I was co-habitating but the rule was never defined, I still don't know what the rule is. All of a sudden I was getting kicked out for it. There was just some things in there I never thought about. That was really my kick in the pants because all of a sudden it hit me, I'm going home. I looked at myself and what I'd been doing and forgot maybe a little bit about fighting and clashing with everybody above me and around me and thought, "What can I get out of this program?" We had a big meeting and I said that I would change and that's what I've done. After this meeting at Larouche, I started working more ...

J.H.: That meeting had to do with you especially?

Michael: Just with us. I guess you don't know too much about it.

J.H.: No, but it doesn't matter really. It matters only if it is important to you.

Michael: Yes, well it's quite important to me.

J.H.: So it was not a meeting about you alone?

Michael: It was about me, me and Carol Ann for co-habitating, so that's why it was an important meeting.

J.H.: You were afraid of being out, both of you?

Michael: Very afraid, and that made me realize what this program was. So after that I started working a bit more, I didn't really work too much in Larouche.

J.H.: Finally, at the end of the discussion, they decided to give you a chance?

Michael: Yes, they appeared to.

J.H.: The group did?

Michael: Yes, they gave me another chance, really a second life. I told them I would change and I did just that. I got put into a different group, but I'd had a lot of trouble with the group leader. He and I had a personality struggle. There was always a conflict between the two of us. I couldn't stay in his group and so the people switched me into another group which at that time was considered the worst group. But it turned out that that was the best group, and I finally had to deal with the people who I had avoided, like I just hadn't thought about, and they had to deal with me.

J.H.: Was it tougher for them or you?

Michael: It was tough for them, I guess you talked to Peter. Peter and I have done each other a world of good in this program because Peter didn't know a lot of longhairs and people like that at all and I didn't know people like workers and stuff, I just thought "stupid bats." We finally got to know each other and we found that we were a lot the same, so he's changed a bit and I've changed a bit. He's had a lot of effect on me, he really has and the same with most of my group. Peter and Kathy and people like this, but Peter the most I would say and Robert too because they've been really good friends, we're very close friends and it's all founded on respect because I respect Peter very, very much and Peter, I think respects me quite a bit and so we really got along and he's really on top of it all, just things like picking up the garbage instead of watching it and letting someone else do it and things like that.

J.H.: So after the lazy bit in Larouche ...

Michael: I started working a bit, I worked on the teepees, but I really wasn't working too much then. I still lived with this group and I wasn't working. It was more having a good time.

Wilcox, Saskatchewan

J.H.: Your change came about in Wilcox.

Michael: Suddenly, I wasn't with Carol Ann all the time, which made a big difference too, and I wasn't with these four other people. I was just by myself and I was faced with this group which ... like I didn't know these people, I really didn't know them, I didn't have any idea who most of them were or what they thought or anything like that. They were getting used to me and I was getting used to them. Everybody predicting the big fight and as it turned out, like we had this workshop in Wilcox, I saw the workshop and I didn't work much there for the first two or three weeks, but then I decided I wanted to take the challenge for once, to face it and see if I could do it, to go to the workshop every day and work hard and learn something from it. I did it a lot with Peter because Peter would stay late at night and I started staying late at night, working and getting things done; everything had a little challenge then, all of a sudden. It took a long time for me to change; it took a good two months for me to go from someone who wouldn't do the dishes in a million years to someone who did the dishes. So I worked on that.

J.H.: Was that the workshop for the college there?

Michael: Yes.

J.H.: Were you doing carpentry work?

Michael: Yes, I was working with Ed, the foreman who's quite a carpenter.

J.H.: Did you know something about carpentry?

Michael: My father had taught me a bit, he taught me not to be totally useless but not to the degree that Ed taught me. I went in there and I thought that someday I want to build my own house, like I want to do my own stuff. Eventually, Ed put me in charge of two other people and that, for me, was great. It really meant something, like people were starting to respect me. I came out of Larouche and I had no voice at all in the group anymore because I'd been bad, I'd just had no right to say anything. I never worked, never earned anything and then all of a sudden I started getting my voice back, and that's what made me go faster. With the help of people like Peter and things like that. I started to really work and I enjoyed it and I guess I just kept going. I haven't changed too much, I still drink and stuff like that. I'm changing from things like that again, like I never would have thought that in a million years I would stop drinking before and now I think I'll end up stopping drinking. One thing I've gotten into is natural foods. Right at the beginning of Larouche, I became a vegetarian because I wanted to do that.

J.H.: Why? Because other people were doing it?

Michael: Because I wanted to do it, there was just something in me, I guess. I wanted to try it, and so I tried it out.

J.H.: Was it just for health reasons?

Michael: Yes, and because I don't like the killing for meat because it's sort of wasteful. I don't want to get into it too much, but there is a lot of wasted protein in meat and so I became a vegetarian because I can take the wasted protein and use it. I started learning more about cooking, healthy foods, a balanced meal. I've been learning more and more all the time. Our meals here are a lot more balanced than they were in Duchesnay or even in Larouche. Living with other people who know more about it, you pick it up, you pick up ideas, like vegetables and things like that. I started getting into that in Wilcox.

J.H.: So in Wilcox you really worked hard?

Michael: Yes, I worked hard myself.

J.H.: Did you have contact with any other people in the town besides Ed?

Michael: Yes, I went curling. It was the first time I had ever curled. I had a little bit of trouble because of my hair then, like I had long hair.

J.H.: People didn't like that?

Michael: It was a Prairie town but basically, I guess, they got used to it.

J.H.: Different from Larouche and different from Brockville?

Michael: Yes. There is a different character out west.

J.H.: In what way?

Michael: Well, they're more conservative, but very friendly people. They have a warmth about them that is all their own.

J.H.: Was it your first contact with the Westerners?

Michael: Yes, I've been across Canada and the United States but just by car. I didn't stop too long. So I'd seen the Prairies but I'd never seen the people. It was interesting, like the climate was different and the people were different and the town was different. I really enjoyed Russell Polcock, our co-ordinator. He was a very good man. He was a very real man, like what he said, he did and he believed in. He didn't say, "I'm going for a walk" and then not go for a walk which I found with the other people. Russell is in the program because he believes in the ideals, he really did and he wanted to do something, to help people. Right from the beginning I really respected him and he started to respect me and so he taught me an awful lot.

J.H.: How is your French now?

Michael: It's gone down quite a bit, but I've an ability with languages which I found out too. My French, I haven't lost it, it's still there, just it hasn't improved.

J.H.: Why don't you use the fact that there are some French people around?

Michael: I do, I talk to them every once in a while.

J.H.: Do you do what Peter does? Study French every day?

Michael: No, Peter is more into it, it's part of his character too, but I'm not quite that heavy about it. I can get along in French quite well.

Grand River, Ontario

J.H.: Okay. So then you moved to Grand River?

Michael: Yes, well I came back early. Carol Ann had a boyfriend who got shot. He had been her boyfriend for three years and he was down in Mexico and got shot to death. When she found out about that she was really upset, so I went home with her for the funeral. After Larouche, our house in Cambridge was just like heaven, having three rooms for ten instead of two for thirty. The house there, I really like it. Then we came to Galt and, well you've seen it, it has the upstairs and the downstairs and there are three bathrooms.

J.H.: So what did you do as far as work was concerned?

Michael: We started working at the GRCA. The first week was a settling-in period if I remember right. Then we went for a day of orientation at the Grand River Conservation Authority. There was this really big wood pile which we had to split. The Katimavik thing was really the picnic tables because they started those from the beginning, so we stained those and we helped cut the holes in them and finished them off, and then we started assembling those.

J.H.: How much wood and how many picnic tables did you work on?

Michael: Well, the wood pile is still there, I think it's just as big as when we started. It's one of those things that just seemed to be going on and on, it's about a football field worth of wood. They're draggging it out of the bush, it's the trees that are dying or they're thinning it out. For the picnic tables, there were 200 in all that were done by us, thirty Katimavikers in various stages. Our group put together, I guess, maybe fifty or sixty:

J.H.: Were you working hard?

Michael: Yes.

J.H.: Michael was proving himself.

Michael: Well, you see I farmed before and I worked hard and I always enjoy working with my hands, getting out there and working hard. That was one of the reasons I joined the program because I wanted to work hard. The work itself was boring. It was good working with someone, it was great and we had a good time. The people we were working with were good. I don't like the GRCA, but who likes their boss really. But we had a really good time, I did anyways, working hard. I'd always shied away from physical activities for the last few years in Brockville, because I sort of got into the thing of being a freak and then there were the jocks who were always going to the Y and playing sports. Finally, in Katimavik I started realizing how stupid I was, because I really enjoy swimming and saunas and things like that. In Wilcox we had a good opportunity because at the college we were working in, there was a gym and so I started lifting weights, well not too much, it was more for fun. Playing basketball, I've always liked basketball and I'd just go out there every few nights and that was really good just running around again and starting to feel healthier again with eating. Basically I was mentally feeling better and getting healthier, working myself back into shape. I started really getting into my body, like I enjoyed using my body. I was also working with the YMCA on Wednesdays. I worked with Robert swimming with old people. It was really neat because we'd help them and we'd talk with them. It was really quite fun and it was interesting for me because I worked in Brockville for a year and a half, part time in a nursing home doing the dishes. That nursing home was really bad, like you watched the people come in and you watched them get old and you watched them die. But this nursing home was something entirely different, they were really doing things with people.

J.H.: Did you have anything to do with the radio station like some of the others?

Michael: Yes, we haven't got our program done yet, we're doing a drama on nuclear disaster.

J.H.: When you say, "we," who are you doing it with?

Michael: With Robert. Peter is doing something with Kathy on the nuclear thing too. We were going to do it, the four of us together, and I guess, we might put our programs together. I really enjoyed the radio station because I like music and going in there and talking with the people about the radio station, it's been really good.

J.H.: That radio station seems to have been an important factor in your staying in Ontario.

Michael: It's been very good. I really like Galt, I've really liked the project. The only project I didn't like was Larouche. Wilcox was good because ...like any project is what you make it, and if you want to make it bad then you make it bad and I made Larouche bad and then I grew up a bit in Wilcox and ...

J.H.: You matured in Galt.

Michael: Yes, I finally started using the program and all of a sudden our group was becoming much tighter and much more together. I've had some really good talks with people and everybody is pretty open and honest about things. The people are really good for me. What I like most about this program are the people. Like each one of those people in my house are very special.

J.H.: How do you think of them?

Michael: It is like a family in a way, they're like brothers and sisters and they've made my life richer. They really have.

J.H.: Did you make their life richer?

Michael: Oh I think so, I hope so. I've really enjoyed my group.

J.H.: Do you think this friendship will last for long?

Michael: Oh yes I think so, for sure. I can see it sort of falling off with some people but never really falling off, if you know what I mean. I can see these people being a part of me for a long, long time.

J.H.: For the rest of your life?

Michael: Oh yes, like I can see someone like Peter and Robert and Kathy is very important to me. Kathy and I are interesting because she hated me, like she really hated me and I didn't like her too well. We had a spat one morning, a sort of an argument and we were sort of nasty to each other. We didn't know each other and it was, "Grrr I don't like her," and she didn't like me. But we finally sorted it out and now she's very important to me. There are a few like Robert who has always been a very good friend, very good because, well, he's shown me a lot of things, he's a very good guy and he's an honest friend, he isn't silly or anything like that, he's more of a real friend. Peter has been ...we've had a friendship based on respect, where we've always both grown together because we found that we're both from the same background, father being German and his is German too, we're both from the same kind of rigid background, German background, so that's really been interesting. So Peter is really important and I guess I'll keep in contact with him and Kathy.

J.H.: What kind of feeling does it give you now to have friends — very close friends and more or less close

147

friends — in some cases spread all across this great country from Vancouver to Newfoundland?

Michael: Oh it's nice. I really enjoy the idea ... I know I could go to a town now pretty well anywhere within Canada, and within a range I'd have a friend somewhere, really. I now have friends out East, I have friends out West, I have friends in Edmonton and around me. I have friends who were my good friends in Brockville and I go back to visit them. They're still in the same place, still going to the bars and they're still, I guess, happy, but they're not going anywhere, they're just sitting around stagnating. They're scared of leaving, they're scared of getting away. So I think I've finally done it. When I started Katimavik I thought I'd never go back to Brockville, but now I think I will, not to go back to get to know the people or anything like that. I want to maybe finish my school and get that over with or I might work, but I'm going to use Brockville instead of having Brockville use me.

J.H.: You started saying that you were almost a bad boy when you got into the program.

Michael: Not almost, I was.

J.H.: How are you now? In what way have you changed so much?

Michael: I changed ...

J.H.: Well you cut your hair, that's a simple thing.

Michael: Well it's symbolic, I guess in a way. At the beginning I would never have cut my hair. There was no reason for me to be growing my hair except, I don't know, I was just growing it. Then one day I just realized, you know, what am I doing, it's getting in my way, it's hard to keep clean, it's just sitting there and not doing anything. So I cut it. In the beginning I was a mixed up kid really. Before I left for Katimavik, I was just boring to talk to. Everything I said was boring, very "I know what I don't like" sort of thing. Now I know what I don't like, but I also know that I can change it and I'm starting to do things with myself and be consistent and just basically getting healthier.

J.H.: They won't recognize you in Brockville ...

Michael: I went back just the other weekend and my friends have a hard time dealing with me now, really hard. I don't know how to really talk to them anymore. They're good people but they have trouble dealing with me because I'm talking about this and that and they don't have any idea about, like eating well, about working really hard. Their idea of working hard is to get money, work enough so that you're keeping your job, and my idea of working hard is having pride in your job and doing it and getting something done. It doesn't really matter about the money too much, as long as I'm getting food.

J.H.: You learned to live, really.

Michael: Yes. I go back and I think they're very young, that's one thing. The first time I went back after Larouche, once, just overnight, I saw my friends and it just hit me how young they were. I thought, look at all this I've been through, all this changing and everything, and I'm just starting to become something. These people are still so young. They have false happiness. Being drunk might make you happy, but you're not really happy.

J.H.: I remember when I saw you first in Larouche, you didn't look really happy.

Michael: I wasn't, but I am happier now, I'm starting to be happy with myself.

J.H.: Katimavik was a good idea for you?

Michael: Oh it was, for all my complaining. I was thinking when I was talking at the beginning about Larouche, how negative I was. It has a part in my whole story, being negative at the beginning, because there is a lot of negativeness in this program. If you were going to write a book or something I don't think you should hide that.

J.H.: The funny thing is that other participants told me exactly that, there are a lot of negative things in the program, but, "It has been very positive for me." Well if it is true for everybody ...

Michael: Yes, but the negative things, like what people are really forgetting is that the negative makes the positive. If you look around you will find some very happy people.

J.H.: Well, I cannot think of anyone who is not.

Michael: Except Gordon maybe.

J.H.: Well, yes, that's ...

Michael: There is a lot of ugly ... I'd like to tell you some stories, but they shouldn't go on tape, I guess, really.

J.H.: You decide that.

Michael: Yes, there are some things that just ... like some of the people that Katimavik chose to be our leaders just amaze me.

J.H.: Yes, I know very well what you're talking about because that was my worry from the very first day of this year. It started so quickly and it would be a long story to tell you why it started that way, but anyway, we were caught and at one point we had to start. We had to improvise everything. The staff hired the people very quickly and those people were not fully qualified. We looked and we had fifteen days to find, I don't know how many dozen group leaders, etc. So it is true, but next year I think we will improve a lot.

Michael: I think Katimavik has got to stop being afraid to kick people out.

J.H.: Yes. Well maybe they would have kicked you out on that principle!

Michael: Yes, okay. But give people a chance to change ...

J.H.: Michael, in spite of all its mistakes of this first year, I would feel good about Katimavik if only because of what happened to you in ten months ...

13 *Kathy Ophel,*
Age 17,
Deep River, Ontario

I come from Deep River which is a very strange environment. You know Chalk River near where the nuclear reactors are? There is an atomic energy agency and also a nuclear laboratory. The Ottawa valley is a very depressed area, very poor farming with high unemployment, but Deep River is professional, middle class. My father is a scientist; my friends are all very career-oriented, going into science. It is fairly isolated. My mother stays at home but she does volunteer work. One sister is in her fourth year of medical school, one is an economist working for the government, my brother is studying engineering. So, everyone in my family is career-oriented, as well as all my friends from Deep River.

J.H.: Before Katimavik, what were your own plans about the future in such an environment?

Kathy: I went straight from grade 12 to university. I've always been a very good student, with top marks and I always knew I'd go to university, but I've always had a dilemma about a career because I really enjoy writing and I enjoy music. I play the flute. I've always been very good in math and sciences so I spent a year at Carleton University in Ottawa doing chemistry, but I knew that wasn't what I wanted to do.

J.H.: Did you travel at all when you were younger?

Kathy: My family is Australian. I was born in Canada, my parents and my sister were born in Australia, so we went back when I was five. We've been to the Atlantic provinces, and I used to play competitive tennis from when I was in high school, so I travelled around Ontario and Quebec and once to British Columbia, but I'd never really seen the West, the Prairies, and I've never been up north.

J.H.: What was your idea of Canada in those days?

Kathy: I thought it was all very much the same, it was just the land that changed. The Prairies were flat, but the people were the same as in Ontario, with the same sorts of goals, the same ideas about things.

J.H.: How did you hear about Katimavik?

Kathy: Like a number of people, I read about it in *Canadian Magazine*. I'm always interested in opportunities like that, so I applied and then forgot about it until I found out that I was accepted for the interview.

J.H.: What was your first impression when you got to Duchesnay?

Kathy: I was really boggled; I didn't know what to do. I had always spent a lot of time by myself and being with ninety people just blew me away. I didn't know what I was getting into at all, and all through Duchesnay I was really wary of Katimavik. I was not ready to commit myself to it totally. I'd say to myself: "Oh, I can quit, I'll just see what it's like and then I can still quit if I want to."

Larouche, Quebec

J.H.: But it really started in Larouche with your first program. There were a lot of challenges. You had to live in a house not meant for that many people; how was that?

Kathy: The first two weeks in Larouche I was really, really unhappy. That was the lowest point for me in Katimavik. When we first got there, there wasn't much to do and I had expected a fairly structured work program, something to do for the community. I went to a farm for the first three weeks and that was a complete change. It was the happiest time in Katimavik for me. I loved it. I was with the

Tremblay family. Diane Tremblay impressed me so much — she's one of those people I'll remember for a long time. I really admire her because she is so independent. She's about thirty-five or so and she lives with her family, but she built this beautiful log cabin all by herself, in her spare time. We talked a lot about being a woman and being independent, the things we wanted, what society wanted of women.

J.H.: Was it your first experience on a farm?

Kathy: I'd been on a farm, but never to work. I'd done things like ride horses and spent a lot of time outdoors because Deep River is near Algonquin Park and there are beautiful places to go hiking, canoeing, etc.

J.H.: Was it your first contact with a French-Canadian family?

Kathy: Yes. I learned a lot of French there and certainly gained more confidence in speaking French.

J.H.: Did it change your mind about what the French Canadians were like?

Kathy: Yes, we talked a lot with the family about the problems of Quebec, about the problems of having a farm around here, and I really got a different look at things. All of Katimavik, the farm, and everything was a complete shock to me ... Where I grew up and when I went to university, everyone was in a "rut" of sorts. It was a shock to me to find out that not everyone wanted to go to university. They just thought it was useless.

J.H.: Did you keep in touch with them?

Kathy: Yes, I've written to Diane since I left.

J.H.: Do you think you will ever see them again?

Kathy: That's hard to say. I know that if I'm ever in Quebec City I'd go up.

J.H.: What did you do in Larouche besides that?

Kathy: I worked on the greenhouse a lot. There weren't many of us constantly but it was good. When I got back from the farm things were a lot better for me because we had the greenhouse to do and I felt I was doing something useful. Because I was happier, I found it easier to be with people. I had calmed down a bit on the farm and had a chance to be away from the group. I helped with the teepees as well as working on the greenhouse. I got more involved with the group life which was good. I started going out with people and getting to know them. My first impression of some people was bad: I thought they just wanted to lie in bed and get drunk at night, but I realized there was a lot more to them when I actually sat down and talked with them. Larouche was good for me for that reason — just realizing that my first impressions of some people had been wrong.

Wilcox, Saskatchewan

J.H.: From there you moved to Wilcox where everything changed in the sense that you were living in small groups of nine or ten, and it seemed all of a sudden almost family size.

Kathy: It was good in most ways. A group of ten is probably a better way to live but sometimes I missed the group of thirty, because on the whole a group of thirty is more fun. But it's much more stable, calm, and more normal living in a group of ten. I really love my group.

J.H.: Could you describe them to me?

Kathy: In my group there is Peter, Yves, Lise, Jo-Anne, Angie, Michael, Robert. On the whole I like our group because everybody contributes something different. We had troubles at various times, but people took their share of responsibilities. We like things to be fairly organized although all the houses are different. Some, like with meals, are more casual. In ours, we have the three meals and we sit down to them together and I really enjoy that.

J.H.: What did you do in Wilcox?

Kathy: First I worked on the curling rink with Carol and the farmers from around the area. That was a good way to start because when I came I didn't know what to expect. I really liked the people there. For me the best part of Katimavik was meeting the people of the community. We had a lot of fun doing that rink and I met a lot of people. It was just before Christmas so that was great. They gave us little Christmas presents and we gave them some and that was fun. Then I worked in the workshop for most of the time after that.

J.H.: The workshop that was being built for the students?

Kathy: Yes, for the college. I worked on finishing up the café and everybody helped with that. During the week I also taught physical education classes at the college, two afternoons a week, but it was more like supervising. In the workshop I did a lot of painting. Mark and I had a lot of fun doing designs on the walls, so we made the best of something that wasn't too exciting. The work in Wilcox was not exciting, but meeting the community and curling were great. I just got to be a curling addict. There was a gym and we used to play basketball and things like that. I had a lot of fun there.

J.H.: Was it your first contact with the Prairies?

Kathy: Yes, and I was shocked when I saw how flat it was. At first, I just hated the flatness; I'd look out and it was just so empty; there was nothing there at all but by the end you saw ... the skies were just incredible and at night the sunsets were beautiful. Sometimes you would see mirages and we could see the lights of Regina about thirty miles away.

Grand River, Ontario

J.H.: Then after three months you moved closer to home?

Kathy: Yes, but still quite far away from Deep River.

J.H.: Yes, to the Grand River project. Where were you?

Kathy: I was in Cambridge. I wasn't that pleased at being in the city. I don't know if it's a good idea or not, although there are a lot of facilities there like the library. I really enjoyed that. I spent a week on a project in Belwood and it was nice to be in the country, I would have liked that.

J.H.: What did you do in Cambridge?

Kathy: We worked at the GRCA, doing the picnic tables, chopping wood, and then planting trees. I worked one day a week at a day-care centre for retarded children and then at the radio station one day.

J.H.: What did you do at the radio station?

155

Kathy: I was doing a documentary with Peter about the sale of nuclear reactors to Third-World countries. That's been interesting. I knew a few people to contact, so that's been handy. Peter is very organized and a good person to work with. At the GRCA, I really enjoyed working outdoors.

J.H.: What did you do mainly?

Kathy: I spent a lot of time chopping wood. After a while I really got bored with it but planting trees was the best part. It's too bad that it came right at the end because that was another place we met some nice people. I liked the people we worked with. They were students and that was a nice job even though it was a ten-hour day — we worked from 7.00 a.m. to 5.30.

J.H.: What type of links do you have with all the people in the group?

Kathy: I guess it's different for each person. Some people I still feel I don't know very well even after ten months, but I consider them good friends. Some people, those that I've shared something special with, I feel definitely are like brothers and sisters. Maybe it's crazy but a couple of us are interested in farming eventually, having a small farm and practising organic agriculture. So, some people I am going to see, definitely, in the future, even if we never do that. I think there are some people I won't keep in touch with after, just because I haven't got to know them.

J.H.: But out of the twenty-six, how many do you think you will keep in touch with, writing or maybe seeing?

Kathy: To start out, I am sure about half of them, but I think in the end, maybe about five or six. Some of the people I know I'll be friends with for a long time, others I think I'll write to for a couple of years and maybe I won't see them and it will just die out.

J.H.: What does it feel like to have friends of different degrees spread out across the whole country, friends from the West, Centre, North, and East?

Kathy: It's a nice feeling, because almost anywhere you go you can find people that you know, and also knowing that the Katimavik project is all across Canada. I always get the feeling that if you needed a place to stay you could go to a project and say: "I used to be a participant and I just don't have a place to stay."

J.H.: And you can count on them if you need them?

Kathy: Yes, I hope so.

J.H.: What will you do right after Katimavik?

Kathy: I'm going to go home first; and Mark, and later Cindy, are going to visit for a while. Then I'll just see a few old friends and go to see my sister; I haven't seen those people for a while. I've been accepted for something else for the summer, a two-month program in the Northwest Territories called Frontier's Foundation. It's for people from all over the world which really excites me, because I wanted to go on Canada World Youth at one time.

J.H.: And after that?

Kathy: I've been accepted for university in Guelph but I don't think I'm going to go this year. I'd like to work for a year and I'm looking into an apprenticeship in woodworking. I know I'll go back to university, but not until I'm really sure why I want to and not just because I felt that I had to.

J.H.: If you go to university, do you have any idea what area you would go into?

Kathy: Yes, I think I'll still be in the sciences but probably agriculture. I'd like to get involved in doing work in Third-World countries so I think agriculture is a good field for two reasons — because I'm interested in it.

J.H.: Why the Third World?

Kathy: Because I've always been concerned. I did a course in high school on the Third World, called Revolutions and the Third World. I had an excellent teacher. She got me very interested in different issues and I won a prize in that course and got a subscription to the New Internationalist magazine on Third World issues. Reading that made me more aware and Katimavik reinforced those ideas.

J.H.: Did you talk about that a lot?

Kathy: With some people I did. In Wilcox, Peter, Carol, Lise and I had a Third World discussion every Sunday night, showing films for the community and that stimulated my interest more.

J.H.: But finally Katimavik was a good idea for you as well?

Kathy: I think so. There were times when I've really been down on the program and I was really unhappy at different points, especially at the beginning of Larouche, but it's been really excellent for me. I think I've come out of myself a lot instead of spending so much time alone. Now, I feel much better about being with people and I think I've opened up a lot. I have a lot more fun that I ever had before.

J.H.: So you have changed?

Kathy: Oh, I've changed a lot and people have noticed too. My family have noticed it. The first thing they said was, "You look so happy." Even when Katimavik was not happy, I was happy with myself just because I feel I've become a better person through Katimavik. I don't know if it's a good idea for everyone, I still have reservations, but I think if you're willing to put a lot into it, you can change yourself and contribute something. It's a good program but it needs changes.

J.H.: You bet!

14 *Lise Coulombe,*
Age 19,
Laval, Quebec

My family's very ordinary, very happy parents. An ordinary background, nothing extravagant ... My father's been working for the Montreal School Board for twenty-five years, I think. My mother stays at home now. Before, she used to work from time to time, here and there. I have two brothers, one older and one younger, two ordinary brothers, we squabble. ...

J.H.: Where were you born?

Lise: Montreal. I moved to Laval later. Around Saint-François, I don't know if you know it? It's in the east and still quite rural, though there's been a lot of development lately. It isn't Montreal, there isn't as much pollution. It's green, with cows and farms. I had a quiet childhood. I had quite a few friends at school. I've always enjoyed school. I like going to school but I've never been very studious. But the time comes when you have to study. At CEGEP for instance. And that was my mistake. I got bad marks because I wasn't used to studying hard, probably.

J.H.: Before Katimavik did you have the chance to visit other parts of Quebec, or other parts of Canada?

Lise: Before Katimavik, no. Quebec a little. But I didn't really know Quebec.

J.H.: What's the farthest you'd gone in Quebec?

Lise: Baie Comeau. Which is really quite something! A trip to Manicouagan organized by the school. Afterward we spent four days at Baie Comeau.

J.H.: So for all practical purposes, before Katimavik you hadn't left the Montreal area very much? What idea did you have about Canada?

Lise: I saw British Columbia as a sort of dream. And the East too, Prince Edward Island, that part of the country. I thought it must be very beautiful. It was just a dream, I wanted to go there some day, that's all. I didn't even think about provinces like Alberta or Manitoba or Saskatchewan. I'd never thought about them. The important thing for me was one end of the country or the other!

J.H.: When you thought about your life, your future, what kind of dreams did you have?

Lise: Before? I don't know, it was a little vague. I wanted to study administration, have a business career.

J.H.: Why business?

Lise: I don't really know. But I saw myself travelling with my suitcase ... It was travelling that attracted me in particular, and all the papers, I really thought that was what I liked ... So I ended up studying administration and I discovered I didn't belong there. But even then I wasn't sure because I'd left CEGEP after two years, and went to work in a Caisse Populaire. I liked it, not because there were papers and money and all that, but because we saw people. That was where I started thinking that maybe it was relationships with people that I liked better than paperwork. But I didn't have any definite ideas. What I wanted to do most of all was to travel. I saw myself going away, getting on the plane, spending one week here, another week there ... It was more a dream than anything else.

J.H.: And then Katimavik came into your life.

Lise: I remember, it was in April — somewhere around then. I was looking for a job. I'd gone to the banks and I was waiting for answers. Then I saw the ad for Katimavik. "Okay, that looks like fun and everything!" But that was all, I applied. It would mean travelling. And meeting people. And then there was the business about appropriate technology. I think overall it was living in a group that interested me most, because I've never had the chance to go to summer camp or anything like that. That was what attracted me most. The work too. For me it meant a chance to do something besides going to school or being a teller. Work outside ... I saw myself in big boots ... ... I didn't really know what it was. It was like a sort of dream I saw on paper ...

J.H.: And the dream started to take shape at the training camp in Duchesnay?

Lise: It was really new. I had to adapt to it. So many people! From all sorts of different backgrounds. And I'd never had friends who spoke a different language. Until then all my friends spoke French.

Larouche, Quebec

J.H.: You'd never had any Anglophone friends?

Lise: No, not really friends. Acquaintances, people who lived near me, that's all. We didn't talk. "Bonjour, bonsoir ... " But nothing more than that. So for me that was different. And when we got to Larouche I'd learned a little but it was different again. There, we were in a house we thought was big but, in fact, it was small. We had to put up with one another. What was hard was having so many Anglophones. We were stuck in the house and we weren't really living in Quebec. It was pretty well Anglophone. At a certain point there was a little crisis in the house with the Anglophones. Because there wasn't any French being spoken in the house. And that was pretty difficult.

J.H.: Afterward, did the situation get better?

Lise: Yes, it changed. We had a meeting and talked about it. It changed after three weeks, a month. When we got to Wilcox it was settled. I think that was a problem for most of the groups. There was too much English.

J.H.: There were more of them, so of course ...

Lise: Yes, that's true. But none of them, practically none of them spoke enough French to talk with us.

J.H.: I'm thinking of Peter ...

161

Lise: Yes, he's an exception. He never stops speaking French and he works hard.

J.H.: Do you have Anglophone friends now?

Lise: Oh yes! I'm not angry because of the people but because of the situation. But I've got good friends who are Anglophones. It isn't because we aren't friends ... But I really don't like it when English dominates at the meetings in particular, when we talk about business, when we talk about serious things. It doesn't bother me to speak English with friends. But at meetings, important things, it's always in English. Even though I speak English I've always had trouble understanding ...

J.H.: Did you speak it at the beginning?

Lise: A little. I could get by.

J.H.: And now?

Lise: Yes, I can speak, but it still isn't my language. And I don't know it · perfectly, I make mistakes. And if somebody's talking either too fast or about a subject I don't know, I have to pay more attention or I'll miss some of the words. And that makes me mad because often it's important. I either have to make them repeat themselves or ask somebody. And that's what I don't like. Maybe that's why I got angry, because I don't understand too well. I don't know, but I think it's a bad situation, and not just for our group. A number of groups were like that. There weren't enough Francophones, I think, it should be half and half. But I don't know, for the tax-payers ...

J.H.: Aside from that problem, was living in a group easy for you? Did you have to change your behaviour somewhat to adapt to so many people?

Lise: Yes, I had to change. It was easy sometimes but ... Okay, you have to adapt to the needs of the group. The group is very important. It's not several individuals but a group. So, you have to change a little. Sometimes it was hard. Okay, I'll change a little; but on the other hand I got a lot out of it.

J.H.: Did you notice that the others changed too?

Lise: Yes. Everyone changes.

J.H.: What kind of work did you do in Larouche?

Lise: At the end, I did a lot on the greenhouse because we had to finish it.

J.H.: The greenhouse was very important for your group?

Lise: It had a meaning for us. It was for the village, so they could grow vegetables even in the winter. I don't think we took the idea far enough. It was the building, learning how to build a greenhouse ...

J.H.: And aside from the greenhouse?

Lise: We worked at the dump. With everybody. I liked that because it was fun. The whole group was together, we enjoyed ourselves. But it isn't a job I'd want to do for very long because it was pretty revolting! And I worked in the library, I cleaned the church with the women. I made some friends with the women in the village.

Wilcox, Saskatchewan

J.H.: When you got to Wilcox did you feel disoriented?

Lise: Yes and no. We were in smaller groups. It was more like a family. Personally, I felt lost outside. I found a refuge inside the house, with my friends. So I didn't feel so disoriented because we were often in the house. I met some really fun people. In fact I met more people in Wilcox than in Quebec. I thought they were very nice, maybe because I had the chance to get to know them. I found them nice. Our neighbours, the people we met at work would invite us to their places ... The first time we met they'd tell us, "Come over for coffee." I really enjoyed that. They were especially interested in the people from Quebec. They liked to argue ...

J.H.: Did you work hard in Wilcox?

Lise: Yes and no. Not as hard as I could have. I think I've done the most work here, in Cambridge.

J.H.: What work did you do in Wilcox?

Lise: I worked at the day-care centre, with the mothers. I went to the library and worked there with the students. I worked on the student café and in the carpentry shop. In the café, we plastered the walls, painted, redid the ceiling ... I worked mostly in the shop. I learned quite a lot

163

of things. How to make a windowframe, a doorframe.

J.H.: Now would you take the risk of making a doorframe or a windowframe?

Lise: Yes, I'd take the risk. That doesn't mean I'd succeed! But I'd try. I've learned how to do manual labour, which I hadn't done before. Now I do a little more. I'm not really wild about it but I like the results, when my day's work is done.

J.H.: After Wilcox, would you say that Saskatchewan has become something special for you?

Lise: It's very impressive to see the Prairies. The big fields ... The people's attitude too ... I like Saskatchewan a lot!

Grand River, Ontario

J.H.: After Wilcox the whole group moved to Grand River.

Lise: My group went to Cambridge.

J.H.: To the old, old historic house that's going to be demolished?

Lise: Yes. It's terrible, it's so beautiful. With the Grand River Conservation Authority I worked on the picnic tables. Staining them, dipping them in a big vat of stain, assembling them. In the forest I transported wood because I can't cut down trees. And I planted trees in the parks too. But mostly I did community work, and the day-care center, with handicapped children, at the YMCA where I taught swimming. ...

J.H.: Do you like that kind of work?

Lise: Yes, I like it a lot. The people I work with are fantastic. I work in the school too, at the high school. I teach French as a monitor. We have discussions and I lead the discussions. And the students are, oh! they're really fun! And the teachers!

J.H.: How old are they?

Lise: The students are eighteen.

J.H.: About the same as you ...

Lise: Almost, yes.

J.H.: Are they interested in speaking French?

Lise: Ah! They're very good. Yes, that really surprised me, I can't get over it ... Some of them hardly understand at all, but some of the others, if I speak a little more slowly than I'm speaking now they understand almost everything. We talked about marriage, divorce. We've talked about Quebec, about politics in Quebec. I talked about Katimavik. About life on the farm, city life. A whole bunch of things. They asked me questions, I answered, I'd ask them questions, they'd answer.

J.H.: After ten months in Katimavik have you changed in any way?

Lise: Yes, I think I've changed. The way I live ... I've discovered simplicity. Before, I was a city girl who just thought about behaving like everybody else. I've changed in that respect.

J.H.: What do you mean by simplicity?

Lise: For example, I don't really care about having money ... Money to buy dresses ... Spend just for the sake of spending, buy this, buy that, the way I used to before. Now it doesn't interest me.

J.H.: Why not?

Lise: Because I don't think money's a real value. I don't know if it's just the influence of the group ... Someone sends out an idea, it makes us all think ... One of the participants, Peter, made me think a lot about all that.

J.H.: Who'd have thought that one day a guy from Edmonton would have such influence over you ...

Lise: I'd never have thought it. It's Peter and some of the others who made me think about a lot of things. I started asking questions about myself. In any case, I hope I've changed. I'm waiting to get back to Montreal, to see my friends, to find out if I'll fall back into my old way of thinking, or if I've really changed. Maybe it's just superficial, but I hope not. I don't think it is.

J.H.: You don't trust your conversion?

Lise: Yes, but it's because I'm not in the situation. Here, there aren't any stores next door, I don't have any money. Maybe it's because I just have seven dollars a week that I think this way. I don't think so but we'll see ...

J.H.: In two weeks you'll have $1000.[1] in your pocket. What will you do with it?

Lise: Put it in the bank and take a trip this summer. And the rest is for my education.

J.H.: You've decided to go back to school?

Lise: Yes.

J.H.: But you'd left school for good.

Lise: For good. Because I wasn't interested in school. I wanted to find out what it was like to go out to work.

J.H.: You seem to be saying that Katimavik brought back your interest in school.

Lise: Because I'm going in a different direction. I don't want to go back to work in a Caisse Populaire or a bank or some place like that ...

J.H.: And what about your dream, with the papers and the suitcase and travelling?

Lise: I'm still interested in travelling. Even the suitcase is all right, but not the papers! What I'm interested in is meeting people, living in new situations, to feel useful, not to make some company's profits go up.

J.H.: You're moving from accounting to sociology?

Lise: Back to CEGEP first, to finish certain courses and take some sociology, then some psychology courses too. Because I'm a little bit interested in delinquency. I'm interested but I have no experience. So this summer I might get a job as a volunteer in a milieu like that. To see if I'm really interested.

J.H.: How would you describe your group — which you'll be leaving in a few weeks?

Lise: It's really a big family. And when I think we'll all be leaving soon ... It hurts me more than when I left my own family. Because I knew I'd be back with my family in ten months. But our group won't get together as a group most likely ...

J.H.: Perhaps ...

---

1. The last day of the program, each participant receives $1000.

Lise: Okay, perhaps ... But it'll be harder to go to Vancouver or other places. We'll be travelling, but there's always the matter of money ... And if you go back to school you can't travel. Maybe we'll see each other again, but there's some people in the group I'll probably never see again.

J.H.: Won't you go to Saskatoon to see Bruce?

Lise: If I'm in Saskatoon, yes ... But I don't think so, unless I've got money to spend ... Ah! Maybe I'll go to see Bruce just to see Bruce, but I don't think I can do that with everybody.

J.H.: I mentioned Bruce just at random ... I could have mentioned Mark or Carol Ann or Robert ... Now to conclude, would you say that Katimavik was worth it to you?

Lise: Yes, yes. In spite of the bad times. Yes. There were so many good times, it was worth it. I lived so much during Katimavik. And the people I've met — I'd never have met them if I'd stayed at home. And the work! I'd never have had the chance to make a window frame! I think that's good, because Katimavik is full of possibilities.

J.H.: It's nearly over now; in a few days you'll be leaving one another ...

Lise: I don't even dare to think about it. I know there's going to be a lot of tears. Sometimes Jo-Anne and Angie and I talk about it, we make jokes about it, but we've all got tears in our eyes whenever we think about it! In two weeks ... Soon it'll be an hour, half an hour ... I know it's going to be terrible.

15 Robert Yee, Age 18, Vancouver, British Columbia

I was born in Vancouver, I spent the first six years of my life in a suburb of Vancouver, then I moved to Vancouver in the fall of '65 and I have lived there ever since.

J.H.: Is your family big or small?

Robert: I have two brothers; they still live at home with my parents.

J.H.: What kind of childhood did you have?

Robert: I didn't do that much as a kid. I wasn't really involved in anything like churches, organized sports, I sort of went to church every now and then and I played sports on my own, with the neighbourhood kids. My schooling wasn't that high. I was never a good student, schooling just didn't turn me on.

J.H.: Until Katimavik, did you travel at all?

Robert: Well, my family went to Montreal for Expo '67. We flew and we took some small driving trips around down to the United States every now and then and around the province and we drove down to Disneyland, I guess seven years ago.

J.H.: You can say that you knew little of Canada until recently?

Robert: Yes, I would say I knew very little of Canada.

J.H.: How does it look from British Columbia?

Robert: It's ... Well, I think I remember Diane Tremblay

who lives on a farm outside of Larouche where we had our first project. She felt that Paris, France, was closer to Larouche, Quebec, than Vancouver, British Columbia. I guess she is right. Vancouver is a long way from Eastern Canada and that is where most things happen, I guess.

J.H.: Were you still in school when you heard about Katimavik?

Robert: Yes, I was going to a community college in Vancouver, taking a university level course in sciences.

J.H.: What were you planning to do then?

Robert: I didn't really have any concrete plans, but I was sort of nudging toward getting into UBC and maybe getting a degree in a biology-related field.

J.H.: And then you heard about Katimavik?

Robert: Well, I was just looking in *Weekend Magazine* and I saw the advertisement.

J.H.: What struck you in the few lines of the advertisement?

Robert: Well, the ideals. I liked them immediately because I was sort of searching for that sort of alternative at that time and I have always wanted to move into some log cabin on the hills, like everybody else and live off the land and be self-sufficient and just cope. Actually, everybody has that dream, I think.

J.H.: Well, not everybody!

Robert: Not everyone, a lot of people. But like I read the advertisement and it appealed to me 'cause those sort of ... the ideas of Katimavik I liked, you know.

J.H.: The idea of group living, was that something that you were looking for?

Robert: Well, I guess I wasn't really like "gung ho" about it but I wasn't really scared either.

J.H.: So, one morning you arrive in Duchesnay, Quebec, and you met almost one hundred young people from all across the country. What kind of shock was that?

Robert: I guess it didn't hit me that hard, for some reason. It was certainly something I'd never gone through before and it was a strange experience. I kind of liked it the first week, it was really fun, because ... there was a lot of good feelings and good vibes going around.

Larouche, Quebec

J.H.: But it really started in Larouche, which is a small town in Quebec.

Robert: As far as I could see, Larouche wasn't that great. A lot of time and energy and money was wasted that could have been put to better use. I thought that Wilcox was much, much better than Larouche, and Cambridge maybe just a little bit better than Larouche for me.

J.H.: Let's start with Larouche. What did you find good in Larouche for yourself?

Robert: Well, I thought the living in a group of thirty in that little house was something you could really learn something from. I learned how to get along with people, I learned how to get to sleep while other people were snoring, I learned how to cook, I learned how to build a greenhouse, I learned a little bit about teepees, I learned a lot about Francophones. I think I'd met one Francophone in Vancouver that I can recall. So, I learned quite a bit about French culture and French people, which is good.

J.H.: Was it very different from what you'd thought in Vancouver?

Robert: No. I found that certainly the French people have different values and ideas than the people in British Columbia but I also found that we shared a lot.

J.H.: You were on a farm for some time?

Robert: Yes. The Tremblay farm. I spent three weeks there, with Mario and Michael ...

J.H.: I remember seeing you there milking a cow! Was it the first time you'd done that?

Robert: Yes it was. It is the first farm I'd ever been on. I like milking cows and it was nice living on a farm. I didn't even mind shovelling the shit, you know. The people there were really good.

J.H.: So you learned about farming?

Robert: Yes, a little bit.

170

Wilcox, Saskatachewan

J.H.: So, from Larouche, you moved to Wilcox and that was quite a change?

Robert: Yes. The first day I got there, I was walking around with a light parka and jeans on and I was really cold. But Wilcox was really a change, of course, the mentality of a small Prairie town is very different.

J.H.: In what way is it that different?

Robert: I didn't get to know the region of Larouche that well, so I couldn't really tell you what the mentality of small town Quebec people is, compared to Saskatchewan, but I got to know the Wilcox people just a little better. It was just during the winter, when nothing is happening except curling, but they seemed to be, you know, laid back, easy-going people, not in a rush to do anything. My kind of pace. And they are really friendly.

J.H.: What kind of work did you do in Wilcox?

Robert: Mostly construction. We were converting the Legion Hall into a workshop for the Notre Dame College there, who was our sponsor, and we built work benches, we tore up old floors and laid new ones, sealed old windows, insulating.

J.H.: Were you familiar with that at all?

Robert: Yes, because my dad, he builds houses and I have worked with him a bit.

J.H.: So, you didn't learn a lot but you worked a lot?

Robert: Well, I learned quite a bit actually because I worked a lot. It was fun. Wilcox was my favourite project.

J.H.: Tell me about it.

Robert: Well, our co-ordinator was Russell Pocock and I really admired him because of the lifestyle that he lived, and his attitude toward everything. And I liked the work, although it got a little bit boring, and I liked the people. I had a good time. We played a little hockey, we did cross-country skiing, which is one thing we didn't do a whole lot at Larouche, physical activity. I am the sort of person who really feels restless if I don't get some sweating exercise and I learned cross-country skiing, which I'd never done

171

before. I also got to know certain members in my group better and I'll always remember the good feelings between those people and me. I liked the library too! I learned to ski at Wilcox and that was a lot of fun because it is really a good feeling and we camped, winter camped.

J.H.: In that weather?

Robert: Yes. It is −20⁰F. or something and that was really fun. Nine people went out and camped the first night and of the nine, I was the only one who stayed the second day. But the second day, they had some other people coming. But that was really a strange experience, that was fun. I really felt high on the way back, just the fresh air, the sun, the skiing.

J.H.: Did you like this type of flat country, coming from Vancouver?

Robert: It didn't bother me. I thought the sunrises and the sunsets were just magnificient, there is none other that compare.

J.H.: No trees?

Robert: Well, I guess that was a bit strange. There were some trees around Wilcox because people planted them.

J.H.: Did you do any work in the community?

Robert: I worked in the school cafeteria and I got to know some of the people who worked in that cafeteria quite well.

J.H.: A moment ago, talking about Russell, the co-ordinator of the Wilcox project, you said that his lifestyle impressed you?

Robert: Yes. He lives on a farm just outside of Coaticook and he is a very well-educated man, which doesn't mean he has got all his degrees, but he is a very knowledgeable man and the farm that he runs is an organic farm; he avoids pesticides, chemical fertilizers and he is a very back-to-nature man.

J.H.: That is one of the things that you were dreaming of doing?

Robert: Yes, for sure. That is something that I would like to really check out.

Grand River, Ontario

J.H.: And from Wilcox, you moved to Grand River, to Cambridge in the case of your particular group?

Robert: Yes. Well Cambridge was a rough time for me because I had, I think I had trouble adjusting to a big city again.

J.H.: Is it such a big city?

Robert: Well, Cambridge has a population of 70 000, it is not a small town. The house that we lived in was right next to a major street, so I went to sleep to the sounds of motorcycles and big trucks going past my window. And a lot of people got ill for some reason at the house. At one point, Yves got pneumonia, Peter had scarlet fever, Kathy had something that she was on penicillin for, everyone else had colds. For one month there, I was really having a rough time because it was stressful. Anyhow, during the last two, three weeks, it has been really nice, I've liked it. It is only during this past week that we have been having some real interaction with some of the people that we work with, for instance, people from the GRCA.

J.H.: What kind of work were you doing?

Robert: At first, we were doing a lot of "joe" jobs ... painting lawn mowers, and chopping wood, and staining picnic tables and putting them together, picnic tables ... and we really got disenchanted with our work. No one likes to do that stuff every day for eight hours. It got a little boring and then, we eventually got into the water-quality lab. Yves and I went fish stocking once or twice and we collected water samples and did "ethnic" studies and things like that. Other people got to tree-plant, go out in a boom truck and do sort of landscaping jobs. It's not utopia but it is kind of nice to do that sort of thing. I really enjoyed the work at the YMCA too!

J.H.: Did you learn something there?

Robert: For sure, yes. At the water-quality lab, I thought I learned quite a bit.

J.H.: What about the people there?

Robert: They are good, really good. Almost all the people

that I have worked with down at the GRCA are really nice.

J.H.: So, in a short time you discovered three different parts of Canada?

Robert: Yes, and I feel good about that. I am happy I have gained knowledge. I have always known that Canada was a really big country and had some really diversified places and now I know it is really true.

J.H.: Do you like it better?

Robert: Yes, I think Canada is the best place to live in the world. It's got the most opportunities, it's got everything going for it.

J.H.: Have you changed at all in the process?

Robert: Tremendously. I think I have matured quite a bit and my outlook, my way of thinking, everything had really evolved. I think I have gained some skills that will really help me, you know; not only how to hammer a nail in right, but how to solve a problem, how to initiate myself, how to discipline myself.

J.H.: Did you learn that mostly through the projects or through the participants in your group?

Robert: I would say both, because our work projects taught me how to, you know, drag myself out of bed and go down to the greenhouse when it is −10⁰F. and then work on the greenhouse and sit back later and say: "Wow! I did that!" It is a good feeling, you know, and you remember those good feelings so next time the alarm clock rings at 6.00 a.m. and you say: "Do you want to get out of bed?" and you say: "Yes, I want to get out of bed because I want to work," and it is ... you know, it is those sorts of things that you learn from, plus interaction with the other participants. I think my motivation is something I have really developed, because before I came here, I was really not that motivated a person, because, you know, if I like something, I would say, "Yes, I will do that some day," but I never got around to it, but things that I like to do nowadays, I am doing. Discipline too; I guess those two things are related.

J.H.: When you look at your group, at the whole group, what is your feeling about them?

Robert: I think it is a sort of family, but I don't know if commune is the right word, it is a commune team. I have looked at some other projects, and I have looked at ours, and I think that living in a group of thirty, with all the participants under one roof, provided you have enough space and a good place to live in, can be a lot more fun than maybe a group of ten.

J.H.: Do you think that these links you have with your ... well, brothers and sisters, will last long?

Robert: Yes, I believe so. I think we are all making efforts to keep those links because it is something you share. I guess it is my philosophy, it is something you should keep up, you know. There will be a lot of people in Vancouver that will be passing through. I will probably be seeing quite a few of the participants.

J.H.: Will you write?

Robert: Yes, I will see them and I'll write. It will be interesting with what happens to some of the participants after we get out, I am curious to know.

J.H.: So, on the whole, was Katimavik a good idea for you?

Robert: Yes, it was a real good idea. I don't regret joining Katimavik at all. I think that if people coming to this program are willing to give a little bit of themselves then they will do OK, because people who give a lot, they will get a lot back. I remember Russell saying, "The people who are really having a good time in Katimavik are usually the workers, who really give a bit of themselves."

J.H.: Suppose you meet a friend who would ask you about Katimavik, "Say, what do you think about it, should I go?" What types of arguments would you give him?

Robert: Well, if he is asking me, "Should I go?" I will tell him that, if you have the right attitude, sure, go ahead and you probably won't regret it; but, if he is just going in there to, you know, run away from his family, maybe he has got a hassle from school, and he just wants an escape, he just wants the party, that is not the right attitude to get in Katimavik with. Even though he would probably lose that attitude quite quickly.

J.H.: Because we have to admit that some of the participants in your group came in for exactly the wrong reasons you have just mentioned.

Robert: Oh yes.

J.H.: But it turned out well in the end?

Robert: For sure, yes. But it is better, you know, to go in with the right attitude. Then, some people in this program just haven't got a whole lot out of it. Maybe that is because it wasn't right for them, maybe Katimavik didn't have a lot to offer them.

J.H.: Well, I haven't met one yet who told me he didn't get anything out of it.

Robert: Well, I know everyone has got something out of it. That's for sure.

16 *Yvan Gagné,*
Age 18,
Ste-Thérèse, Quebec

I was born in Longueuil, which was called Montreal-Sud at the time. Then when I was two we moved to Ste. Thérèse, where I spent the rest of my life until now. I went to elementary school in Ste. Thérèse, and to high school partly there and partly in Deux-Montagnes. I went to CEGEP in Ste. Thérèse too.

J.H.: Tell me about your family

Yvan: There's three of us — two girls and me.

J.H.: What kind of childhood did you have?

Yvan: As far as the family was concerned, it was perfect, a fairly pampered childhood.

J.H.: A little bit spoiled?

Yvan: Spoiled — I don't think so. Only son, an affectionate father. That was something I had to fight against a little.

J.H.: What does your father do?

Yvan: He's a worker, in a company that makes lasts for shoes. He's really a guy who's sorted things out in his life. Because of his work ... I hope I've got some of my father's blood in my veins.

J.H.: I get the impression you're very fond of your father.

Yvan: Yes, I admire him a lot. He's got the Gagné determinism.

J.H.: When you were still in Ste. Thérèse, before Katimavik, did you think about your future? What you wanted to do with yourself?

177

Yvan: No. Never. It was never important for me. After Katimavik, yes, but not before.

J.H.: And afterward, it came all of a sudden?

Yvan: Yes.

J.H.: A sort of awareness of the future?

Yvan: Well! I've always been aware of it, I knew there was some reason why I was on this earth, but I didn't think about it all that much. I didn't start worrying about that sort of thing until after Katimavik.

J.H.: Had you done much travelling before Katimavik?

Yvan: In Quebec.

J.H.: Never outside Quebec?

Yvan: No.

J.H.: What did Canada mean? A sort of vast snowy sea?

Yvan: Canada was a big country, but I didn't think of it having such a small population. And with so few "typical" Canadians. It's a new country, after all, with lots of people who are Canadians, but with very different origins. I didn't know the Anglophone way of looking at things. I had a bit of an idea, no more than that.

J.H.: You'd never had any Anglophone friends? That didn't happen in Ste. Thérèse?

Yvan: I didn't have any Anglophone friends like the kind I got to meet through Katimavik.

J.H.: You say you didn't think about your future, but still, at your age, you're ... ?

Yvan: Nineteen.

J.H.: At nineteen though, people start thinking about things, you want to change the world ... Didn't you have ideas like that?

Yvan: Yes, I even had the impression I was doing it! The impression ... I mean I'd done everything I wanted to do. Partly.

J.H.: For instance?

Yvan: Well, there was no café for the young people in Ste. Thérèse. So some friends and I started one; when I get interested in something I go all the way. Or I tried!

J.H.: How did Katimavik come into your life?

Yvan: It's strange ... It happened when I'd finished

178

CEGEP. That was really the peak for me; everything was going fine, things couldn't be better. Friends, plans, everything. Then suddenly I got this feeling that I had to go away; I had some ties that I though were too strong.

J.H.: Your family, other people around you ...

Yvan: The family, yes, there was that too. My friends, it was just too good. And since I don't believe that good things last forever ... I got a kind of message: "It's time to go, take a trip somewhere." It happened one morning in the cafeteria at the CEGEP. A friend came up to me with an application form for Katimavik, and she said: "Here I've got something for you!" So I applied and I was accepted. Just before, I'd applied to Canada World Youth, but I was refused. So Katimavik was my last hope. That's how it happened.

J.H.: So one day there you were in the training camp at Duchesnay. With a whole crowd of people you'd never seen before! With whom you probably had some problems communicating ...

Yvan: The first night I got to sleep around five in the morning. I wasn't used to meeting people like that. I was a little tense. Anyway, it was a big discovery. All the dreams I had before I went away were coming true: lots of people, everybody talking to each other, everybody nice ... Anyway, all my dreams were coming true. For the first month everything was wonderful. As far as human contacts were concerned I had everything I'd ever dreamed of. Oh, everything was great! It was so easy! It was fun! No problems!

Larouche, Quebec

J.H.: Once you were in Larouche, with the group of thirty, were your dreams still coming true?

Yvan: I was overwhelmed, they weren't dreams any more.

J.H.: It was reality, perhaps?

Yvan: That's right: What I'd dreamed was real now. So then I didn't know what I wanted any more, and instead of being satisfied with what I had, I started looking for something else.

J.H.: How did you react to the communal life in the house?

Yvan: It was quite amazing. Thirty of us in two dormitories and one kitchen. It was very hard, but still I was glad to have that experience. Very glad.

J.H.: How were your first contacts with the Anglophones in the group?

Yvan: They were excellent and I tried to keep them that way all through the project.

J.H.: You didn't speak any English?

Yvan: Just a bit.

J.H.: But still you managed to understand each other?

Yvan: Oh Yes! It was really weird.

J.H.: When you *want* to understand, language becomes almost secondary ... I can remember long, friendly conversations I've had with desert Bedouins ... But that's another story. Was living with a group important for you?

Yvan: Yes, it was super!

J.H.: In Larouche you really had the ultimate experience of group living. With thirty of you, it must have been hard ...

Yvan: It was a discovery.

J.H.: The fact that all the people in the group came from different provinces, different social situations — some very humble, others more well-off — some of them university students, others young workers: did that cause problems?

Yvan: No. Differences in background, education, age — that worked out pretty well. Whether a person was seventeen or twenty-one, there wasn't really any difference. The people were at the same level. The only thing that mattered was your personality, what you were.

J.H.: You're right, that really is quite amazing.

Yvan: That's what I think. And it's very rare to experience something like that.

J.H.: Did you live with a family in Larouche?

Yvan: Yes, with the Lessards. For three weeks.

J.H.: Was that your first contact with farm life?

Yvan: No, there were farmers on my mother's side of the family. But it was my first experience with a family who had that way of looking at things.

J.H.: What was so remarkable about the Lessards' way of looking at things?

Yvan: There's seven boys in the family, and the father and mother. "The poor downtrodden woman," the children with their roles all set out in advance ... But the experience made me realize that those people were happy with their lives. If you don't think so, all you have to do is arrange things so you can live differently. But you don't have to bother anybody. You have to respect other people.

J.H.: You've just said something profound, and that's not very common. We always have a tendency to want to change other people, convince them what we think is the truth ...

Yvan: Everyone has his own truth. When I was with the Lessards I watched the way they live. It wasn't my way of living, it was theirs. And I could see they were happy. But that's what life is. They accepted me as I was and I did the same.

J.H.: Did you learn things about farming?

Yvan: Of course. Getting up in the morning, milking the cows, working in the field, cutting wood.

J.H.: You did other things in Larouche. When I met you, I remember, you were painting garbage cans blue, and then you were going to distribute them around the village.

Yvan: And aside from that there were the signs the village asked us to make: "Watch out for children," things like that. And I worked a little in the greenhouse too. There were cross-country ski trails to lay out, the road to the aqueduct that was widened. And there was ...

J.H.: A little stone wall somewhere?

Yvan: Ah, yes! Yes. That was for the house for the golden-agers. I worked there too. I found it very interesting to have contacts with older people.

J.H.: Have you gone back to Larouche since then?

Yvan: Yes.

J.H.: Why? Who did you go to see?

Yvan: No one in particular. Larouche ... I saw the priest again because the person who drove me to the village when I was hitching a ride was on his way to fix the furnace in the church. I was just going back to see Larouche again, a year later.

J.H.: To stir up your memories ... You must have thousands. I don't have as many, and they aren't as fascinating. For instance, I remember the time I made cakes with you and Cynthia. I was a little preoccupied about you, remember? I was from the outside of course, and I tried to be as discreet as possible, but in spite of everything I felt that something was going on, that you were tempted to leave the group, to leave Katimavik. It wasn't really any of my business, it just concerned you, but the whole group — including me! — felt concerned. They'd talk about it to me in a corner, "It's awful, Yvan's thinking of leaving," and so forth. What was it that happened then? In your head or in your heart?

Yvan: In my head, everything was fine. But it's hard to explain. First of all, I lived according to a peculiar kind of discipline. A sort of goal, a certain way of living. And I realized that perhaps my way of seeing things was taking over because of Katimavik. But the experience was a good one, in spite of everything. I knew I was there because I had to be there. Group life was really marvellous, but there were some things I missed, like my own discipline that had fallen by the roadside. That was what made me say, "Okay, I'm leaving, I'm going to do something else." But in the end I decided to stay in Larouche, because I realized I was a little bit wrong. There's one part of you that has ideas and another part that lives the life of Katimavik.

J.H.: Had you stopped being what you wanted to be when you arrived at Larouche?

Yvan: That was because I'm a fairly weird kind of guy. I didn't do it because it would have been too much trouble.

J.H.: Whatever the case, too much trouble or not, you finally made the decision ...

Yvan: ... to stay.

J.H.: Because of pressure from the group a little?

Yvan: Mmmm ...

J.H.: You knew all your friends wanted you to stay?

Yvan: I'd explained my decision to the ones I was closest

to. It was official, almost official, that I was going. And I saw how people reacted: some of them took it well, others took it badly. But even if I went away I wasn't really going, I was still there with them in my heart. I wasn't dropping anyone, and not Katimavik either ... It was really for personal reasons. Then at the last minute I decided to stay.

J.H.: And we were *all* glad! So you went to Wilcox with your group. What was your first impression when you got there?

Wilcox, Saskatchewan

Yvan: I was knocked out. I wrote to one of my friends and told her I was feeling optimistic. About all the ideas and projects they had there.

J.H.: What did you do in particular in Wilcox?

Yvan: I worked in the carpentry workshop for the college. And I did some work at the day-care centre, and at the student café too. The Katimavik group before us had started the work. We just had to seal the joints.

J.H.: Had you ever done that before?

Yvan: No, never. I was knocked out by Wilcox. I loved the little village and I thought it was a little mysterious too. The college, the little house out front, the cafeteria, all that ... It was very appealing, interesting. And the people in Saskatchewan have a rather mysterious nature. They keep a lot inside. You can tell there's really something there. But they don't express themselves the way other people do.

J.H.: It's good that people aren't all alike. Otherwise, why travel to India, to Nepal?

Yvan: Yes, that's true. See what's behind that difference. I could have got to know them better. That's what I thought about most when I came back. I missed a lot of things and it was my own fault. I know very well it isn't anybody else's fault. They day-care centre, for instance. I'd always dreamed of working in a day-care centre. When I came back to Montreal, that's the kind of job I looked for. I really think I was a jerk to drop that project and go and look for a job in a day-care centre! Another job I really liked was helping out in the college cafeteria.

J.H.: Why?

Yvan: I was interested in the way the students looked at things, the college too, the structures. I saw a film about that before I left. It was called "YES" and it took place in a British College.

J.H.: Yes, I saw it too.

Yvan: It was almost the same atmosphere I found at the college in Wilcox. It made me laugh; it was really funny.

J.H.: Do you feel that you learned a lot in Wilcox, in the short time you spent there?

Yvan: Yes. The more I saw different things, things that were new to me, the more I saw myself. I wanted to get a grip on myself, ask myself: "All right, what's going on inside me?" Get my bearings, ask myself why I still wanted to leave. I always did my best to see the real reason. Why I was critical of the rules and structures of Katimavik ...

J.H.: You were in a group of ten then. Who were the other members of your group?

Yvan: There was Lise and Yves, the Québécois, and there was Jo-Anne, Kathy, Michael, Robert, and me.

J.H.: A good group, quite well-balanced.

Yvan: Yes. We were the "buffer" group.

J.H.: What do you mean by that?

Yvan: People who wanted to have a good time and not upset anybody. When we talked it was always level-headed. We never had any conflicts with other people.

J.H.: But finally, in spite of everything, after a month and a half in Wilcox you decided once and for all to leave.

Yvan: Yes, I did. In fact it happened in Larouche, I was aware of that. But from Larouche, I would have been running away. I'd decided to see it through to the end. Then there was the business of the group leader, the one who came to replace the one we'd left behind at Larouche. He arrived with a knapsack with the symbol of the Mother[1] and I saw that as a sign.

---

1. Eminent Indian disciple of Sri Aurobindo.

J.H.: Providential?

Yvan: Almost! I understood that it was time for me to leave. I'd gone a way with Katimavik, learned the things I had to learn. And there were conflicts with the group leader. It was my fault as much as his, but that's forgotten now, it's over. At the time, though, it made me decide to go. Then there was a coolness with the co-ordinator and then the valve burst. Stupid things, really; now I can say that I was stupid, but at the time it wasn't that.

J.H.: Everybody's told me that the day you left was a very sad day. In the end no one blamed you. They respected your reasons. That's what I found quite surprising. As far as they were concerned you weren't a dropout, a guy who abandons his friends. You stayed close to them, you wrote to them in Wilcox and you even came to see them twice at the worksite in Grand River, Ontario.

Yvan: Well, that's what Katimavik is!

J.H.: You weren't there in body, but you were in spirit.

Yvan: Yes, it's true that I was there.

J.H.: Now everything's over — though it isn't really over, because that's what's wonderful about Katimavik, it's never really over. I'm seeing you a year later, so you have a perspective the others didn't have when I interviewed them. For instance, I asked them, while they were still in the program, "Do you think you've changed?" What about you, Yvan?

Yvan: Yes, I've certainly changed. Absolutely. I've changed. I've also changed my way of seeing Canada. I've had the chance to discover this enormous country, with its scattered population.

J.H.: How do you see Canada now?

Yvan: More concretely. Before, I had an idea that was more ... intellectual. Now, it's more concrete. Thanks to my group I have a more positive view of the people in this country, despite all our differences of opinion. And I'm very glad about that. The problem is the lack of communication. Everybody had personal opinions, I had mine, the others had theirs, but in our group I thought that was really fantastic. The exchange ... what was exciting was that everybody had personal opinions. Everybody listened to everybody else's opinions and there was a lot of goodwill; we wanted to understand things and even when we didn't manage to agree at least we always ended up understanding the other person a little better. The people from Ontario didn't really understand the situation of the Québécois, because of a kind of gut reaction. But in the end they understood us all the same. There were the people from Vancouver, from the West ... It was a *rapprochement* of the different provinces and different ways of looking at things, it was really marvellous, you know.

J.H.: How do you think of your group? As a big family?

Yvan: Maybe not a family ... Of the thirty there were some I really liked, others I didn't like as much. But "didn't like as much" — I don't really like that expression!

J.H.: It can happen in a real family.

Yvan: So why shouldn't it happen in a group like ours? Anyway, I can say that with the twenty-six participants who were there, I'm positive that if we sit down to talk about Katimavik in thirty years or fifty years it'll be as fresh as yesterday. Even now after a year, nearly two years in August, we still talk about it when we get together. Sometimes we say, "All right, we won't talk about that any more; after all, we've come a way since then."

J.H.: Moved on to other things?

Yvan: Yes, that's right. But in spite of everything it keeps coming back. When I'm with friends who weren't in Katimavik I try not to talk about it any more, to keep from getting on their nerves, but it keeps coming back all the time. It was a big bank of feelings, a pure, beautiful experience that had its good points and its bad, you mustn't forget that, but deep down it's made us more open.

J.H.: You're free, but you're still deeply attached to one another?

Yvan: There are ties, but still you're free, but ... the relationships are different from the ones with friends you make in everyday life. It's another level. The friends you make at school or in your neighbourhood are friends ... But the friends you make at Katimavik are different, it's not part of the ordinary world. Friends from CEGEP are friends at an intellectual level if you want to stop there: a contact is made, you have the same ideas, everything's fine and wonderful. But it isn't that in Katimavik. Here's a silly example: in the morning you're eating toast and jam and the guy across from you is eating toast and jam too. Silly, isn't it? But I mean the ties are made in terms of the way we live, in terms of what we are, not what we think we are or what we'd like to be ...

J.H.: After a while you couldn't hide anything from one another!

Yvan: That's right!

J.H.: You can't play roles.

Yvan: That's right. At Larouche, I realized that before, I'd been myself, but maybe it was a notion I had of what I was. Lots of times I wasn't really what I am because that just wasn't done. When you live with twenty-six people you have to be satisfied with being what you are and accept the way you are.

J.H.: What did you do after Katimavik?

Yvan: I got a job in a prison. I was a clerk in the socialization department, in a socio-cultural program. Helping the prisoners do crafts, for example. I worked in the prison library for a month.

J.H.: After that you went to university to study Sociology. Why Sociology?

Yvan: I applied in Psychology and I was refused. Sociology was my second choice, so that's what I took. I like it anyway, it's interesting. In CEGEP those were the two things that really aroused my interest, Sociology and Psychology. There's a lot of things I wouldn't have done if I hadn't been with Katimavik, like ... There are things I'm finding out at this very moment, as I talk, that I hadn't even thought about before.

J.H.: So have I; I've discovered a lot of things too.

17   *Jo-Anne Lennard,*
Age 21,
Islington, Ontario

I was born in Toronto in 1956 and I lived there for three years, then we moved to Vancouver. I lived there for about seven years and we moved back to Toronto where I have been ever since.

J.H.: Do you have any brothers or sisters?

Jo-Anne: I have one brother who is eighteen.

J.H.: When you went to Vancouver were you old enough to remember it?

Jo-Anne: Very well. We moved there when I was about three and I left when I was about twelve. If somebody were to ask me where I was from I would prefer to think of myself as being from Vancouver. I have very fond memories of Vancouver and it's a beautiful place.

J.H.: Have you ever been back?

Jo-Anne: No. I've sworn for the last two or three years, "This summer I'm going back," but now I have a good opportunity to go back because I know people in Vancouver too. Dorle and Robert and Lap are from Burnaby or Vancouver so it gives me a twofold reason ... to see them and to sort of look up the old neighourhood, and some of my old friends.

J.H.: What kind of idea did you have about Canada?

Jo-Anne: It was very narrow. I had very good feelings about British Columbia, about the coastal life. The East coast really intrigued me because I've just seen pictures, and the Northwest Territories was a place I've always wanted to go to. Not very many people have the opportunity to go there because of the expense and the distance. I hadn't travelled much before Katimavik, but I want to go see people and some of these other places I haven't been to. I want to spend some time in Quebec too.

J.H.: So you went to school in Toronto and Brisith Columbia.

Jo-Anne: Yes, I finished school a year and a half ago.

J.H.: What have you done since then?

Jo-Anne: I worked for a major company for four months and I had a title even: Marketing Research Analyst.

J.H.: Did you have any experience in that field?

Jo-Anne: No, the only requirements were that you be good with figures, and I was good in Math.

J.H.: Did you like it?

Jo-Anne: I did like it. I got this job for four months and I was asked to stay on for a year, but I decided I would go back to school. It was better because afterward the computer took over my job anyway so I wouldn't have been there very long.

J.H.: What were your plans for the future before you heard about Katimavik?

Jo-Anne: I had wanted to go into theatre or music. I wasn't sure whether university, or college or theatre was exactly what I wanted to do right after school and I was feeling very low about what I wanted to do, where I was going. I had started to think, at that point, about society and some of the wrongs of society. It's funny, since I didn't feel as though I fit in ... I didn't feel comfortable. In school I was very much a loner. I didn't agree with a lot of the things that were happening in society, like the material things, people wanting bigger and better things, the little social games that people play and all sorts of things like that. When I heard about Katimavik, it seemed like a lot of the ideas that Katimavik had were some of the ideals that I have or I wanted to have. Katimavik seemed like a good idea.

J.H.: So you came to Katimavik and one fine morning you arrived in Duchesnay, Quebec; you opened the door and saw a hundred people there. What was your reaction?

Jo-Anne: I was just so happy to be there. First of all, back in May or March when I saw the advertisement in the *Canadian Magazine,* I sent that questionnaire in. I didn't hear anything and I had planned to go camping. I didn't, so I wrote a letter explaining some of the reasons why I wanted to join Katimavik and my enthusiasm. Two weeks later, I had left for camping, and I phoned home and my mother read the telegram to me over the phone, and I just started jumping up and down and the people I was with were looking at me as if to say, "What's wrong with her?" I had to explain about this program. I felt very happy about being in Katimavik. I felt very privileged too by the fact that I had been chosen among thousands of young people.

Larouche, Quebec

J.H.: So, now let's go to the first project in Larouche. How did it strike you, this first French-Canadian village you'd ever seen?

Jo-Anne: For the first while I was very unhappy and very frustrated, because I felt that what the project was going to be, the ideals of Katimavik, fell very short and a lot of other people in the same group felt the same way. There was a lot of tension, a lot of frustration. Larouche did not offer as many work opportunities as it could have.

J.H.: I agree with you.

Jo-Anne: But it was very important in getting to know the group of thirty.

J.H.: What about living in this house, all packed in there?

Jo-Anne: It was crowded and at times I felt just like screaming, like getting out and being by yourself and I'd do that a lot, just go for a walk by myself or with one or two other participants. It was hard living with other people. Now with the group, we are like a family, but at that point we were sort of trying to become a family. But it had its advantages. I think that's one of the reasons why we're so strong.

190

J.H.: Was the language problem a big thing?

Jo-Anne: It wasn't really a problem, it wasn't a boundary, it was something I could overcome. What I think was very difficult was that we all have very different morals and values and at times I feel, and I think other people felt, people infringe on the morals and values of others, without thinking about that other person. The whole thing was the house. It wasn't a very good thing and caused a lot of problems. That's something we all learned from about Larouche: we were living in a group of thirty and had to be that much more concerned about what another person was thinking.

J.H.: Did you know any French then?

Jo-Anne: Very little. I took French in high school from grade 9 through to grade 12 and I was good in it but I found out when we were in Duchesnay and Yvan came up to me. He was the first French person who spoke to me and he knew very little English and I thought I knew more French but when it actually came down to speaking it, I knew very little. I remember, too, the first conversation I had was with Christine. She in her broken English and I in my broken French were trying to communicate. We managed pretty well. That is the only way to learn any language: to be put into a situation where the desire is there but you are also forced to communicate. It was very good that we were in Quebec for our first project, because it helped us a lot to use our French throughout the two other projects.

J.H.: Did you work on the greenhouse, or anything else?

Jo-Anne: No. I worked on the teepees and I did community work. A couple of days we helped build a rock wall along the bank of the river. We also painted garbage cans and distributed them along the town.

J.H.: Were you on a farm? With what family?

Jo-Anne: Yes, the Lessard family. I liked it because I had never been on a farm before. I'd seen them from a distance and that was it, so it was really a good opportunity for me. I have a lot of respect for farmers and the kind of life that they lead is very different from city people's life. They have a commitment to that farm and they can't break it; they have to get up every morning at 6.00 a.m. and they can't take weekends off and they can't take holidays the way we can. It's a very hard life but a very good one. If I had the opportunity, I would like to live on a farm.

J.H.: What did you learn from them?

Jo-Anne: As far as the family life is concerned, I don't know whether their family was typical of that region but they were very, very conservative. Mme Lessard did all the cooking, all the dishes. Mr. Lessard wouldn't touch that, it was women's work. Mme Lessard was not allowed in to milk the cows. For the first three weeks I was there, I asked if I could milk the cows to really learn what the farm was like ... but the second time, I think Claire and Serge were there, they were asked not to milk the cows because it was considered man's work. That is an example of some of the conservative attitudes they have. They were a very close family though, with seven children. They were very nice people, very kind, very open. For the first couple of weeks it was hard for me to communicate, I found, and I heard other people say the same things, the accent and they speak very, very quickly. But when I went back the second time for the week and a half, maybe a three-week lapse between the two, I'd learned enough French to carry on a conversation and I could understand what they were saying too.

J.H.: What was the highlight of your stay in Larouche?

Jo-Anne: The farm, I think, our group life. We had a very strong group because for the most part we didn't have a work project so we spent a lot of time with each other, getting to know one another, doing things together, learning different crafts and different skills from one another. That was important to me.

Wilcox, Saskatchewan

J.H.: Then after three months, you moved to Wilcox, Saskatchewan. How did it strike you?

Jo-Anne: Beautiful. Even now when I look out in my mind

and see the Prairies, it just looks like water to me. It reminds me of driving down the Gardiner Expressway and looking out and seeing Lake Ontario, just flat, just reflections, but it's beautiful.

J.H.: What about the people?

Jo-Anne: In the town where we were, the people were very conservative. It would have been nice to have been on the farm there to try to compare the different styles of farming. Farming there would be a lot different too because it's more agricultural, while where we were in Quebec it was more dairy farming. The people were very nice. I found that Regina was very conservative, very behind-the-times in many ways. There was a lot of prejudice against the Indians too, which I found very disturbing. There are a lot of problems out there between the Indians and the white people. It was the same thing with the Hutterites: we tried to billet in a Hutterite community. I can understand it too, they don't want people to be there just for the sake of being there, they want people to be there who are devoted to their religious beliefs, but we went on a tour for two days and that was interesting.

J.H.: What type of work did you do?

Jo-Anne: There was a lot to do. We did work at the workshop which was to be used by the students of Notre Dame. We also worked on the café for the students, plus every week we would send a different person to the cafeteria to help Gino, the head cook there. Angie and I worked at the library mostly, but it didn't get rolling until about a month after we were there. That I found interesting.

J.H.: I'm told it was an amazing library.

Jo-Anne: Oh, it's beautiful. The second last day we were there, Peter, Lise, and I went there and the Dean of Arts opened the vault for us — beautiful books — the Nuremburg Chronicle dated back to the fifteenth century, letters that had been written on leather and bound with leather, all sorts of different bibles in different languages. It was incredible.

J.H.: What type of work did you do at the library?

Jo-Anne: I typed. The books have to have card catalogue numbers and I typed those and stuck them all on the file cards. I cleaned off one whole wall of books before I left.

J.H.: What did you learn at Wilcox?

Jo-Anne: Tolerance, mostly tolerance. We did a lot of w．r'. for the college, the college was our sponsor, yet they gave us very little in return. They would take and they wouldn't give. We would talk about it amongst ourselves, yet in the morning we would get up and still go to work. I learned tolerance and patience.

J.H.: But the work you did was useful?

Jo-Anne: It was useful, but in many cases they took advantage of us. Many times they would ask us to do so-called "shit" jobs and we wouldn't do them because that's not what we were there to do. We were there to do constructive work, work we can learn from. I learned a lot working in the workshop — I had never done any building or any construction at all — so, I learned a lot, like how to put legs together, levelling things.

J.H.: Could you build a house now?

Jo-Anne: I don't know, I'd like to build a log cabin, and I'd like to build my own furniture too. Right now those are just dreams.

Grand River, Ontario

J.H.: From Wilcox you moved to Grand River. What town were you in?

Jo-Anne: Cambridge. It was much more structured than the other two projects. In Wilcox, we had to seek a lot of the contacts ourselves and find a lot of work. We were given the café and the workshop was our only project. For the first while we did that we got tired, so we started looking around for other things. But when we got to Cambridge everything was pretty well set up for us, there was a very good selection of work; the GRCA, two different day-cares centres to work at, swimming classes, the radio station.

J.H.: What did you do yourself?

Jo-Anne: Mondays I worked at Christopher House, a day-care centre for physically and mentally handicapped children and that was a very good experience. I like children and I've done a lot of babysitting and stuff and I did four years' volunteer work at a hospital. Tuesdays, of course, was the radio station.

J.H.: What did you do at the radio station?

Jo-Anne: We produced our own programs if we wished. We're producing a program on aspiring musicians in the area to try to give them an opportunity to become better known. Wednesdays and Thursdays, I worked at GRCA. Fridays, I worked at another day-care centre, for so-called "regular" children, but there were a few who had problems.

J.H.: What did you do at the GRCA?

Jo-Anne: Most of the time we were building picnic tables and then chopping wood. Before we finished work last Friday, we were planting trees, and I just enjoyed being outside. Planting trees is something I've never done before so I was learning a lot about that. As far as chopping wood and building picnic tables I don't want to see them again, I've done enough.

J.H.: What were the people there like? They were not unfamiliar because they were not too far from Toronto, where you live.

Jo-Anne: The people we worked with directly were very nice. We've since had them over to the house a few times and got to know them. One man that I worked with came last night; he plays guitar, so he had dinner and played guitar for us. A couple of the other people come over a couple times a week and just sit around and talk.

J.H.: Now we are getting to the end of the program, do you feel you have changed a lot?

Jo-Anne: Oh, for sure.

J.H.: In what way?

Jo-Anne: I've become more confident of myself. Confidence is something I lacked a lot and I still have a lot more to learn, but I've come a long way. I've learned tolerance and patience. I've learned, of course, the French language. I'm very happy because it's something I've wanted to do for a long time. I've learned so many things. I've learned how to relate to people. I've been exposed to so many different kinds of people now, and a lot of the people I've met here, I doubt I would ever have had the opportunity to meet. If I had seen them from a distance I would have classified them and said, "Oh, stay away from him," but now that I have been exposed to them, I have a better insight. We all have different images we put on, yet down deep we are very similar. Another thing that I've learned is that there is a different kind of love. Love is a very hard word to define, at least it is to me, but being in this program, I've been doing a lot of thinking about the last little while. I've become so dependent on the people that I've been living with, my group of nine. But our group of thirty, even though we haven't been living all together now for several months, just knowing they were there and being able to talk with them and thinking of special times, it's going to be very hard to leave that. There's a strong sense of security among all of us.

J.H.: Do you consider them like brothers and sisters?
Jo-Anne: Yes, definitely.

J.H.: Do you think you will write to them and visit them?
Jo-Anne: Yes, for sure. I hope they will visit me too.

J.H.: Do you plan to visit anybody soon?
Jo-Anne: After Katimavik is over, I'm going home, and I hope, I haven't heard yet, but I hope to be accepted for an immersion course in French in Trois Rivières.

J.H.: Somebody told me it was difficult to get in.
Jo-Anne: Oh, I think that's for the bursary program. I applied for the bursary too. When I'm finished the program I would like to stay on for a while. Lise, Yvan, and I are thinking about sharing an apartment together. I hope it works out.

J.H.: Where?
Jo-Anne: I think in Montreal, because Yvan has applied to Trois Rivières and he's also been accepted at the University of Montreal for sociology and Lise has also made an application for CEGEP but she hasn't heard yet.

J.H.: That would be in the fall. So you mean that after Katimavik you would go to Trois Rivières?

Jo-Anne: The program begins on July 3 to August 11, six weeks to be exact.

J.H.: Have you been to Trois Rivières before?

Jo-Anne: No.

J.H.: Will you be alone or is somebody else going with you?

Jo-Anne: No, I'll be alone. I heard that Lap was accepted for Trois Rivières.

J.H.: He was, so you won't be alone?

Jo-Anne: If I'm accepted, yes, but he might be in a different level than I am. There are three or four different levels.

J.H.: So your French is not bad but you want to improve it?

Jo-Anne: Yes, I want to be bilingual. There's a French heritage on our side — my grandmother was French and when my mother was young she learned the French language, but she's lost it. It's a part of Canada's culture and of my culture and I'm very proud of it and would like to know more about it. To live in Quebec for a while and learn more about the culture and the music and all those things are important to me.

J.H.: Then after Trois Rivières you plan to go to Montreal?

Jo-Anne: Yes, hopefully if things work out with Lise and Yvan. I'll find a job more than likely until January and then in January I'm going to apply to the National Theatre School for the following year. I'll find a job and my French, I think, will be an asset. If things don't work out with Yvan and Lise, I'll probably either go out to British Columbia or go back to Ontario and try to use my French and maybe get a government job where I can use my French.

J.H.: So, Katimavik was not a bad idea for you after all?

Jo-Anne: No, it was a very good one. There have been times when I've really thought about leaving.

J.H.: I guess all of you did.

Jo-Anne: The people have held me together and each project has offered different things. There have been ups and downs in each project but for the most part Katimavik has been very good. I've grown a lot and I'm more sure of my ideals and values now. One thing I'm really worried about is maintaining those after Katimavik, trying to fit back into society. That's going to be the hard part, because right now the way we're living it's very idealistic. It might be realistic to us, but to go out and live this kind of life in society, it's going to be something else. Let's just say that it's going to be an adjustment, and an adjustment for the families too, seeing how we've changed.

J.H.: What do you plan to do in the distant future?

Jo-Anne: So many things. I've said I'd like to build a log cabin in British Columbia. I'd like to live on a farm, I've been thinking about having a farm of my own on a very small scale and have a few animals. I've also thought about having another group-living experience. I really like it, living with people that you are not into at all. Just being shut together has been a very good thing. I'd like to do that.

J.H.: Do you think you learned more from the other participants than from the work projects and communities?

Jo-Anne: I'd say half and half. I've been more open to different attitudes and ideas because there are so many of us here and each one has different ideas. As far as the work is concerned, I've learned a lot of things. A lot of the work we have done, the outdoors work, the physical labour is something that I know that if I had not joined Katimavik, I never would have even thought about doing.

18 *Peter Splinter,* Age 19, Edmonton, Alberta

I was born in Edmonton and lived there all my life except for two trips to Europe to visit my grandparents. My father's family comes from Germany, and my mother's family comes from Yorkshire in central England.

J.H.: What does your family do?

Peter: My father is employed in the federal government in Public Works Canada — that's what we call it now — and my mother is employed by National Health and Welfare in a federal hospital — but it's since become a provincial hospital. She is a nurse there.

J.H.: What kind of childhood did you have?

Peter: That is a question that I don't know how to answer. I suppose that having met other people the past year and having seen and heard about the way other people have been brought up, I'd say I had quite an ... average isn't the word ... quite an uneventful childhood. My parents were quite strict, my father, especially, set down the rules and those were the rules ...

J.H.: More than three rules?[1]

Peter: Oh more than three rules, but they weren't so much rules as, more of an understanding, such as with drinking, there was always an understanding. It just would be something that wouldn't occur among the children, myself or my two brothers.

---

1. The three rules of Katimavik: no drugs, no hitch-hiking, no co-habitation.

J.H.: An uneventful childhood could be called a happy childhood?

Peter: Oh yes, I can't say that I had an unhappy childhood. No, basically, it was just like everyone else's starting from age one, starting from birth until getting ready to leave home. It's a pretty sheltered life, like my parents wouldn't give me everything I wanted, that was another understanding. If I wanted anything I would have to work for it, but it was always sort of working within the family. My dad comes from a family that was very close, and after the last war they were broken up, and now he looks forward to having a close family again now. Because of that I haven't seen much of the world outside of the family.

J.H.: That is to say, not much outside of Edmonton?

Peter: Outside of Edmonton, no. About the rest of Canada, I knew very little, just what I read in newspapers. I read newspapers avidly but a newspaper impression could be quite distorted or quite oversimplified.

J.H.: Obviously you never lived with a group before Katimavik?

Peter: No.

J.H.: Before Katimavik, what were your plans for the future?

Peter: I plan to go into law and ...

J.H.: You've been interested in law for some time?

Peter: Only since I was about fourteen. There was a lot of encouragement from my father to go into law but it was also my own idea. Just going into that to help others.

J.H.: To help other people? Money wasn't that important?

Peter: No, not in a sense. I found that one thing in our family that's never been important is money.

J.H.: You had enough but it was not important.

Peter: That's probably why it wasn't important. We always had enough when things were tight. My mom has always had her job so it never became too difficult with money, it never became an important goal. I know my father, many times he was offered jobs where he could have tripled his income and he refused them because of the many changes it would have made in the family.

J.H.: You would have had to move for example?

Peter: Yes.

J.H.: When you say you want to help people, do you think law is a good way to do that?

Peter: I think to help people you have to have a capability to do it, you have to have some tools, whether intellectual tools or physical tools. If you can't take care of yourself and you don't have anything to offer, I don't think you can help people; you can have the best of intentions but intentions aren't enough by themselves.

J.H.: Just talking people away from their troubles is a rather simplistic way to approach things.

Peter: I think so. Right now ... I've been very down in the hole about the way society is going; there is a heavy emphasis on materialism and I'd like to change that. It's obvious that one person, ten people, twenty people, maybe a thousand, whatever, are not going to change a society if that's what they are going out to do.

J.H.: How many thousand do you think would be needed to change it?

Peter: It depends who they are and what leadership capabilities they have. Take agriculture. *"Nous ne pouvons pas cultiver assez de nourriture pour nous-mêmes. Et pourtant nous avons assez de terres pour cultiver la nourriture pour la population. Aussi, le Tiers monde a des problèmes avec le sous-développement. Je crois qu'une grande part de ça, c'est parce que les pays de l'Ouest exploitent les pays du Tiers Monde, on n'a pas assez de terres agricoles pour cultiver la nourriture de ces pays-là, les gens doivent vivre dans de mauvaises conditions. Ce n'est pas nécessaire d'importer la nourriture comme le sucre. Nous n'avons pas besoin de beaucoup de sucre. Je crois que la meilleure façon, c'est de cultiver la nourriture soi-même, je crois que c'est une bonne idée."*[1]

J.H.: I really feel what you have just mentioned is one of

---

1 Spontaneously, Peter started answering my questions in French. I had to insist that these interviews would be translated anyway ...

today's main problems. We should change that or there'll be a catastrophe before long. At the same time you mentioned that your involvement in society would be through law because you think that is more suitable to you?

Peter: Mais maintenant, je pense que ce n'est pas aussi important que l'agriculture.

J.H.: Tu as changé d'idée?

Peter: Oui.

J.H.: Okay, so all of a sudden Katimavik came into your life. How did that happen?

Peter: I just finished my B.A. at the University of Alberta, and I wasn't ready to go straight into law school. I wanted to take a year off. I had originally planned to work. What happened was, I heard about this program, seeing other parts of Canada, meeting people from other parts of Canada, getting to know them and their ideas. I also liked the idea of a simple lifestyle, not so consumer-oriented. That's how I interpreted it and I played with the idea. At first I thought it was just a bunch of crap, just another silly government program.

J.H.: Thank you very much!

Peter: Sorry, but that's what I thought. It stayed in my head and I thought that perhaps something like this was worth having a try at. It's easy to sit on the outside and say something is lousy, but you could say that about anything. You could say that about a university, that the university was no good, that one is no good, and spend one's whole time saying everything is no good. I had nothing specific to do, Katimavik was an opportunity and I decided to take it.

J.H.: How did the family react?

Peter: My mother said if that's what I wanted to do, go ahead; that it sounded like an interesting concept. My dad said something to the effect that: "You've got to be kidding, be serious about this, this is a year of your life, don't waste it on something like this." He continued to say that until I left, but in the first letter I received from him after I left home he said he was happy I'd taken this opportunity, that perhaps I was ready to go out and start taking a look at other parts of the world. So in the end I guess...

202

although my father had doubts and my mother didn't express any, they both seemed to accept it as a good idea.

J.H.: Okay, so you joined finally and you were in a camp in Quebec called Duchesnay with two other groups, about a hundred altogether.

Peter: Ça a été un grand choc. Le français, ça a été un grand choc pour moi. Moi, je viens d'Alberta.

J.H.: Tu ne parlais pas français du tout?

Peter: Du tout, pas du tout. Peut-être un signe sur la route, c'est tout. Ça a été un grand choc de vivre dans le même édifice avec les gars, les filles, à partager tout. Ça a été un autre choc pour moi. Les gens de toutes les parties du Canada, de Terre-Neuve spécialement, j'ai trouvé beaucoup différents de moi.

Larouche, Quebec

J.H.: Let's not talk about the training camp, which was so-so. Let's jump to the first project in Larouche.

Peter: Je me suis senti gêné, à cause que je ne peux pas parler français, je ne peux rien parler. Je me suis senti gêné. Les gens là ont voulu parler avec moi et je voulais parler avec eux, mais je n'avais pas la capacité. Je pense que c'est le premier sentiment que j'ai eu.

J.H.: You were now thirty people together in a small house. What was life like?

Peter: It's funny, at that time it was hell, it was really hard to live with thirty people, especially thirty people I didn't know and who didn't know me. I think we had quite different values. At that time I was very unprepared to accept other people's values. I came to Katimavik expecting to do work; voluntary work in small communities across the country, things which would not otherwise be done in those communities. At Larouche I had this expectation in my head, but I got there and at first there was nothing to do, really. We'd sit in the house, stay in bed until noon, we'd read books and write letters, have meetings and after about two weeks I began to wonder if this was Katimavik. It shocked me, that's all. I thought if this is Katimavik, it's a farce, I don't want anything to do with it. It's just another government program.

J.H.: The first two weeks were lousy, but what then? You did something, I saw you working?

Peter: Well, after a while we started building a greenhouse — myself along with Kathy, Carol and Lap, Daniel and Serge; that was a big project. We got together on that and we went out and we weren't quite sure how to build a greenhouse. We had these plans for a greenhouse, we threw in ideas and finally set to digging the foundations. When it came time to pour the cement, again, no one knew quite how to do this. We all threw in ideas. Daniel knew a man there who lived in Larouche, who came and gave us advice. So he'd be there and we'd all be throwing in ideas on this, "Okay we'll do it that way." Then we poured the foundations. That was a really good time for many of us in Larouche. We were out at midnight pouring cement foundations for this greenhouse. Daniel had to go in the van with Matthew, a group leader, and find some cement, we had run out about three-quarters of the way through the foundation. It's not a good thing to let concrete harden and then pour on top of it and we wanted to get it all done at once. Daniel and Matthew went to ask people in Larouche if they had some. One man had seven sacks and lent them to us and Daniel came back with the cement. Here we were at midnight mixing cement and everyone was coming out of the house. Until then only a few people had shown an interest in the greenhouse, only six of us, as I mentioned. But that night everyone was coming out and everyone had such a good time, throwing them together and laughing. So we built our greenhouse.

J.H.: You were very, very proud of your greenhouse finally.

Peter: Yes, but I was unhappy we didn't finish. I was very happy we got it as far as we did, got the frame up and covered it, but we hadn't finished the insulation. I thought we could have done more but I was proud of what we did finish.

J.H.: What else did you want to say about Larouche?

Peter: Again, I'll be negative. After two weeks I felt that I really had enough, but then Michel, our co-ordinator, found some families who were willing to take people for three weeks of billeting and I was among the first group to go. I stayed with the Tremblay family.

J.H.: One of the thousands of Tremblay families in that region ...

Peter: I suppose so. I don't know Mme Tremblay's name. She was an older lady who was in charge of the house, I guess, and she had a daughter and a son living with her. The daughter, Diane Tremblay, was thirty-five, and Jerome was fourteen. We'd go out and milk cows, help Diane finish off a chalet, we'd sit down and just talk. Diane was so very open, so willing to try to make this a good time. She helped me with my French; I was having an awful time with French. I went to the farm and tried to speak away and she would say, "Well, try this the next time, it's like this." She continued to do that, it was such an encouragement and that's what encouraged me to continue learning French and made it possible for me to continue with Katimavik, just as one sideline. After we'd left Larouche, I found out that Diane spoke English and that came as a shock to me because she never spoke English once while I was on the farm. She knew that Carol, Kathy and I wanted to learn French and I'm sure that at times it must have been awfully difficult for her to understand what we were trying to say. It would have been much easier to ask in English but she didn't.

J.H.: Did you keep in touch with her?

Peter: Yes, I write letters and I want to see her once more. When I go to Montreal, I would like to go and visit the Tremblay family.

J.H.: You kind of like that family?

Peter: Yes, quite a bit.

J.H.: Was it the first French-Canadian family you'd ever met?

Peter: I visited the family of one of the participants, Lise's family in Montreal, for one day. Other than that, yes, the Tremblay family was the only one I ever had contact with.

J.H.: Did you have some other contacts with the community?

Peter: We worked in the library in Larouche. There was a contact with Gilles, the man who helped us with the greenhouse. We helped for a while to clean the town dump. Actually we cleaned up the town dump and no one from Larouche was involved in that except, as we were finishing off one day, Robert Peron came by with his tractor and offered to help us. In Larouche, what struck me was sort of the easy-going sort of way of life, no big rush to get anything done, take your time and do it, if it got done, it got done; if it didn't, it didn't. At the time Mr.Champigny, who owned the house where we were staying, he did a lot of work around the house. When I first came there, I throught, "Gee, look at the way he's building this house, he's not building this house right." My father was in the construction industry and he's taught me various things but after a while ... like now I look back and I think that while Mr. Champigny wasn't building things right if you go by the CMHC code book, the house was fine. It didn't leak and it was warm enough. We had good times. Mr. Champigny also built a woodshed that I'm sure will stand up as long as any shed you want to build; even if it's not right according to the books. Now I look back and I see that I seem to be more relaxed in that type of life. That's a funny thing. I'm only beginning to understand it now and I think it will take a long time for me to fully understand it. Although I found the people there to be very different, something attracted me to the life there. It was easy-going, spontaneous. For instance, a couple of times there were baseball games with the town, and once there was a dance. I found the people to be so open, so spontaneous, they didn't hang back and wait for us. We sort of hung back but they were outgoing and welcomed us in. Like the Tremblay family did. I felt it was real hospitality. Sometimes I felt that the people were doing it just for the sake of doing it, but I imagine that happens everywhere. On the other hand, many times, with the Tremblays, the Simards (another family who billeted participants), and other families that some people were billeted with, their generosity was so outstanding.

J.H.: Did it change the view you had of Quebec before you got there?

Peter: Yes and no. For instance, before I came to Katimavik, the big issue with Quebec, of concern to Alberta, was separatism. Quebec wants to leave the country. Of course with that in my mind I often asked about separatism, and in talking with Diane Tremblay and people in the group and just observing, I suppose I began to think about the issue more. For instance, one thing that struck me personally, again, was the fact that I couldn't speak French. Here are these people in a small community within Quebec and many of them could speak enough English to communicate with me and I couldn't do the same for them in French. Before I asked why Quebec should want to separate, look they're getting all our tax money, all ... everything keeps getting thrown into Quebec as they write in newspapers. I never thought of the human level. It struck me so much that if this is really one country I should be able to speak their language and should be able to communicate with them. Perhaps there is an issue with separatism, perhaps it's not so much Quebec saying, "You're not babying us." Perhaps they do have real complaints and that's when I began to think that these people have a culture; it's being overwhelmed, they're different from us — the dances, the small farms, the easy-going life; it's different from what I'd seen in Alberta from the money, money, money — go out and get a job — work hard type of life I've seen. So perhaps with television and with everything in North America, much of North America being controlled by American companies, industrial economic units and United States with English-speaking Canada, perhaps they really are threatened. These people knew English; why? because they had to know English. There was a real threat there. I think I began to feel that... these people's concerns were not like what I'd been led to believe before.

Wilcox, Saskatchewan

J.H.: And you moved to Wilcox. You were getting nearer your home ...

Peter: The scenery was a shock. I've never seen anything so flat in all my life. I found the people much more conservative, although Wilcox is only 700 miles from my home. I lived in a large city and Wilcox is only a small town. I found there was a definite difference in the way people thought in a small town.

J.H.: But wouldn't you say the people were Westerners like you?

Peter: It's funny, sometimes perhaps I'm being self-righteous but I found them to be much more conservative than myself.

J.H.: Well, Wilcox is a small town.

Peter: People are conservative in the West but I was really shocked by how conservative.

J.H.: But it's not a typical town, although 1 don't know Saskatchewan that well ... It's a college town really, there's more people in the college than in the town.

Peter: It's a very special town. I am sure that there are few others with a comparable history in the West.

J.H.: What work did you do in Wilcox?

Peter: Like everyone else I helped to renovate an old Legion Hall, make it into a workshop for the college. Also I worked on the café toward the end of the program. We decided as a group we wanted to finish a café for the students of the college. And I also helped to draw up some lifestyle courses wherein people came from Regina to talk about subjects such as problems of the alternate technology. Another group looking at the Third World was separate from the lifestyles, but it involved the same people basically. Lifestyle courses were about energy, appropriate technology, the food we eat, nutrition and consumerism. In these courses new ideas were introduced and although the courses were very elementary, they were very eye-opening.

Grand River, Ontario

J.H.: So what about your next project, Grand River. What town were you in?

Peter: Galt, Cambridge. There we worked for the Grand River Conservation Authority. I hate to be so negative, but once again I felt it was like another eight-to-four job; get up in the morning, go to do your job, and come home.

J.H.: But that wasn't the only thing you did. The week has seven days so you were four days working manually, doing things that were useful, I suppose?

Peter: We really shouldn't talk about this because it's a big mess. I think the people in charge there wanted us to chop wood which their employees could buy to sell again at a higher price. That is one thing they were doing. That was really sour ... of course on the other hand it doesn't come out that it was a bad experience working with the people in the GRCA. There were many very, very friendly people, many people were very outgoing in their effort to improve our stay with the GRCA. There was Connie the foreman of the department of GRCA where we worked; he went out of his way to help us and so did many other people who worked with us.

J.H.: Making a hundred picnic tables is not useless work. People will be using these tables some day.

Peter: That's true, but I think I came into Katimavik expecting to learn and perhaps I was a bit naive. Perhaps I should have realized after Wilcox that that was not what Katimavik was about. I didn't mind making a hundred picnic tables for the first month. I thought, well, people will be able to go to parks and wooded areas and enjoy the country. Perhaps they will begin to realize the value, I could rationalize that. But on the other hand, toward the end of this month I began to see that's all the GRCA wanted from us. I didn't come here just to save the GRCA X and X number of dollars, that type of thing.

J.H.: Yes, but besides them — they were probably so involved in their own work that they saw you that way — there was also a community and you had some contact with it. What did you do in the community besides hard work?

Peter: We had a project with the radio station at the University of Waterloo.

J.H.: Did you do something there yourself? a program?

Peter: Yes, I haven't finished the program yet. I'm hoping to finish it during the last week we have here because that week will be free.

J.H.: What is the title of it?

Peter: I'm doing this with Kathy and the title would be "Canada should not sell nuclear reactors to Third World countries." Basically, we're trying to present both sides of the argument, but ... to come down to it, well we're saying that Canada should not. It's going to be in the fall; if it turns out it will probably be a fifteen — or twenty — minute program.

J.H.: You did some community work also in Grand River?

Peter: Yes, I worked in a day-care centre and the YWCA taking care of ...

J.H.: Handicapped children?

Peter: At the day-care centre, Christopher House, that was part of the work, helping take care of handicapped children. At the YWCA we sort of organized sports, activity days, for when the children had a vacation from school.

J.H.: What do you think of that community?

Peter: It's funny, I got two different impressions. The people I worked with at the day-care centre were very concerned about themselves. They had a job to do and that was it. I felt they didn't really care much. They did a good job, but on the whole, and that doesn't mean everyone, I felt they just looked upon it as something to do and who cares, just get it done. People at the GRCA we worked for in Forestry felt they enjoyed their jobs. They were sick of the politics of the GRCA but they liked their jobs. So I saw two sides of the community; I saw a community that was aware of working with nature, aware of some of the responsibilities of the people taking care of this world, aware of the differences among people. As an aside, I should just say this, about one man from the GRCA. He was talking about the people of Quebec and I was telling him that he'd seen the people in our group from Quebec were very discouraged — no one spoke French, they always had to speak in a language that wasn't their own. This man sat and thought about it for a few minutes and said, "I don't know French but I play the guitar and I know a few songs by Harmonium, a group from Quebec. How would it be if I came and played, do you think that would cheer them up any?" It came to pass about a week later, he came and he sang these songs by Harmonium, three songs were all he knew. He sang them in French and did them very well and Lise and Yves enjoyed them. This was a guy who was willing to take his own time one evening and come and play his guitar.

J.H.: That was nice. Did other things like that happen?

Peter: Day to day we had fun, nice things happened. We'd often drive to go to work and the GRCA guys would take back roads instead of the highway. It would take them longer but they'd show us the countryside and they'd say, "Well, look at this over here. Do you know about this? This has a history, this little place here." Things like that. That was one side of the community I saw. The other side of the community was Christopher House. Not to blame anyone because it's not an issue where we can attach blame, the way they were with the job was get it done, finish it. They expressed gratitude that we were there, but, once again, when the day was over, the job was done, it was goodbye. One point I wish to make about Christopher House is that we, for whatever reason, never really felt needed.

J.H.: So we are getting near the end of Year I of Katimavik for you. Do you think you have changed in any way through the process or is it too early to ask?

Peter: It's early to ask how I've changed. I think I have changed. I've been shown many different ideas, many ideas I've never had in my head before.

J.H.: You mentioned a few times the things you have learned from the community. What did you learn from the other twenty-five participants that you lived with for the entire period?

Peter: I'd have to think about it, but off the top of my head, I've learned that I have to be a lot more tolerant, I learned that my ideas aren't necessarily the best ideas, I learned I'm in this world with other people, I have to live with other people and accept them, enjoy living with other people, not really finding it a chore. In Larouche, I sometimes felt it was a chore to live with twenty-five other people counting the group leaders. Now when we go, as you were saying, it is going to be a very emotional experience. For myself, I think that it is true, because now I feel very close to many of these people.

J.H.: What kind of links would you call that? Do you feel that you're like brothers and sisters or special kinds of friends?

Peter: Brothers and sisters I think would be too much, but special kinds of friends, yes. Before with friends, friends were people, people I'd do things with. We had interests in common. For the last ten months I've been sharing a life with these other people and that's quite a bit more than just being friends. I can't say what it will be like five years from now, how I'll feel, but ...

J.H.: But do you feel you will stay in touch with most of these participants?

Peter: No, to be quite honest, I think I'll start out trying to keep in contact with most of them, but with time I won't be able to keep up as many contacts, perhaps contacts that will last a lifetime.

J.H.: Suppose you go to the Maritimes for some reason, would you contact the people there from your group, will you go and see them?

Peter: Definitely. It's the same when I'm back in Alberta or wherever I am. If anyone comes they're most welcome. I hope that my parents will share that view with these people.

J.H.: Has your view of this country changed somewhat, living with young people who were really representatives in their own way of all parts of the country?

Peter: That I find a very difficult question to answer because something like Canada is very nebulous ... What is a country? A country is the people and if I look upon the people across the country, I'd say Canada is a very terrific thing because the people in it are terrific. They're people, they have their lives, I have my life but we have many things in common, we share many things, we share many beliefs.

J.H.: Do you have the feeling now that people are not that different?

Peter: I don't think I ever believed before that people were that different. Perhaps now I really see the people more than I did before. Perhaps now I feel that people are not really different. However, the lives they lead are very different. Jobs are one example; the fact that we all talk now about what we're going to do in the summer, what you are going to do in the fall. We talk about getting jobs and/or going to school and get to talking about the unemployment situation, or the schools in different parts of the country. You begin to see that people in different parts of the country have different priorities and different opportunities. For instance, talking to people from the Maritimes about jobs, you realize there aren't that many jobs there. That's an everyday worry in these people's lives.

J.H.: Which is not true for somebody from Edmonton?

Peter: No, presently no, not in this part of my life. Perhaps five years that I've looked for jobs, they've always been there, easy to get. I see that's not part of life in the Maritimes. It's a real worry and although these people aren't very different, they have different concerns. For instance, "Should I go into law, would it lead to politics?" Not that I plan to have it lead there. I realize that when someone from the Maritimes worries about fish quotas or whatever, coal mining, they're not just worried about some trivial little thing. Alberta, okay they've got a problem, but having met people from there, you see this is an important part of their life. It's like ... it's very important and it touches people. Before, I'd always think of big issues — the leadership, the French issues — but it's people that are really touched by government, by society.

J.H.: Do you communicate as easily with people from the East, from the West, from Central Canada?

Peter: Oh yes, on a person-to-person basis, yes I think I could. I didn't find that it was that great a difference by region. Between Anglophones and Francophones, it was a difference of language, but once one starts to have a feel for the other's language, communication isn't that hard. I'm just a person like they are, we have common interests, some common ideas. We can talk and there's no need to shout at each other.

J.H.: The question that was asked so many times among yourselves about what you are going to be doing this summer — what *are* you doing next fall? What will you do with your life?

Peter: Myself? Oh this summer I'm going to go back home. My father has asked me if I could help him out with a tree farm that the family owns, so that's what I'll be doing then. In the fall I've been accepted by McGill University to study law. I plan to go ahead with that, to start studying law. I don't think I'll finish it. I'm beginning to seriously think about giving up law to study agriculture. As I was saying earlier, people should be able to feed themselves and we should take care of ourselves so the world will be able to take care of itself.

J.H.: And if we could produce more, we could share it.

Peter: Yes, and take only what we need, share more.

J.H.: Re-arrange the world, make it a bigger and better place for everybody. You say you will take law but you will not finish it, you will jump to something totally different, agriculture?

Peter: I have considered agriculture, but it wasn't until the last couple of months that I began to very seriously think about it and by that time it was too late to enter the agricultural college that I wished to attend, I'd been accepted by law, so I'm going to law school. It will be an education, perhaps, having studied a year of law. I'll learn a bit about learning.

214

J.H.: There's nothing wrong with studying law ...

Peter: Perhaps it will broaden my horizon a bit and then I can find out if what I feel right now is sincere or if it is just the pressure of the last ten months.

J.H.: You will find out if it is a Katimavik complex ...

Peter: Yes, it could be. I can say right now that I don't think it is, but how can you really know until you've been away for a while.

J.H.: Why did you choose McGill in Montreal instead of, for example, Simon Fraser?

Peter: Before Katimavik, I looked upon law as an end in itself but I never understood why. I wanted to study international law. I know it sounds funny, but I wanted to help out with underdeveloped countries and thought maybe if I took international law, I could work with the government or the United Nations and somehow show my personal beliefs and use the law as a tool. Queen's and McGill are the only two universities in Canada that teach international law in any depth. I chose McGill over Kingston because I figured that if I was in Montreal, I'd have an opportunity to learn French and if I was going to work either at the UN or with the Canadian government, I should be able to work in both French and English. This country is a bilingual and bicultural nation.

J.H.: Do you think Katimavik was a good idea after all? In general, and for you in particular?

Peter: I think Katimavik is a good idea. In some ways I feel that it could be better but then, as you said yourself, this is the first year. Of course, there are going to be problems, but I think it will improve in many ways.

J.H.: I want to talk about the absentees, because they are gone and I won't be interviewing them.¹ I think it's a good sign that your group started with twenty-six, because we cannot count the ones who dropped out of training camp, that's part of the selection process. But you were twenty-six and you are now twenty-three which means that

---

1 I changed my mind later and interviewed Yvan and Gordon.

three have left. One of them was Robert and I don't think we can call him a dropout as he was promoted to group leader and I heard he was doing a good job. Then Yvan left and I was there when he was undecided at the end of Larouche. What do you think of him?

Peter: He was in my group but at Larouche we didn't live in groups. In Wilcox we were together for about a month. He seemed to be a very creative person, although that is stereotyping. He has artistic tendencies, he is very expressive and I found that he didn't have a chance to express himself, to use his creative ability. He was becoming very frustrated, feeling very trod upon having to go out and work in this workshop and never be able to express his creative ability.

J.H.: He's not really a dropout in my view, because he still keeps coming to see you ...

Peter: Yes, he's kept in touch and he'll be coming back in a week to see us. He left the program but I don't think he's a dropout. He left to continue what he believed in. He was working in a prison in the rehabilitation centre, he was teaching inmates art and he was procuring supplies for them.

J.H.: Maybe we shouldn't talk about the case of Gordon because it's very touchy, but generally speaking, what do you think of him?

Peter: I missed him and I was very sorry he left because I enjoyed talking with him. He's a very rebellious type of character and was always in a revolt. That was a good deal of the reason for his dismissal. What happened was, it was a joke that went sour. I miss talking with him because in his rebelliousness he thought a lot and he was stimulating to talk with. I knew some of what he was thinking and he wasn't scared to say what he thought. There happened to be some arguments.

J.H.: One day, I was telling Gordon about the three-day meeting the board was planning to discuss the program for Year II. It would be representative of the whole Katimavik. Howard Nixon and I, the two co-chairmen, would be there, many people from the Montreal staff and the five regional directors plus one representative of the co-ordinators and one of the group leaders, and I stopped there. And Gordon said, "A moment ago you said that the most important thing at Katimavik were the participants and you seem to have forgotten them." I said he was quite right, not that we forget about the participants, we are doing the whole thing for them. But we'd forgotten to have some of them for our three-day meeting and when I came back to Montreal I acted quickly and two participants — one Francophone, one Anglophone, one from the West and one from the East — were invited. That was probably the best idea we had. During this whole conference, the two participants were always consulted because it dealt with things that concerned them directly. You said that Gordon was rebellious. Well, it is very stimulating to have people like that.

19 *Angela Hodge,* Age 17, Nitro, Quebec

I was born in Lachine, Quebec, and lived in Nitro. I have three brothers, two older and one younger.

J.H.: What did your father do in Nitro?

Angela: He worked for the CIL plant.

J.H.: I know you have travelled to most of the provinces of Canada.

Angela: All, except Newfoundland and the Northwest Territories and Yukon. One of my friends has a van and we just drove across. We camped out every night... for a month.

J.H.: What kind of ideas about this country did you get from this trip or from your previous life?

Angela: It's a nice country. It's really beautiful. It's so great because of the differences in culture and that.

J.H.: Before you got involved in Katimavik, what were your dreams about the future, what you wanted to do with your life?

Angela: Get back to the country and raise horses.

J.H.: Horses?

Angela: Yes.

J.H.: Still have the same idea?

Angela: Yes. More so.

J.H.: For other reasons?

218

Angela: Well, Katimavik has brought me closer to nature than I was before.

J.H.: So one day Katimavik came into your life. How did that happen? How did you hear from it?

Angela: My mother saw posters about Katimavik and she knew I was looking for something to do, so she told me about it and I applied. I worked and I wasn't planning to go back to school, so I needed something and a change.

J.H.: A change? Were you getting away from something? Or getting into something?

Angela: Getting into something. I just needed a different atmosphere from going to school.

J.H.: But what was in your mind from what you heard or read about Katimavik?

Angela: Getting to meet different people and seeing parts of the country and living with people, because I am not used to it.

J.H.: Did you like people?

Angela: Oh, yes, I really did.

J.H.: How is it that you are not used to it? There were some people in Nitro as well.

Angela: Being friends with someone is different from living with a bunch of strange people and trying to make a family out of it. Everybody has different ideas.

J.H.: All of a sudden, you found yourself in a place called Duchesnay, with almost a hundred young people from all across the country, one third Francophones and some of them speaking only French, Anglophones only speaking English. What was your first impression? Was it a shock?

Angela: Yes it was. Before I even got to Duchesnay, getting into the bus stop in Montreal all the Francophones were there, I was the only Anglophone and I was scared since I thought I would be stuck for a month with ninety people that speak only French. And it scared me a lot.

J.H.: Why did it scare you? After all, you knew some French ...

Angela: Well, I knew French, but it was just the idea that I had never lived with somebody who is French, nor have I ever spoken that much French.

J.H.: But in Nitro, what is the proportion of the French population there?

Angela: It's about 99 per cent French.

J.H.: Well, then, you were used to it.

Angela: Yes, but most of my friends live outside of Nitro and they're English.

J.H.: What was the most difficult thing besides this problem — which was not really a problem, because when you got to Duchesnay, you realized that you were, as a matter of fact, in the majority, because two-thirds of the participants are Anglophones. Besides that, what were the problems that you encountered being ninety or a hundred young people, so different in many ways?

Angela: Just trying to talk to them ... at the start I was very, very shy and I wouldn't go out and talk with somebody.

J.H.: Are you still shy?

Angela: Not as much. After all, when you are put into a situation with a group of people, you really have no choice but to open up.

Larouche, Quebec

J.H.: Finally you started the first project, in Larouche? A French-Canadian village, partly farmers, partly workers. You were assigned there with your group of thirty — well, three groups of ten but living in the same house. I know the house, it is not a big house. How did you feel being stuck in that house with thirty people?

Angela: It was hell at the start.

J.H.: In what sense?

Angela: I will just say people who were, you know, like vegetarians and non-vegetarians. It just started off, you know, little things like that which turned into big meetings that lasted till 3.00 a.m., which was real hell.

J.H.: But it seems to me that most of the participants are now more or less vegetarians, or at least they go for natural food. Were you concerned about that before?

Angela: No, I was a vegetarian. It was nothing new to me. I couldn't understand the problems, I faced it back in my own house but it was just the idea of having to have meetings about it. And everything that had a straightforward solution, (to me anyway), turned into a long, drawn out fight.

J.H.: Because in your own house, you are the only vegetarian, the rest of the family is not?

Angela: Right.

J.H.: Of course in the Larouche project, there was not a lot of work to do but, besides that, what did you do for the community or for the group's house?

Angela: In Larouche, I didn't see too much of the group, I was on a farm for seven and a half weeks.

J.H.: How do you explain that you were the only one to wish and to succeed in living so long away from the group in a farm? There is nothing wrong with that because every participant should live either on a farm or at least in a family, but it has not been structured well enough this year. It will be better next year. But how is it that you persisted so long living in a farm, where normally other people were there for three weeks?

Angela: I went the first time, then the second time came around when one of the girls who was supposed to go on the farm that I was on previously decided she didn't want to go. I said that if nobody else wanted to go, then I'd go. Nobody else in the group wanted to go so I was lucky enough to get on again.

J.H.: You say lucky because you thought, you seem to think that it was the best part of Larouche for you?

Angela: Oh yes. I really enjoyed it.

J.H.: What family was it?

Angela: Lessard.

J.H.: Talk to me about them?

Angela: Seven boys in the family and I was the only girl, except for like the other participants. We lived their lives. Got up at 6.00 a.m., milked the cows and everything. Whatever they did, we did. It was lots of fun.

J.H.: What else did you learn from living with this family? Did you learn anything about Quebec that you didn't know before in Nitro?

Angela: I learned that for them, their farm is everything whereas at the other farms that I have known, it was just like a hobby.

J.H.: What was particular about that family that made you like them so much?

Angela: Well, they accepted me as sort of their daughter. I wasn't like an outsider coming into their family.

J.H.: And you, did you think of them as your parents in some way?

Angela: I considered them like a home away from home. Their family is now part of mine.

J.H.: And what about your seven "brothers"?

Angela: I like them all. I probably like them more than my real brothers, because they aren't my brothers and I didn't have to live with them for that long but ... they treated me just like a sister and things like that, even little fights. Quite an experience.

J.H.: What did you learn through that long stay, about the mentality of this little region of Quebec?

Angela: I found it was very similar to the area where I come from. When strangers do come in, there is a sort of hesitancy to go up and meet them and talk to them. But after they got to know us and found out what our goals were and what we were really like, their whole attitude changed.

J.H.: What other kind of work did you do?

Angela: I did a bit of work on the greenhouse and the teepees.

Wilcox, Saskatchewan

J.H.: After three months, the whole group moved to Wilcox, Saskatchewan. That must have been somewhat different from Nitro and Larouche!

Angela: Yes, quite a bit.

J.H.: In what way?

Angela: We weren't wanted, Katimavik wasn't really wanted in the community.

J.H.: As much as it was in Larouche?

Angela: Yes. And most of the people, with the exception of two or three, never got to meet many of the people in the community until the last few weeks or the last few days.

J.H.: But you were involved in a lot of work though, physical work?

Angela: Yes. Building the workshop and the café for the school. It was hard but in some cases rewarding.

J.H.: Were you involved in the building?

Angela: Yes, I really got into construction. I was the official painter there. I painted the walls, work benches, saw horses, etc.

J.H.: You worked regularly during that whole period in Wilcox?

Angela: Yes. We worked 8.00 a.m. to 4.00.

J.H.: That was tough. But did you like it?

Angela: Well, yes and no. Like when we got the café finished, I went back later and there was a really good feeling inside me.

J.H.: It was a café for the college?

Angela: Yes. We finally accomplished something that would be used promptly, for the students, give them some place to go. It made me feel good.

J.H.: Do you think the students were happy about that?

Angela: Yes. We had the open house for them and the band from Hull came up and they were really happy, like the place was just packed. Afterward, they said how much they appreciated it.

J.H.: So for a group that was not wanted, you achieved something because they were happy with what you did?

Angela: Yes.

J.H.: Were you involved in anything else in Wilcox? Social work?

Angela: Yes. We worked at the cafeteria and I found work at the school library as well as teaching gym classes a couple of afternoons a week.

J.H.: They have an extraordinary library there?

Angela: Yes. A lot of very interesting books. The original BNA Act was there in a safe and books from the 1400s.

J.H.: Did you get a better idea of what Saskatchewan is about through Wilcox?

Angela: Yes. At least a little bit. The most striking thing was the scenery, it was really totally different. It was flat.

J.H.: Do you think that you could live there?

Angela: No.

J.H.: Even to raise horses?

Angela: No, it's too cold for me. Maybe it was just a bad winter or something but it was really cold out there. It's a lot warmer in the East.

Grand River, Ontario

J.H.: So let's move to Ontario. There were three communities but we always called it the Grand River project. Where were you? In what community exactly?

Angela: Cambridge (Galt).

J.H.: You were involved in the work project? What was that?

Angela: Putting together picnic tables and chopping wood for the Grand River Conservation Authority.

J.H.: How many picnic tables did you finally do?

Angela: We put together 200.

J.H.: Do you have any feeling at all about these tables? Do you see them, for example, in the future with a happy family around them and think, "Well, they don't know about that but I did them."

Angela: I thought of that but I also thought of the agony and boredom that I went through building those stupid picnic tables and how monotonous it became because I wasn't learning anything. I was there for a month and I was still putting together picnic tables. I wasn't getting any other experience out of it except a lot of patience.

J.H.: Well, learning patience is something. You always learn something in the worst situation.

Angela: Yes, but I feel that nobody has to learn patience in that kind of situation.

J.H.: So you did not have much chance to communicate deeply with people, in these regions except the Lessard family in Larouche. What about the participants in your group, the big group and the small group? What did you learn through this experience with these young people coming from all across the country and from all walks of life?

Angela: How to be patient and understanding and change myself so, not to please them, but so that we can find some meeting place in the middle where we can all be happy.

J.H.: What are the things in yourself that have changed, do you think?

Angela: Everything changed, my whole lifestyle. Getting out and working on a forty-hour week really changed me. It also changed my eating and sleeping habits.

J.H.: You mean to say that you were not very disciplined before?

Angela: Oh, I was disciplined to have good manners and be polite to people and things like that but I was never disciplined in the sense of getting along with people.

J.H.: But even if you had been told, that's the kind of thing you have to experience ...

Angela: Yes, you have to.

J.H.: I know because I visited your group a few times, that you spent many hours each night and in the afternoon, and on weekends talking to each other. What did you learn, for example, about the different parts of the country?

Angela: The different types of cultures, the different beliefs. Like for Lap, his religion, what Hong Kong was like. What he finds different between the two places. Finding out how nice it must be to spend winters out in British Columbia.

J.H.: Do you have a different feeling about the Maritimes because of the people from there in the group or through the exchange you have made?

Angela: Yes, actually being able to talk with them and find out ... like Joyce, coming from Newfoundland, the seal hunting business which I'm totally against. Just sitting down and talking with her, I realize now they need to do that because of shortage of jobs and unemployment. I'm still against it but I understand their situation better.

J.H.: So you wouldn't go out on the streets and shout against that?

Angela: No, I wouldn't, but I will continue to protest it in other ways.

J.H.: Did you learn about other parts of the country through the participants themselves?

Angela: I'm a geography freak so I know quite a bit about Canada, but just reading it out of the book or something never satisfies me. I have to talk to the people and verify it.

J.H.: What is your feeling about the other participants? Do your consider them as a big family of which you are part?

Angela: I think I am closer to them than I ever had been to a brother or sister.

J.H.: Do you feel that the links will remain?

Angela: I think they will, but maybe it's just wishful. There are certain people that I will keep in close touch with. Others I'm not too sure about.

J.H.: Obviously you like certain people more than others, which is true in a family too.

Angela: Yes.

J.H.: But you have brothers and sisters spread all across the country. Does it give you more roots in the country, feeling that you have friends or brothers?

Angela: It makes me feel more that Canada is my home and not just a place to live in. I know all the people across and if I ever happen to end up in that area then I have somebody I can talk to. It just makes you feel a little bit closer.

J.H.: You know that if you are in British Columbia, there is Lap and Robert and, who else?

Angela: Mark, Dorle.

J.H.: Do you plan to go and visit them sometime?

Angela: Yes, maybe next fall.

J.H.: What do you plan to do this summer?

Angela: I hope to get work aboard a vessel but that's pretty indecisive yet because Canadian shipping lines are not taking female workers yet.

J.H.: Why work on a boat? For someone who is dreaming about horses?

Angela: I want to get my first-class pilot's licence so I can drive boats like through the St. Lawrence, Great Lakes, or wherever. But before I can go to school to get my training, I have to spend two years aboard a boat.

J.H.: Do you plan to go back home?

Angela: Yes, for a while and then I'm going to leave again for a while, just get out and be by myself.

J.H.: And where are the horses in all that?

Angela: They are at one of my girlfriend's, who has racing horses. We're going to go riding up at her camp, spend a week or so riding in the mountains in the Laurentians.

J.H.: Do you think Katimavik was a good idea for you after all?

Angela: Yes, it's really a worthwhile experience.

J.H.: So you are not shy anymore?

Angela: No, not really.

J.H.: In what other ways have you changed?

Angela: I'm really concerned about people. If somebody hurts himself, I become really nervous, just like an old mother.

J.H.: Because you like them?

Angela: Maybe. It was never like that before. They would be the concern but not as deep as it is now.

20 *Carol Ann Letty*, Age 18, Brampton, Ontario

I was born in Brampton, Ontario, and lived there for eighteen years. There were three girls in my family and my sisters are much older than I am, married with children, so I'm basically an only child.

J.H.: You went to school in Brampton?

Carol Ann: Yes, just down the road, up to grade 13.

J.H.: Before Katimavik, what were your dreams for the future?

Carol Ann: I was seriously thinking of going into teaching, but with the situation with teaching jobs right now, I thought it would be silly. I'm thinking in other directions.

J.H.: Did you travel at all before Katimavik?

Carol Ann: Yes, I've been to Europe, to Mexico, and down to the United States a bit. I haven't travelled much around Canada and that's why I opted for Katimavik.

J.H.: How did you learn of Katimavik?

Carol Ann: The newspaper and articles.

J.H.: What struck you besides the fact that you would discover new parts of the country?

Carol Ann: I guess the idea of a different lifestyle, group living; like it would have been hard but a good experience, the travelling and the work outdoors in the woods and social work. It all sounded very interesting. The change in

228

lifestyles and also looking at different aspects of alternate technology.

J.H.: So, with all that put together, you really fit into the program.

Carol Ann: Yes, it was exactly what I have been looking for.

J.H.: You applied, you received a telegram one day and you said, "Well, now I'm off for Duchesnay, Quebec."

Carol Ann: Yes, and I got nervous.

J.H.: What was your impression when you got to Duchesnay?

Carol Ann: A lot of people. My biggest worry was, "Oh my, what am I ... " because I'm a sort of loner.

J.H.: Are you shy?

Carol Ann: No, I just like to be alone.

J.H.: And you were not there?

Carol Ann: No, you were not alone.

J.H.: And, well, one-third was French-speaking. That was another problem, for you, was it? Did you know any French?

Carol Ann: No, not at all, I was turned off, very much so in grade 7, so I didn't take it in high school.

Larouche, Quebec

J.H.: After Duchesnay you finally got down to a smaller group, a group of thirty, which is still probably quite a lot, especially as you were in a house that was good for perhaps ten or twenty people.

Carol Ann: There were times, like when I wanted to go to the bathroom to be alone, yes that was my little place, and I took a book. The thing was also the group meetings. We have thirty different people with different philosophies, backgrounds, deciding on something that everyone will feel unanimous about and it just doesn't happen. A lot of times you find yourself giving in, but other times a lot of people give in to you.

J.H.: In Larouche, was the language a big problem?

Carol Ann: Yes, it was very much the French on this side of the house and the English on the other.

J.H.: But it didn't stay like that for long though. Were you on a farm at one point?

Carol Ann: Yes, with the Lessard family. I enjoyed the family. One of the things was that they had five children and one of my faults is that I'm not that fond of children, so I didn't enjoy that too much, but I enjoyed the work and the people were very good people. One thing that bothers me very much is that in high school, for instance, you're learning American history, not Canadian history, you're really not learning about Canada at all. So, it was really nice being in Quebec, seeing people's feelings, people who have been there; like a lot of the crap we read in the newspaper — the French are not like that at all. They are built up as monsters sometimes.

J.H.: So, you changed your mind a little about Quebec?

Carol Ann: Oh yes, like the FLQ and everything shows Quebec people as monsters, but then you look back and you see that it's just a whole built-up sort of thing. French Canada is something I want to learn more about, I want to do more research into it, because I really don't know anything.

J.H.: Did you learn as much about Quebec from the participants from Quebec as from the fact that you were with a French family in Larouche?

Carol Ann: You did, but you didn't because I think a lot of the participants are very ... well they don't want to talk about it too much. I guess they have been asked so many times, just because they're French; people say "What do you know about this Quebec situation?" I guess they get sick. Also, we have been teaching in high school in Saskatchewan and in Ontario, and some of the French were going and helping people with their French classes; of course the first question is: "What is the Quebec situation, what's happened?"

J.H.: What did you learn in Larouche besides that, besides a better knowledge of Quebec? Did you do some work there?

Carol Ann: Yes, working on a greenhouse. I didn't do an awful lot, and that, of course, was interesting. I haven't done a lot of carpentry work, so it's opened an interest there. We were cutting trails and learned how to use a chainsaw, which I'd done before but not too much. The biggest thing in Larouche, though, was emotional — relating to people, and becoming much more responsible, knowing you have responsibilities to the group, like having your days of cooking and cleaning and just having to get along, getting up in the morning and spending the day with thirty people. It's really a big adjustment. Another thing I found very interesting was building a teepee. I did a lot of it; you sort of get used to working with your hands and getting back to the feeling of how things used to be done, like how today things are just spit out of a machine. At the end there is that gratification of, "WOW, look what we've made!"

J.H.: It was really the group that was building itself?

Carol Ann: One thing also is that now we're in groups of ten and like, for example, Christine, who I don't really know that much but I feel something very strong for her, because of that experience we had; you had to or you would just fall apart. There were a lot of really bad times but then there were a lot of good times too.

J.H.: You have something to share for the rest of your lives.

Wilcox, Saskatchewan

J.H.: After the three months in Larouche you moved to Wilcox.

Carol Ann: It was really a good experience, the Prairies.

J.H.: You didn't know about the Prairies at all?

Carol Ann: I've just seen movies. People have been there and told me about it. Everyone told me I was going to hate it, I'd get sick of it, but I loved it.

J.H.: What did you love about it?

Carol Ann: The physical sense of it; I find it very free and very open. I met quite a few people from there who said they've been to Quebec or to B.C. and found the hills very confining and they had to come home because they couldn't stand it. There was a lot of wildlife there, and the sunrises and sunsets. The town I was in was Milestone. Very friendly. It was really like reading a book: an old general store, you're all wrapped up in the middle of winter when there was blizzards and you walk in and they joke and you can talk with them, really nice people.

J.H.: So you could relate to the population of the town much better than in Larouche?

Carol Ann: Well, we lived around the corner and we had an interest right in town, which was not the case in Larouche.

J.H.: Didn't they find it strange that a group of "hippies," as they may have called you at the beginning, lived there?

Carol Ann: They took a lot of interest in us. They had organized a day-care centre and all the mothers went to the meetings, they said what they felt and what they wanted. You know, it's something you wouldn't get in a bigger town.

J.H.: Were you involved in the day-care centre? In spite of the fact that you don't care for children?

Carol Ann: Well, I've worked with children before and I can appreciate them, but I don't want any of my own; I like them for an hour, because then I can say, "Goodbye, go to mom."

J.H.: What did you do in Milestone besides that?

Carol Ann: Oh, everything. First of all we worked in Wilcox, I helped build a roof on a curling rink, then I went to the day-care centre and taught macramé and I did music lessons with children in the public school. We worked a lot on the coffee house for older people in Milestone.

J.H.: Did you see it in use at the end?

Carol Ann: No. It was almost finished, but we didn't see people use it.

J.H.: The next group will probably finish it.

Carol Ann: They'll have the thing of setting it up, the tables and decorating it. It's too bad but ...

J.H.: You did what you could. Did the people of the town appreciate your work?

Carol Ann: I know we were appreciated in the schools. I'll never forget the first couple of days. We didn't have a group leader and so Dorle and I took it upon ourselves to do something. We went to the high school. They were very down on Katimavik and the principal was not friendly. I talked to him and explained what we were and what we wanted and by the end when we explained we wanted to work at the day-care centre, he said: "Before I didn't want to but now that I know you're going to be working there, I'm going to send my two children," and he became really friendly. It was really nice just to walk away with the feeling that we had changed his impression of Katimavik. There was a lady at the library who was very taken by us and very nice. We did a lot with her as she was the janitor too so we helped her with a lot of library stuff — and social work such as music and macramé.

J.H.: Are you a musician yourself?

Carol Ann: Voice, I love. The other day when we were in Milestone, Lap and I taught in Chinese "I'm a little teapot," and it was really good, the kids just loved it. We taught them French songs too. Mario is very musically inclined and he did all the actions with them and we all had a great time.

J.H.: Do you feel that you will ever go back to Wilcox?

Carol Ann: This summer, on my way to British Columbia. I'll be going through Wilcox. I have some friends and relatives in British Columbia.

J.H.: You have friends all across the country!

Carol Ann: Yes, it's really good when you want to travel.

J.H.: Wilcox was a good project for you?

Carol Ann: It was pretty good, except we had some group problems for quite a while.

J.H.: Yes, you had all kinds of probems with group leaders and all that.

Carol Ann: We were without a group leader for at least a month.

J.H.: How did it work out?

Carol Ann: Very good. That was the problem, we worked very well without one.

J.H.: Maybe we don't need group leaders?

Carol Ann: Well, it's very hard to tell what a group leader is because you're going to have strong-minded participants. Sometimes it seems they are nothing more than babysitters. They are supposed to be resource people but at other times Katimavik seems to be more resourceful about a certain situation.

J.H.: Who are the people in your group, by the way? In Milestone.

Carol Ann: There is Lap, Dorle, Claire, Cindy, Mario, Gordon and Roy. We're a very strong-minded group and that's very difficult.

J.H.: But you managed?

Carol Ann: Oh, yes, we managed.

Grand River, Ontario

J.H.: After Saskatchewan, you moved to Ontario. For you it must have been like coming home almost. You didn't like that I presume?

Carol Ann: No, I would have liked to have been somewhere else, but it worked out all right.

J.H.: Where were you in the Grand River project?

Carol Ann: I was in Belwood, a very small town, I really loved the work and I loved the people, but I don't like the philosophy of working there because I believe that if we hadn't been there other people would be hired. To me one of the most important parts of the Katimavik philosophy is not to take away other people's jobs.

J.H.: I thought you were added to the people already there?

Carol Ann: If we hadn't been there, they would have hired local people. One of the bosses I was very friendly with told me that if we hadn't been there somebody else would have been hired.

J.H.: Did you learn something?

Carol Ann: I learned a lot about working outdoors and about the different kinds of trees. That has always been very important to me, planting trees. We tapped our maple trees and boiled the sap. I've never done that before.

J.H.: You have a few maple trees around your house?

Carol Ann: Yes, all along the driveway.

J.H.: Did everybody know about that or did you have to inquire?

Carol Ann: We did, yes, but we had to know exactly how you found out where to tap them. One of the guys came down and showed us.

J.H.: How much maple syrup did you finally make?

Carol Ann: About a gallon. It takes a lot of sap and you have to boil it and boil it.

J.H.: I tasted it and it was very good.

Carol Ann: We learned about different sorts of trees, about pruning and that sort of stuff. It's very important but I never realized it, to make a tree grow straight. Why they plant certain kinds of trees and all sorts of things. It's silly not to know what kind of trees are around you, it's very stupid. I built shades for trees which was fun.

J.H.: Shades for trees?

Carol Ann: Yes, they put shades over trees so when the snow comes it doesn't weight them down.

J.H.: They must be small trees.

Carol Ann: Very tiny trees, and also, so animals can't get at them. Another thing that I found very relevant was that I learned a lot about the dam which was really interesting. I didn't know anything about the system, or why they made dams, what power they had over the community because of the dams and about building houses and flood plains and what cities have done, because of the cement and the flow off; it's a very big problem and something I never thought of before, having the dam right behind us. It was really interesting. You have to know what to do or you could flood the town, it's quite complicated. I'd like to look more into other conservations, like in Brampton, and I'd like to look into what their philosophies are and what they're trying to do because they are going to build another dam in this area.

J.H.: So you were almost back home. It was not too different, you knew the people already?

Carol Ann: Yes, but Brampton is basically Toronto and Fergus is a small town and Aurora is a very nice little village just up the way. I did a lot of social work there too, especially with the museum, the Wella County museum. It showed me something I wouldn't mind doing in the future, because I'm a history freak anyway. I worked a little bit on displays, cataloguing things. Working with these things is just beautiful and really exciting, the idea of how old things are. I catalogued a lot of books which I just love because then you look into what year it's come from and the family that gave it to you and the whole family background.

J.H.: Were you involved with the radio station at all?

Carol Ann: Oh, yes, every Monday. I did a program on travel in Mexico. I'm not finished, and I am finishing it up and will take it up next week.

J.H.: Now we are getting to the end of the Katimavik program, do you feel that you have changed through it, and in what way?

Carol Ann: I'm much more tolerant of people. One thing that I was very down about was drinking and smoking. I am still against it but I'm much more tolerant. Just living with people which I had never done before and I thought I'd never be able to do. And I, of course, have. Even things like learning to cook: I didn't know how to cook.

J.H.: You didn't know how to cook?

Carol Ann: Oh gosh, no. I could make French toast and that's about all. I've gotten much better and I've learned how to make things.

J.H.: You are now concerned about food?

Carol Ann: Yes, I have learned about nutrition, about myself, about other people, tolerance.

J.H.: So the main change in you is tolerance. Can you see anything else that changed?

Carol Ann: Maybe not being as naive about things. I was very idealistic.

J.H.: Don't tell me you are no longer idealistic!

Carol Ann: Well, no, but I was very optimistic and a dreamer sort of person about the world and the people. Now I see people are pretty silly sometimes.

J.H.: They can be! But nevertheless what is your feeling about your group, the whole group of twenty-three or so.

Because participants told me that you are like brothers and sisters or like a big family. Is that your feeling?

Carol Ann: With most of them. I'll always be concerned and want to know what happened with any one of them. Going through what we've gone through, they're a part of me and especially because we were in Katimavik in its first year when there were a lot of problems and disorganization.

J.H.: So you are pioneers. You had to suffer for it, but you are proud of it?

Carol Ann: Yes, in a lot of ways it's very bad but then in a lot of ways it's brought us closer together.

J.H.: Do you think you will write to many people and visit back and forth?

Carol Ann: Yes, maybe not a lot, but about four or five. For instance, there is one girl I will be spending September and October with. Her aunt and uncle are going to Europe so I'll be there with her to babysit. There are some people I love very much and a few people that I don't.

J.H.: But even the people that you don't love you care about?

Carol Ann: Oh, yes, you have to.

J.H.: What are your plans now and what are you going to do right after Katimavik?

Carol Ann: Hopefully get a job this summer. I've applied for about ten so I've got my fingers crossed that I'll get into something. If not I think I'll go out West and look for a job there.

J.H.: What will you do with your life?

Carol Ann: I want to farm. It was always very strong, like teaching. But it has been much closer to me. It's the only way in this environment I could feel comfortable.

J.H.: You look like a happy girl with no problems.

Carol Ann: Yes, I am a very happy girl. No problems I can't handle.

21 Claire Bellefeuille, Age 18, Pierrefonds, Quebec

I was born in Hawkesbury, Ontario, in Prescott County, near the Quebec border. A Francophone area. But I didn't stay there long, just two or three months. Afterward we moved to Ile Bizard, Pierrefonds more precisely, where I lived for eighteen years. I have four younger brothers and really good parents. I realized that when I was away from them.

J.H.: What about school?

Claire: Oh yes, school. I went to a French primary school, four years of high school in English and one year of CEGEP in English.

J.H.: So you knew English before you started the program?

Claire: Yes. I was bilingual. I was considered bilingual right away and a Francophone called me "the Anglaise," just for fun. In Katimavik they seemed to want the Francophones to speak only French, but I've always been in the belief of trying to help someone in his language if he doesn't understand me. So some of the participants bugged me about that from time to time, just for fun.

J.H.: How did you hear about Katimavik?

Claire: It's very strange; there's a newspaper in Hawkesbury called *Le Carillon* which we get at the house every week.

J.H.: You've kept your Ontario roots ...

Claire: Yes. There was an article about Katimavik in the paper, early last April. I was pretty well fed up with school and it seemed interesting. I sent in an application and on July 13 I got a telegram saying I'd been accepted.

J.H.: So then you went to Duchesnay?

Claire: Duchesnay was quite an interesting experience, with all those people. I noticed a difference between the people from Ontario and the ones from the West and from the Maritimes.

J.H.: For instance?

Claire: Their attitude toward the French language. It seemed as though it didn't bother the people from the West to learn another language. But the ones from Ontario seemed to be saying "Why should I learn it?" There was more ...

J.H.: Reluctance?

Claire: Yes.

Larouche, Quebec

J.H.: So after that first contact you were divided into groups of thirty and yours went to Larouche.

Claire: I remember that Michel, the co-ordinator, told us it was a small house, nothing to write home about. So I'd imagined it was even smaller than it really was. I'd thought it would be just a hole in the wall, but when I walked inside I said to myself, "It's fairly big compared with what I thought!" When I think of it now it seems practically impossible that we were able to live in it ... Yes, it was difficult. When I went to live on the farm I realized that I'd just spent eight weeks in really difficult circumstances. My stay on the Lessard's farm was one of my best experiences. The atmosphere was a little like in my own family because they've seven boys. We've got four. So it was only three more! It makes a difference, but the atmosphere was a little like ours. And I understood that one of the reasons I'd come to Katimavik was that it would help me leave my parents' house. Not all at once, in stages ... Katimavik was a closed environment but you aren't with your parents, you aren't with people younger than you, you're with people your own age who've had just about the same experiences, who feel the same kinds of things, who've left their families for the first time. But in spite of everything I missed my family a lot. Ah! letters were very important, parcels, all that, it was very important ...

J.H.: Was it your first experience on a farm?

Claire: Yes. I learned a lot about dairy production, cows, how a farm operates. I liked it a lot.

J.H.: What other sort of work did you do at Larouche?

Claire: The first week, I helped clean up the municipal dump. Very interesting! Then I built teepees. I went into the woods to look for trees, then brought them back to the house with the tractor, and stripped off the bark. Then I painted the garbage cans we'd put in the village of Larouche.

J.H.: During that time, was the life style of the group being established?

Claire: Yes, we had to learn from one another, you know, learn how to put up with each other, respect the same timetable for everybody, because otherwise it wouldn't have worked. Organize kitchen duty, housework.

J.H.: What have you brought back from Larouche?

Claire: I learned a lot about myself, and I discovered an area I didn't know – the Saguenay and Lac St.Jean. I visited it with my parents when they came to see me one weekend in October. I liked the area very much. And I was very happy to realize that a lot of Anglophones learned a little more about Quebec; it opened their eyes. I liked living with thirty people. Sometimes I'd have preferred to be by myself but I felt I couldn't leave the group.

Wilcox, Saskatchewan

J.H.: After Larouche you moved to Wilcox – or in the case of your group of ten, to Milestone, near Wilcox. What did you do in that little village?

Claire: We worked, we helped the people. There was an old café the people in the village wanted to change into a café for the old people in the community, because there were a lot of old people. So we did the construction, we tore down walls, put up new ones, then we put in a ceiling, nailed, sawed, plastered.

J.H.: Had you done that kind of work before?

Claire: No, so I found it very interesting. And then we worked as volunteers, we gave music lessons, macramé lessons; I usually went to the high school to work in the library. And I went with three other participants to help the Protestant minister, who was a woman. Once we even helped her conduct services! That was quite interesting too. You know, observing another religion ...

J.H.: Can you describe the people in your group? Without emphasizing their bad points too much!

Claire: There was Mario.

J.H.: Mario's from Beloeil, I think ...

Claire: Yes, he is. Mario, you know, he's really full of life! You can have a really heavy argument with him, but next day he's forgotten about it and he's just as good a friend as before.

J.H.: He plays the flute ...

Claire: Yes, he's full of life, but he's always ready to help out when he's needed. And then there's Lap, from Vancouver; he's Chinese, and he's only been in Canada a year. He's full of life too...

J.H.: Too much?

Claire: Yes, sometimes, really too much! And, you know, he jumps around too much, and it drives you crazy! We'd say, "Calm down!" He's too active but he works hard, he likes to cook, he always put in his two cents' worth, if I can put it that way. Then there's Dorle from Vancouver, and she's very nice. We became very good friends. And Carol Ann, who's very lively too. A kind of person I'd never met before. She's very interested in nature, she never wants to live in a city. She taught me a lot too. And Cindy, I had some conflicts with her; I felt quite close to her but it's hard to explain Cindy ... Aside from that, there's Gordon, who's gone now. Ah! it really touched me when he left. At first I couldn't get to know him, I didn't think I'd ever understand him; but now I understand him very well. He taught me a lot ... I can't talk about it ...

J.H.: Why can't you talk about it?

Claire: It's going to make me cry.

J.H.: It's true that when he left it was very difficult for everyone ...

Claire: Aside from that, there's Roy. You must have noticed that we're quite close ... We've been close ever since Duchesnay. He has a lot of energy and sometimes, since he's in my group, his energy was often directed toward me. But I tried to see that it was spread around. And in Milestone he had a lot of contacts with the people in the community. He likes meeting people very much. Ah! it's hard for me to talk about him ... He talks a lot and sometimes that bothers people. He's probably the only person I really know, you know, I know about his past, and why he's the way he is today ... But basically he's a guy who gives a lot. I think that especially in the last three months, he's really tried to contribute to the group life, though we criticized him for not doing enough. And I think it was a success ... but maybe my opinion isn't very objective!

J.H.: Can you talk about Saskatchewan objectively?

Claire: I liked Saskatchewan very much and I might be going back this summer. I wrote to a lady, the one I worked with in the library, and she's going to invite me back in August. I'd like to see Saskatchewan in the summer, with the fields of wheat and everything. It's really another world, you know. Completely different from Ontario or Quebec or the Maritimes. I liked it a lot ... And the people in the village were very nice. At the end of our three months we had a supper with them. The mayor was there and all evening people kept telling us, "Thank you! Thank you! Thank you!" I was very pleased.

J.H.: Proud of yourselves?

Claire: Yes. It's funny, sometimes we'd ask ourselves, "Do they think we're doing a good job?" They really liked us, they wanted us all to come back some day, come and see them again.

Grand River, Ontario

J.H.: After the Saskatchewan episode, you came back east, to Grand River. The groups were divided over three small towns.

Claire: I was in Belwood, three miles from Fergus. We were in a house surrounded by trees, fairly far from the road. There were two barns. It used to be a farm, but it belongs to the Grand River Conservation Authority now. At the start some of us went to work in the woods, cutting trees. After that we made picnic tables for I don't know how long; it seemed like months and months! Now we're working in the nursery, putting the small trees in bags with straw. That's for reforestation. Aside from that, we do community work in Fergus and on Mondays we work at Radio-Waterloo.

J.H.: Did you produce a radio program?

Claire: I worked on one with Roy; on juvenile delinquency. It will all be finished next week. There's quite a lot of interviews and everything. He'll certainly talk to you about it. On Tuesdays two or three people worked at the museum. I only went once because a lot of people wanted to go and you had to have a certain continuity. I liked it very much. On Wednesday, we went to the old people's home, Thursdays to the high school. It was really Roy who went there, who helped in the classes on the environment. He gave French lessons. On Fridays, I went to a school for three-and four-year-olds in Fergus. I really liked that ...· Little children, three or four years old, whose parents were divorced. I realized that if I ever have children I mustn't let that happen to them.

J.H.: Did you like the people in the area?

Claire: I found them less open than the people in Saskatchewan. In Saskatchewan you could talk to anybody. The people were very hospitable.

J.H.: Do you feel that you've changed somewhat in the past months?

Claire: Yes, I'm not as awkward as I used to be. When I meet people I can talk to them. I learned not to stick to my first impression when I meet somebody. I've never been able to express myself like some people, but I'm a lot better now. I've learned to do things by myself. For instance, this summer I'm going to the Maritimes for a month, go to see the participants who live in New Brunswick, Nova Scotia, Prince Edward Island, Newfoundland ...

J.H.: You have reference points all over when you go travelling across the country?

Claire: Yes. And I'm thinking of going to see Dorle in Vancouver ... probably for two or three months. If I can I'd like to find a job there.

J.H.: What are your dreams for the future?

Claire: I worked in the library in Saskatchewan and I liked that very much. So I'd like to find work in that area... If I really like it I'll study library science at university.

J.H.: So you found your vocation in Saskatchewan?

Claire: Maybe, yes. I'll find out later when I've worked for a year or two.

J.H.: Most of the participants told me that you were all practically like brothers and sisters. What do you think?

Claire: Yes, we're very close. We realize we've only got two weeks left together ... The separation's going to be hard. Take Gordon: when he left I told myself, "Good Lord, it's just one person. What will it be like when we all go our separate ways!" Ah! it's going to be very, very hard ...

22 *Gordon Inglis,* Age 18, St. John's, Newfoundland

I was born in Vancouver in 1959. I lived there for seven years.

J.H.: So you are not a real Islander?

Gordon: No. It's the longest I ever lived in one place. I consider it my home. So we moved to Toronto and then I ended up here, seven years ago. I really like it here.

J.H.: Do you see a difference between you and a real Newfoundlander?

Gordon: Oh no. I wouldn't say that.

J.H.: You are one of them?

Gordon: Yes.

J.H.: By the way, before we go any further, I should point out that we're doing this interview a year after the ones that were done with the other participants. Except for Yvan and you, I talked to everyone in the group at the end of Katimavik's first year. The group was in Collingwood, for their final evaluation. For some reason, which I'd like you to go into, you were not there ... you had left what ... a week or so before?

Gordon: About a week before the evaluation.

J.H.: I could not manage to come to St. John's before now, but I certainly intended to have you in the story because I think you are a part of it as much as any of the others. Well, would you mind if we talked a little bit about what happened to you at one point, when you were kicked out?

245

Gordon: What happened? For some reason I grew some marijuana plants, not that I went out consciously to cultivate marijuana. I stuck a few seeds in a pot ... and the group leader found out about it.

J.H.: Other participants told me they felt you were not really breaking one of the three rules which has to do with drugs, because these plants do not become potent for many months. According to them, these plants were just like any other weed at the time of the incident.

Gordon: That could be.

J.H.: The other participants also told me that the group leader asked you to destroy them, which you did?

Gordon: Yes.

J.H.: Right away?

Gordon: Yes.

J.H.: Did you think that this was the end of the incident?

Gordon: At the time I thought it was, yes. I was quite surprised when I was told that I was leaving the next day. I was even more surprised because a girl who had no connection whatsoever with this incident was also told that she was going to be leaving.[1] I really didn't know what was going on at that time.

J.H.: How did you feel about that incident? Did you think it was unfair?

Gordon: Yes. I was upset. Quite emotional about it.

J.H.: I think the whole group was quite emotional about it all ...

Gordon: Yes. I felt I was betrayed, because there were no discussions ... The group leader did not talk to me or anything. I felt close to her. I thought we were friends.

J.H.: How do you explain that? She thought it was her duty to react that way?

Gordon: It could be that. I think she was insecure ... she felt that I had betrayed her, I guess.

J:H.: And it happened nine months after the program had started?

---

1. Finally, that participant did not leave.

Gordon: Yes. But she had been with us for only six months at the time. She was a new group leader.

J.H.: I was with the group shortly after that incident ... a week after. I must say it shook up everybody there. You certainly had a lot of friends among these people.

Gordon: We were all friends.

J.H.: O.K. ... but let's not forget the fact that our present discussion about Katimavik is taking place one year after I spoke with the other participants. So your perspective may be somewhat different from the others. It may be interesting to see how different it is. Anyway, let's start at the beginning. How did Katimavik get into your life. Did you read an ad somewhere or ... ?

Gordon: I went to university for one semester and had only one or two dollars, so I had to quit. I went to work and I was at a sort of a dead end. I didn't know where I was going. My father saw the ad and gave it to me. I applied. I didn't think I'd get in, but I did.

J.H.: What was in that ad that attracted you?

Gordon: The search and rescue exercises. I had a vision of myself saving beautiful girls!

J.H.: Which did not happen very often!

Gordon: No, that's right.

J.H.: Were there some other things about the program ... the chance to work with a group, the chance to see other parts of the country ... that may have attracted you?

Gordon: I wanted to travel. And the alternate technology aspect of the work also interested me.

J.H.: Were you getting out of something, or getting into something?

Gordon: It was a mixture of both. I was getting out and getting in.

Larouche, Quebec

J.H.: So let's talk about this whole year. It all really started in Larouche, a small village in Quebec where I am pretty sure you had never been before. What was your first impression, getting into that house with thirty people?

247

Gordon: It was an interesting thing. When I first arrived I was very sick. For the first month, I was coughing. I had a cold. It was all disorganized. We had practically nothing to do. I don't know how I felt, really. At the time, I guess I enjoyed myself.

J.H.: Was it your first contact with a French-Canadian community?

Gordon: I guess it was my first, yes. I've been through Montreal and Quebec City but it was my first attempt to learn the language.

J.H.: Did you succeed somewhat?

Gordon: Well, I guess I am 100 per cent better than I was before. It helped, yes ... to learn the basics and do something with that.

J.H.: The group life part of it, how did you react to that?

Gordon: I don't know. I don't get too close to people, especially strangers, so I felt there was a bit too much emphasis on the group life. But, it was interesting to see how people reacted.

J.H.: You say "strangers." The participants were indeed strangers the first day but after some time they were not any more.

Gordon: No, after a few months.

J.H.: During your stay in Larouche, you spent some time on a farm. How was that experience?

Gordon: That was really interesting.

J.H.: Which family did you stay with?

Gordon: The Lessard family. A small dairy farm. About forty cows. It was good to see the life on the farm and I liked the work.

J.H.: You had never seen that before?

Gordon: I'd seen it but, you know, I have never lived it. I didn't realize how much work they do on a farm.

J.H.: Did you have a good rapport with that family?

Gordon: Yes. They had two youngsters and two older boys about my age, I guess. I enjoyed myself and we managed to communicate somehow. They didn't speak English and I didn't speak French. So ...

J.H.: You communicated nevertheless?

Gordon: Oh, yes.

J.H.: How did you do that?

Gordon: Just looking up words in the dictionary.

J.H.: Back to the group ... what did it feel like to be with people from all over Canada?

Gordon: Well, that was not really new to me because I had lived in Vancouver and in Newfoundland. Just the French Canadians were strange to me. I had not come across them.

J.H.: Strange?

Gordon: Strange in a way that I couldn't really communicate. I mean, we could communicate, but on a superficial level. I found it hard to talk and express myself to people in English so when they were French it was still more difficult.

J.H.: That must have been truer in the first week than it was in last months.

Gordon: Yes. As we progressed, we began to get closer.

J.H.: What kind of work were you involved with in Larouche besides the farm?

Gordon: There wasn't much. We cleared some ski trails and cleared a road going to a dam. We built a greenhouse as well. I don't think we were prepared.

Wilcox, Saskatchewan

J.H.: After three months you moved to Wilcox. How was that for a change?

Gordon: Well, it was quite a change. The Prairies are very strange. So flat. I never had experienced −40°F. temperatures before. That was a bit of a shock. The work there was pretty interesting. We learned a lot about carpentry. I found it was so cold, you couldn't get out.

J.H.: You learned about carpentry?

Gordon: Yes. It was really very good. The instructor was really great.

J.H.: You were working at what project exactly?

Gordon: We were renovating an old café for the senior citizens' groups.

J.H.: That was in Milestone?

Gordon: Yes, that's right, Milestone. So we were tearing down walls, putting up new ones, insulating and so on ...

J.H.: Things you hadn't done before?

Gordon: I've done them but not the way I did them there. This guy was a professional so I learned proper ways to do them.

J.H.: In Milestone, were you more involved than you were in Larouche with the community itself, and with the people?

Gordon: Yes. I would say so. They were very friendly and we were right inside the town. We went to supper at their houses. While in Larouche we were sort of isolated because we were two or three miles out of town.

J.H.: Did you feel more at ease in a group of ten?

Gordon: No, not really. In a bigger group it's easier to get lost in the crowd.

J.H.: So you felt stuck with ten people.

Gordon: Yes, though I didn't find it too bad. I don't like conflicts and ... I find it easy to get along with people. There were all kinds of conflicts, you know. I tried to avoid them.

J.H.: But, conflicts are part of life.

Gordon: Yes, so is avoiding them.

Grand River, Ontario

J.H.: So, then after three months in Saskatchewan, you moved to the Grand River project, but there again you were in three groups of ten, and in three different locations. Which one were you at?

Gordon: It was Fergus, with the Grand River Conservation Authority. I really enjoyed that project the most.

J.H.: Because there was a lot of work to do?

Gordon: Yes. There was work to do. It was outside, spring was coming, and that makes you feel better anyway.

J.H.: What type of work did you do there?

Gordon: Well, we cut trees in the woods and built picnic tables. We worked in the greenhouse, made snow fences and stuff, so it was pretty interesting. The guy who was in charge of us was a pretty colourful character. Very funny.

250

J.H.: There was a lot of physical work. Did you do any social work at all?

Gordon: Well, I didn't. There were opportunities to do some but I preferred to work with the university radio station. And, at the time, I was working on the solar heater. Did you see it?

J.H.: Yes. I saw it.

Gordon: So I used my radio time to do that.

J.H.: Where did you get the idea for the solar heater?

Gordon: It was in a *Mother Earth* Magazine on alternative technology.

J.H.: You decided that on your own?

Gordon: I was on my own. It was not all that hard. It's pretty easy.

J.H.: I've seen it but it was not quite working yet because you left before it was finished. It was made with an old refrigerator, if I remember correctly.

Gordon: An old refrigerator, a hot water reservoir and copper tubing was all we needed and it would have cost about fifty dollars for material to finish it.

J.H.: Yes. You got the refrigerator for free in a dump or something.

Gordon: Yes, and the water heater was free, too.

J.H.: What did you have to buy?

Gordon: Paint, plywood, nails, stuff like that.

J.H.: Barely fifty dollars. If you'd had time to finish it, it would have produced hot water for the group, do you think, or part of it?

Gordon: It said in the magazine that it would make enough hot water for a shop. So it would not have supplied enough hot water for washing dishes, but it would have provided us with a supplementary water supply.

J.H.: Did you find the people in and around Fergus different from those in Wilcox and Larouche?

Gordon: Yes. We were out of town, so it was different. But Southern Ontario is not as friendly as Northern Quebec or Saskatchewan. It has a big city mentality. Fergus was not a big city but, I don't know, Southern Ontario is almost one big city. You're out of one town and then into another.

J.H.: Maybe it was not the best location for a project.

Gordon: And we were out of the town all by ourselves. We only had contacts with the people we worked with. It's not that the Ontario people are less friendly, but we had less opportunity to meet them.

J.H.: I remember the house. It was in the middle of a field?

Gordon: Yes, it was in the park itself.

J.H.: It was the last project. And for you it ended a little earlier. We are talking one year after the fact, but would you say that, through Katimavik, you have changed in any way?

Gordon: I definitely changed! I mean, you grow a lot. You have to react to new situations ... living with ten people you never met before is an experience. And travelling is experiencing.

J.H.: You changed in what way? Is it for the better do you think?

Gordon: I think so, yes. It helped me realize that there is a lot to do in this world.

J.H.: You want to change things?

Gordon: Yes.

J.H.: Change the world maybe?

Gordon: I want to do something constructive or creative.

J.H.: Which you were not planning to do before?

Gordon: Well, yes. I think ... I didn't really know.

J.H.: And you found out? What did you find out for example that was more precise in the way of doing something creative and constructive and useful to society?

Gordon: I found out for myself that I needed a lot of knowledge and that I have to work harder. I feel I can do a lot.

J.H.: How did you see your future before Katimavik?

Gordon: I wasn't thinking about my future. I don't know if I would have realized those things on my own. Probably... maybe I would have but... well, Katimavik was also a very safe, easy way to get away from home. If you are on your own you have to sort of do all those things on your own. I did not have to worrry about that in Katimavik. I guess it was good. I didn't have to worry about those things. I got a chance to learn more and more.

J.H.: About yourself?

Gordon: Yes.

J.H.: What did you learn about this country through living in three different provinces, in three different kinds of surroundings, living with thirty or with ten people who came from all over the country?

Gordon: I didn't learn about my country that much. I've travelled across Canada. I did learn an awful lot about Quebec.

J.H.: More about Quebec than about the other provinces?

Gordon: Yes. I learned a lot. I understand the separatist thing better now.

J.H.: How would you qualify the kind of links that obviously exist between all you people? For example, when you left, the other participants had a terrible shock, as if someone in the family "had died," as Bruce put it. What do you think about that?

Gordon: I don't really know what it is between us. I feel that I am very close to them. I know that if I meet some of them even ten years from now, it would be like ...

J.H.: ... like yesterday?

Gordon: Yes.

J.H.: Do you realize that this feeling is common to each and every one of you?

Gordon: Yes.

J.H.: Now that it is all over, what is your general feeling about Katimavik in spite of the fact that something happened to you at the end?

Gordon: My expulsion did not alter my feelings about Katimavik. You break the law and you have to pay for it if you get caught. That did not bother me. It bothered me but it didn't alter my feelings about Katimavik. I had a lot of feelings at the time. Sometimes, I really hated it and sometimes I really liked it. I am glad I was in the program.

23 *Dorle Kneifel,*
Age 17,
Burnaby, British Columbia

I was born in Vancouver and I lived there for thirteen years. I really liked it. My dad decided he wanted to move to Burnaby which was only ten miles away.

J.H.: Ten miles is not that far ...

Dorle: Yes, but things change when you're not there. Like your friends go to one school and you go to another school and things do change, but I got over it.

J.H.: Are you from a big family?

Dorle: No, there are four kids. I've got an older sister, an older brother and a younger brother.

J.H.: So you went to school partly in Vancouver and partly in Burnaby?

Dorle: Yes, I spent seven years at a Vancouver elementary school and in Burnaby I went to a junior high and I took grade 11 just before Katimavik. I haven't graduated yet. I'm considering doing it when I get home in the summer.

J.H.: What were your dreams for the future? What did you plan to do in life?

Dorle: I've always known what I didn't want to do. I never wanted to work in an office. Job-wise, I'm really interested in prison reform. I did a report two years ago on the prison system and what happens to prisoners and I really feel that a lot has to change there. I have this dream of having a farm, like a half-way farm, so that people coming out of

254

prison come onto the farm and work there. Hopefully, if I am established enough in it, I could get jobs for them, or they could work on the farm and get adjusted somehow or at least have a place to go instead of having to go back to where they came from originally, back to all the crap they started off with. I've thought about this idea fairly recently but I've always wanted a farm too.

J.H.: How long ago did you start thinking about that?

Dorle: Three years ago. Before that I always wanted to be a teacher but that sort of faded with the bad job situation. I've always been interested in forestry. But to get into prison work I would need to get a degree to be a probation officer or whatever, whereas in forestry I would be taking a completely different road — I'll have to decide soon which one to take.

J.H.: What kind of idea did you have about Canada from Vancouver?

Dorle: At one time Dad was going to move us all to Germany. We fought this and ended up staying so I really, well, wanted to stay in Canada, but how much did I know? Vancouver is all I knew ...

J.H.: You were born here, but your family is from Germany and they are still German citizens too, so you are a first generation Canadian.

Dorle: Yes and I'm also a German citizen according to German law right now, so at twenty-one I choose where I want to stay.

J.H.: And so then you heard about Katimavik. How did that happen?

Dorle: I was going to school and I had two jobs at the same time. I didn't want to continue school because I was doing really crummy and I wasn't really interested in it at all. I was working at the racetrack in Vancouver and it was okay except I didn't like the people I was working with. I worked at a gas station too and I didn't like the people because I had certain interests and everybody that hung around there didn't share these same interests. They were into their cars or their horses. I like cars and I like horses, but my life isn't a car any more than a horse. So when I

255

heard about Katimavik it sounded really good because everything I heard was something that I always wanted to do but never had the opportunity to; from solar energy to working in a forest. In March, while I was doing my homework, I heard it advertised on the radio. I never, never answer ads but I wrote in for an application and I got it on March 27. The deadline was March 30, so I sent it in right away and said sorry it's late but I just got it March 27 and then didn't worry much about it. Then I got a letter saying there would be an interview on June 4. So I went to the interview and I got accepted.

J.H.: One day you arrived in Duchesnay?

Dorle: I can't stand being around a lot of people because I don't like being in large groups. That's why I hated school. When I arrived in Duchesnay with ninety people there, it really scared me. I'm not the social person who will run up to someone and say, "Hi! how are you?" If I get to know them, fine, if I don't, well, we weren't meant to know each other. It was like coming out of a situation where I was the only one my age at home into a place where there were ninety people. I got to know a few people really well which was nice, but it was nice to get away from there too.

Larouche, Québec

J.H.: You say that you dont't like to be in a big group, but you certainly were in one for your first project, in Larouche, Quebec. At least thirty people in a house which would be comfortable for maybe ten ...

Dorle: For me, during that time it was really hard because I'm used to having my own bathroom, and my own bedroom. When I wanted to disappear, I could just disappear in the house, and not be bothered by anyone. In Larouche I had no privacy so it was really hard, but it was nice in that there were enough people around so you could get to know a lot of different people. If things went wrong there was usually someone there to help you out. When I was in Larouche, a lot of times I thought, "I've got to get out of here," but looking back on it, it was really something.

256

J.H.: What impression did you get from your first French-Canadian village?

Dorle: The first thing we did when we arrived in Larouche, was rush off to this conference with the mayor and I couldn't speak any French. I took four years of French in school and I spoke nothing. I could say, "Je viens du Vancouver" or whatever but luckily I had had a very good French teacher though the last year so that I knew my verbs really well. So when we got to the mayor's office, they were all talking in French and I didn't understand a thing. All of us English-speaking ones were standing in a corner trying to find out what we were going to do and drinking our wine, and whoever could speak French would talk to the mayor. I heard that Larouche was going to be an all-French community and we were told that if they were nasty to us not to worry about it; that it was a "separation thing."

J.H.: My goodness, who told you that?

Dorle: Just in Duchesnay, I heard, with this separation going on, they may not appreciate English people.

J.H.: Did you feel any of that in Larouche?

Dorle: No, not at all. I didn't get to know a lot of the townspeople because it took me two months to learn the language, but the family I lived with was just fantastic. I lived with Jean-Paul and France and their little boy. For the first few days I couldn't say anything, but we always got a dictionary out and if they wanted to tell me something, we worked at it until both sides understood. I'd be asking what this was and what that was, what a garbage can was, what dishes were, what the word was for wiping dishes. There were three words in French that I always got mixed up and it was fun trying to figure out which one meant dishes. They were really, really good to me. It was very nice, because at one point we were talking about winning the million dollar lottery, and I asked, "what would you do with a million dollars?" and France said, "I'd adopt you," so it was really nice. It was also nice when I came back to the big house after the three weeks: I could speak French and everybody was so impressed. I remember our group leader just jumping around because I could speak French now so it was fun. Once I got past that barrier of actually starting to speak, it was no problem.

J.H.: Are you still in contact with that family?

Dorle: I've written them once. Right now I've got so many people I've met across Canada that I haven't been able to write again. What I am going to do when I get out of the program is to write them and say that I'm sorry for taking so long to write.

J.H.: You will be writing for a whole month!

Dorle: Yes, well I don't think I'll explain a lot of things, I'll just tell them what I'm doing right now. I want to go back there and eventually study in Quebec. Right now so many things are happening, and it is so hard to tell them everything, plus my French isn't good enough. I can write letters but not well enough to go into detail. The way I am with writing letters is, if I write a letter I write a detailed letter. I hate just writing "Hi, how are you?" and I cannot do that, so I just wrote once. But I do want to keep in touch with them and apparently they're coming out to British Columbia next summer, so I hope they'll come out to my place.

J.H.: What work did you do in Larouche?

Dorle: I worked on the cross-country ski trails a fair amount, then I worked on the teepees because I really like sewing. I made shelves and I did a lot around the house just to make it livable. I worked a day here and a day there on the greenhouse but not regularly at all. We had to paint the garbage cans for the town of Larouche, so a few of us did those. What else did I do? It doesn't sound like much. Oh, we cleaned the dump; two weeks were spent doing that.

J.H.: What did you learn in Larouche?

Dorle: Lots of things. French. A lot about group life, a lot about myself. Before I came there I always thought that the opinion I had was the only right opinion. Then all of a sudden you have somebody sitting down in front of you and telling you theirs and it threatens your own opinion. It takes a long time to learn that there are other opinions that may be right besides your own. A lot of time went into just surviving, getting to know the people around. Then when Michel, our coordinator, was sick, I didn't do very much work because we were taking care of him, being there and feeding him. He was like that for two weeks so we spent a lot of time doing that. When I was with the family I learned how to trap rabbits. Jean-Paul went trapping in the woods and I went along with him certain days. I learned how when the weather was okay, the rabbits come out and how you can tell where they've been by how the branches are broken. That was really interesting. I don't plan on trapping but some day ... you never know, you might need it.

J.H.: So you really know how to do it now?

Dorle: Yes. I almost fainted once — we always picked up the rabbits along the way and sometimes it wasn't too pleasant but it was interesting, a different lifestyle than what I'm used to.

J.H.: Have you changed the image you had of Quebec somewhat?

Dorle: Duchesnay and Larouche changed a lot for me though I've never been prejudiced against Quebec. I really enjoyed French in school and I wanted to learn it because I wanted to have the three languages. I remember the jokes flying around about the frogs and such, and it always used to bother me. When I quit my job at the gas station I told my boss I was going to Quebec and he laughed and made a joke about it. It wasn't vicious, just a little joke. When I came to Quebec, with the separation thing, I got better insight. When I was in Vancouver and I heard about separation I wasn't interested; I thought it was a thing that would pass in a year or two, but when I got to Quebec I realized how serious it was. When I first got to Duchesnay, there were hard feelings, I thought, between the French and English. In Larouche we had a lot of arguments about us English not speaking enough French and it really hurt me because I wasn't there to hurt them. I had nothing against French-speaking people and I realized that due to what had been happening, there were some people who did have hard feelings against me because I spoke English. That really opened my eyes. There were things happening that I hadn't realized in Vancouver.

J.H.: Did that type of feeling, that they didn't like you because you were English, last long in Larouche?

Dorle: It wasn't the community, it was within the group and it just lasted until we got to know each other. When I got to Larouche I didn't know the people in my group because my friends that I met in Duchesnay went to Coaticook and Gatineau so I didn't know anybody and it took time. I got to know most of the French and just getting to know them was really nice; just talking to them, saying that I'm only human, they're human and the only difference is this language thing and this political thing. I've got nothing directly to do with it, I don't understand it, they may not understand it and we're both caught in the middle. So, once you got to know the people ... I can remember Yvan saying that before he came to Katimavik his friends were bugging him, saying that as soon as he came out of the program he'd probably like the English and that really scared them. When he quit in Saskatchewan he was saying that he was happy that he had met us. I visited him in Montreal a month ago and it was really nice. His parents seemed to be separatists but talking to them — I'm from Vancouver, big deal — I talked in French and it was fun. I don't feel now that they've got anything against me and that's nice. I can understand if they do and I don't hold that against them. It's just that it really hurt me.

J.H.: But you say when you start knowing the people, that type of thing fades away, it doesn't exist anymore?

Dorle: No, because I think that you hate or misunderstand when you don't know people; when you generalize. Like in Vancouver, East Indians are hated and that's because they are clumped together; there may be one jerk in the middle but they are all classified as being bad. Yet, there is nothing wrong with the individual, he just happens to be East Indian. I see the same thing happening between the French and the English.

Wilcox, Saskatchewan

J.H.: Then after three months you moved to Wilcox?

Dorle: I call it Milestone, though.

J.H.: I call it Wilcox because it is the Wilcox project, but you were in Milestone, a nearby town. What was it like?

Dorle: In Larouche I hadn't been in contact with the community and all of a sudden here we were right in the middle of the community. Milestone was fantastic. The people were really open to us. Like, I went to the high school and tutored two math students there. It was nice because I got to know them. It was funny, because I was in the staff room so I got to know the staff and I would talk to them, and I also got to know the students, so I was half way between the two. I got to know what the students thought of the staff and vice versa and it was really interesting. Then we worked in the café for older citizens. I really liked that. My younger brother is handy so I've never had to do anything because he would fix it for me. Now all of a sudden we had to hammer and we had to make walls and put ceilings in. I never even thought about what was behind the gyprock, ever, and all of a sudden I know where the insulation was put in, so just learning that was interesting. There were times when it wasn't that hot. When we first came there, the café had been closed down, I think, and there was still salt and pepper on the tables so we had to clear everything out and we had to clear out the basement which was really messy work. But when we came to rebuilding I found that really interesting especially as Gary, the person we were working with, at first he was really shy and never said anything. But once he got to know us he would start talking. It was really fun. We would have a lot of the older people dropping in and they would joke around with us and hammer with us, so we got to know them. It was the nice thing in Milestone because we met all levels and age groups of the community.

J.H.: So you were really busy?

Dorle: Oh yes, almost every night was planned. We could go to Wilcox and do pottery. At night I'd made a point of writing to my parents once a week. I told them everything that happened; every lousy little detail and the letters took me hours to write, so whenever I had free time I would write to them or we would go visit somebody in the community or we would go to Wilcox and visit the groups there. We were always busy.

J.H.: Was that your first contact with the people from the Prairies?

Dorle: Yes, it was incredible because to me the Prairies were always so boring. I saw pictures on calendars of the Prairies and I always thought it was so boring, how could people live there? But it was interesting how really open they were to us. The mayor's wife would come over and bring cinnamon buns; we were invited over for dinner at the mayor's house. We knew the minister, Cheryl Black, really well and we could go over anytime, her house was unlocked, and listen to her stereo. There were four different people who said to come over and use their washing machines whenever we wanted. There was another lady who moved into a new house by herself with her two little boys, so I went over there and talked to her a fair amount. Community-wise it was great and then when I started to get to know the younger people in town, some of the girls came over and gave me snowmobile rides and we went to parties with the other kids in town. I really enjoyed that.

Grand River, Ontario

J.H.: Then after three months of Saskatchewan you moved again?

Dorle: Before I went to Milestone I was really worried about how I would fit into the community, how this would work out. I was always worried. But, by the time I hit Ontario I took things more lightly and whatever happens, happens.

J.H.: What kind of work did you do?

Dorle: We had to work at the Grand River Conservation Authority. I was in Belwood, and the fine thing about Belwood was that one of the girls who was in Duchesnay with us had been in the Belwood house before us and she left a note for me when I arrived saying "It's terrible here, this house is just awful." But when I got there it was great because from what she had described I'd expected something just terrible. My expectations were so low that it seemed great. When we arrived I couldn't believe how nice it was.

J.H.: It was not a luxurious house, as I remember ...

Dorle: No, it's not a luxurious house at all, but I expected a lot worse. So when I arrived I was happy because to me it was like a home; it was a friendly place. When we approached the house, even before we got in it, there were these maple trees lining the driveway. For me that was so nice; it was like an official welcome with these trees standing there. I thought even if the house is crummy, the area is nice, so things couldn't be too bad. We had to work at the GRCA four days a week, five people.

J.H.: That was tough work, I understand?

Dorle: Yes. At first when there was still snow on the ground some people went in the woods to cut trees and I got to do painting. I painted the public washrooms, I painted the office inside, the window frames and the door frames. I liked that because the people who were working there were really friendly. Then we started doing picnic tables. The first two days were fine, and then I really started resenting it.

J.H.: Yes, these picnic tables seem to be on everybody's minds. I heard a lot about them. I don't know how many hundreds you did, but they seemed to pile up to the sky.

Dorle: Yes. I resented working on the picnic tables because we were in a community where there was so much to do, so much community work that could have been done but we couldn't do it because we had this commitment to the GRCA. The pre-school in town wanted to have a playground built and we had to turn it down because we didn't have enough manpower. I really felt that it was wrong because the community, I felt, was more important than the GRCA. Besides, the GRCA was a company and I didn't feel we should be supporting it.

J.H.: But not a private company.

Dorle: Well, it's community-owned but the community doesn't appreciate it. That was another thing. Because we worked for the GRCA, the public had that against us because they didn't appreciate the GRCA. I guess that it's because the GRCA had gotten so big and powerful that the towns are getting scared of it and for us to work there was like — "What are they doing working for them" — so I didn't appreciate working there until we went into the nursery. We worked in the nursery and I just loved it. I was working with different seedlings, figuring how to cut them, learning how to replant trees, then transplanting trees and taking them out of the ground and packing them, putting straw around them and shipping them away. The first day I went there, I remember, it was raining and cold and I got all dirty. I didn't want to get dirty and I resented the whole thing. But a few weeks afterward it was great, tying all these dirty bundles ... I really liked it. I know the last week I really enjoyed it. Being there, you have your own schedule and you do the stuff that's there, you take your break, fifteen minutes in the morning and fifteen minutes in the afternoon; you talk away. The people we worked with ... there was one who's Dutch and one who's German.

J.H.: I met the Dutch guy. A very nice person.

Dorle: Yes, but he talks so much. But he's got a lot to say and it's nice hearing his point of view.

J.H.: He seems to like you all very much. He talked to me for about five minutes and he seemed to be very proud of you all.

Dorle: Yes, Henry is really good. He had his problems with some of the groups and even with us. Even now I can say that I didn't like to work for the GRCA, the principle behind working there, but he knew that and he told us, "I've got nothing to do with your working here, you can't change it so why not make the best of it." With that attitude, that's how we did it. I really enjoyed it.

J.H.: Did you have time to do anything else in the community?

Dorle: There were four days of social work. I chose to help out at the museum. The people there were really interesting, all ages worked there, from all sorts of different backgrounds. There was one lady who looked like the real secretary type, always nicely done up. Yet she's got a farm with pigs and sheep and everything on it — some people even knew how to spin wool — and it was all things that I wanted to learn more about. One of them was into herbs so we would talk about that.

J.H.: What did you do in the museum exactly?

Dorle: We worked in the archives downstairs. There were a bunch of books that had been donated. They'd never been catalogued so we had to take all these old books and catalogue them into files so that eventually it would be open to the public.

J.H.: Was it a library or a museum?

Dorle: It's a museum and the books they have are donated; they are antiques.

J.H.: Oh, they are not books to be lent out?

Dorle: They may be in a while. Once they're all organized the antique books will be open to the public. People come in every day to look up who their ancestors are. A lot of these books had inscriptions in the front like, "1862 Christmas to my Mom" or whatever and everytime we went through these books, we'd read the inscriptions. I just loved it, going through the different things. At the same time we were working, there would be displays going on, so the girls would dress up the different mannequins in old clothes for the different displays and we'd help them with that. It was just fantastic.

J.H.: It seems you loved everything about Katimavik except the picnic tables?

Dorle: Yes, well I like doing things where I can learn or where I get a new insight into something. For me the picnic tables were interesting for the first two days but I don't like assemblyline work. Whereas with the museum it was like it's funny because I usually like dealing with people, the museum was basically dealing with things. It was like dealing with people indirectly. Take these old photographs.

J.H.: You are right; a book is not an ordinary thing, it has a soul of sorts.

Dorle: When you look at an old photograph, you'd see these people in it and you'd wonder what they were like, what sort of life they'd had. One thing that was neat — they had some German books donated as the German population is quite large around there. I went through the catalogue to look for this German book and the title was absolutely wrong; it didn't make sense, because the lettering was coming apart. Because I know German, I knew what it was trying to say, so I had to rewrite it. That was neat, just knowing the language and being able to fix it up. I found the museum interesting because I had never been interested in that at all. All of a sudden I saw the possibilities and the people that worked there told me how to get into the museum on a volunteer basis. What I found really neat was that no matter what you focus on, maybe it's the old folks' home, there is a whole world of old folks' homes. In the museum they've got a whole world of museums where these people know all the connections everywhere, and I sort of got an insight into that world that I normally don't see.

J.H.: How do you like the people in the community there?

Dorle: They're great. Just the other day we went out with a few people from the GRCA and they showed us all around the area. They like their area and they're proud of it and they want us to know what it's all about. A few of them are really helpful, like one day after work none of us was going anywhere. We were going to stay home because we had no place to go for our free weekend. We had been working really hard, it had been raining, it was horrible weather and Claire and I were saying how nice it would be to have a television in the house just for once and sit back, come home from work and just watch TV. One of the girls said she had a TV but it was broken. That night we got a phone call from one of the guys at work who said he had a TV and would be right over in three minutes. He came over and lent us his family's TV for the weekend. We hadn't even talked to him, he had just overheard the conversation.

J.H.: Do you feel that you know your country better now?

Dorle: Yes, a lot of things mean something to me now; today in a film I saw where they mention Gravelbourg or that thing about the Prairies. Before Katimavik I would have walked out on that film. To see a machine cutting wheat was nothing, but now I've lived in the Prairies through the wintertime, and although I've never seen it in the summertime, it really interested me to see what it's like in the summertime. Hearing different names means a lot now. Like Joyce comes from Newfoundland. Newfoundland used to be just a name; to me it was like this desolate rock at the side of Canada. Now if anything happens politically, or say the weather in Newfoundland, I'm interested because Joyce is there and I know whatever happens affects her. Before Katimavik the thing was to go straight from high school to university, then work and that's it. That's all I saw open to myself before too. Now there's so many other things open, at times it gets confusing because there's almost too many things. It's good to see that you have a choice in life.

J.H.: How do you feel about the group?

Dorle: Most of the people I feel very, very close to. I know them better than all my previous friends. I don't write to any people in Vancouver at all other than my family because I see now that I really don't know them. Here, if I'm feeling down I don't even have to say something, they can sense it, they come and talk to me and vice versa and it's nice. It's going to be really strange going away from some of those people because ten months is a long time to have spent with them. Some of them are really different from what I am and I'd never have run into them any other way.

J.H.: And if you had, you would have crossed the street maybe.

Dorle: Exactly. Like I had nothing in common with them and now having lived together with them ... it's different! When Gordon left, I didn't know him that well,

I lived with him but I didn't know him. But the day after he left we were really down and someone mentioned that it felt that he had died, and that's exactly how I felt. He called a few days ago and it was really nice talking to him because there is this person you really care about that called back. I don't know if I could call my group my family because my family isn't even like this.

J.H.: Are they your brothers and sisters?

Dorle: No because I didn't choose my brothers or my sisters.

J.H.: Well, they are friends because they say that a friend is a brother we have chosen.

Dorle: That's true. I can't explain how I feel about them, I only know that some of the people here, I haven't been that close to another person other than my mom, ever. They are the closest to me, which is really nice, considering how I felt when I first arrived in Duchesnay. I thought I would never get to know these people. It's going to be really strange leaving too. What's nice is that two of them are coming to Vancouver to live with me for three months. Carol Ann and Claire are coming out. Carol Ann is from Brampton, Ontario and Claire is from Pierrefonds, Quebec, so it's going to be really nice because I can show off my city. I've seen Montreal, I've seen Toronto. Now they'll see Vancouver.

J.H.: And Larouche...?

Dorle: C'est ça, oui. Carol Ann's been in Vancouver before but Claire hasn't and just to show off my province to her will be really fun.

J.H.: Do you think you have changed a lot?

Dorle: Too much; yes I have and it sort of worries me. How am I going to fit in at home again? For example, Claire and I were talking about this just the other day. Just walking past people and touching them, hitting their head, doing anything, it's so natural, you just walk by and you hug them. When I went home at the beginning of December, last year, some of my friends came over and I reacted the same way and you realize you can't do that because they don't know where you're at, they don't understand that. It is going to be hard adjusting back to them and I think I've changed so much that there are very few people that I knew beforehand that I'm ever going to contact again.

J.H.: You changed a lot, but in what way?

Dorle: My attitudes toward how you can live with others for starters. My parents are going to freak out when I come home because a lot of things they do I'm not going to agree with. I'm not going to try to change them but I know ... for instance with cooking and things ... Wayne has given me some addresses in Vancouver on macrobiotics and I'm going to start looking into that. Mom buys no sugar at all, she doesn't buy any packaged foods, and hopefully she'll start going to co-ops and buying things to stop eating meat around the house. My dad will still want meat but he's really cut down on that. Just seeing that you can do with a lot less and that your way of eating potatoes, vegetables and meat isn't the only way. For instance, going to Mc-Donald's; I won't touch the place anymore because it's a huge corporation that I don't want to support. In terms of lifestyles, I feel that we are really living far too high class. I can't change my parents but I know with me I'm not going to bitch to them about them giving me money for clothing or whatever because I don't need that. I think I'll appreciate things a lot more, like I've been living in houses which are adequate, they're great for me, they're my home. But I'm going to go home where there are rugs everywhere, my own bathroom where I ... it's too much for me but I know I'll appreciate it whenever I'm home. I had lived in an apartment just before I got to Katimavik and I was just running around, always on the go, never sitting down to think about anything. I think I've really slowed down a lot. I can't see how I could relate to some of my friends because they're really into their cars and they couldn't understand how I wouldn't be interested in getting the latest fashions. I can't change them, and I don't want to change them. If they're interested in what I'm doing, fine, I'll share it with them, but I'm not going to push it on them.

J.H.: What will you do when you go back?

Dorle: I'm going to try to get my grade 12 this summer. I'm going to do as much as I can this summer, stay home and try to get to know my family. One thing that's really changed is I appreciate my family a lot more because no matter what happens they're always there. Like when I called home a week ago to tell them I had to leave, Mom didn't yell at me or anything. She said, "Great, it'll be nice to see you three weeks sooner," and it was like they're there no matter what happens.

J.H.: Because you almost left?

Dorle: Well, I was almost thrown out. My dad wasn't living at home before I left and I didn't talk to him or anything. He's back in the house now and he's been writing to me and stuff and I've seen a lot by living with other people a lot like him and I can understand him a lot more now. So I really want to try and get to know him. He's always just been there and I want to get to know him because he is my dad. And with my brothers too. My younger brother I'm fairly close to but my older brother I've never bothered to get to know him. There are different people at home now that I want to get to know. With my dad I've somehow got to find some interest he's got that I can share with him so we don't always have to fight about things that we can't resolve anyway. My mom got a letter from Germany saying there might be a job for me there. If there is I might be going in the fall after Claire and Carol Ann have left, because I do want to get out of the city, I don't want to live there for the rest of my life. Right now my sister is buying some land in northern British Columbia and she's borrowing the money from my dad. I thought that if I worked in Germany, the money there is very strong and if I came back to Canada I'd be worth something and I'd like to put it into land. So right now I'm looking into going to Germany. Otherwise, I'll be going to the school of forestry in Thunder Bay that sounds interesting, otherwise there's Trois Rivières, different places that I'm really interested in. But I think no matter what happens, something will open up for me, so I'm not worried right now. I'd like to go home just to get back on neutral ground and think over all I've done the last ten months and put it into proper perspective. Whatever happens after that, something will work out I'm sure. If nothing else I can study music in British Columbia. I'll think of something ... So, Katimavik was good for me, for sure.

24 *Mario Côté*,
Age 18,
Beloeil, Quebec

I moved to Beloeil when I was seven. Before that I lived in Laval des Rapides. Bust most of my memories are related to Beloeil. I have some older memories, but they're vague ... My family belongs to the petite bourgeoisie. There are three children and I'm the youngest. I have two sisters — one twenty-two, the other twenty-four. My father's a translator, but just for the past four or five years. My mother's a secretary. We're a comfortable family. No great luxuries, but the children have always had what we needed, and the parents too.

J.H.: A happy family, I think?

Mario: Yes, quite happy. My parents never tried to impose their ideas on their children: they've always tried to stimulate our minds and let us find out what might interest us. Sometimes if they might prefer one thing to another, they'll give advice. For example, a few years ago my sister, who was still young, decided to stop going to church. At the time, everybody went to church. There were discussions, but she was the one who decided; they didn't want to force her to do something against her will.

J.H.: What were you doing just before Katimavik?

Mario: I was at CEGEP, studying science, and I'd just finished the year. But I lacked motivation. With two sisters who'd studied science and been very successful and found jobs, I got caught in the system. I was in science, but I discovered this year that it wasn't what I liked, it wasn't what interested me. So during the last session I dropped two courses.

J.H.: You went into science partly because of your family's influence?

Mario: Yes. The advice I was given ... In the last year of high school, when you're fifteen or sixteen and you have to choose between science, the humanities, technical courses — the choice you make leads you to your profession. But when you're fifteen how can you decide with certainty what you want to do later? I needed to see something more, form new impressions, meet other people. And Katimavik came along just in time.

J.H.: It came along just in time, but just how did you come to hear about it?

Mario: My mother's a secretary at the high school, working for a guidance counsellor and in student services. She received leaflets from Katimavik at work and when she found out about it she gave me one.

J.H.: "Ah, that might be a good thing for my son?"

Mario: Yes, that's it exactly. Because I often told her that I didn't like school too much and everything, the educational system as it was operating. She was concerned about my future and all that.

J.H.: What was it in the leaflet that attracted you particularly?

Mario: At the time, I was interested in things like appropriate technology, self-sufficiency ... I'd started reading a little on the subject, and doing some research on my own.

J.H.: Are ecology, appropriate technology, environmental problems some of the subjects that were discussed at school?

Mario: No, it was a personal interest.

J.H.: You were concerned about what was happening in the world?

Mario: Yes. Perhaps less concerned than curious. I've always wondered what man was doing on this earth, I've always been interested in different eastern and western philosophies, religions. And through my reading and the research I'd done on my own I'd become aware of new forms of energy, solar energy and so forth. For me a way of living is a totality. The clothes you wear, your food... I've always looked for a way of living that seemed proper to me, in harmony with nature, in harmony with my own ideas, my beliefs. At CEGEP they put you into a certain mould and send you off to do like everybody else. I didn't want to get caught in the ratrace: get an education, find a job, work in an office, have a house and keep things going that way. It seemed to me that it might not be the best way to live, that there might be something different. And then I woke up to environmental questions and man's self-realization. And I was filled with wonder.

J.H.: What sort of impression does a young fellow from Beloeil get when he arrives at a training camp in Duchesnay?

Mario: It was fine. I liked it. It was interesting. Especially when you start to become a little bored with your own milieu, sick of seeing the same people all the time and not doing very much ... At Duchesnay I certainly met a lot of interesting people. You can talk with each of the participants, discover them. It was fine.

Larouche, Quebec

J.H.: Then one day, along with thirty other young people, you arrived in Larouche, a small Quebec village. Tell me about Larouche.

Mario: There were thirty of us in a small house, a very small house: two dormitories, two bathrooms, a laundry room, a kitchen-dining-room-living-room ... When you're used to having your own room it's a shock when there are thirty of you under the same roof. Sometimes it was hard. Sometimes I just had to go out. One of the only ways to be by yourself was to go outside for a walk! Yes, it was hard sometimes, but other times it was fine too. We had to try to make compromises with our personal tastes and habits because we weren't alone. One person wants to go to bed at midnight and read at night: another, just next to you, wants to go to bed early and he doesn't want any light. So at some point you have to sort that out. At home, mama helped you a lot; she did the cooking and the laundry; but here you have to do all that yourself. You have to clean the toilets and wash the dishes. Those are just details, but ...

J.H.: About half of you were boys and half girls. Did that cause problems?

Mario: No. We always got along well. The only little problems were caused, sometimes, by the people in Larouche we worked with. They might say, "That's a job for the boys and that's a job for the girls." But that never happened among us. We didn't distinguish between boys and girls.

J.H.: Were there any tensions in the group because some of the participants spoke only English and others only French?

Mario: No. That raises an important point about Katimavik — learning the second language. At training camp the English were given French lessons because it seemed that the French already knew a little English and could get by. And also because our first project, Larouche, was in a Francophone area. So at training camp each Francophone had two or three Anglophone "pupils." We tried to keep up with those courses at Larouche but it didn't work out too well at first because the courses were imposed. We were awakened in the morning by "Language course! Language course!" Or: "You have to go to it! It's important!" Or: "You have to! It's obligatory!"

J.H.: But if you hadn't been pushed at all would it have worked out better?

Mario: Yes, I think so. In fact that's what happened later. When people don't want to learn a language, no matter what pressures there are from outside, they won't learn it. There was less pressure toward the end, but the participants were beginning to be motivated. They realized that the community was Francophone and that they'd have to know some French if they wanted any contact at all with the population: and among participants as well, sometimes it become important to be able to communicate.

J.H.: Besides that, you took turns living with families in Larouche for several weeks.

Mario: Yes, we did. So if you were an Anglophone and you wanted to communicate you had to make an effort because those families didn't know a word of English.

J.H.: Besides working on the farms and in Larouche itself, you built a greenhouse near the house, and you made teepees, those beautiful Indian tents.

Mario: Part of the group worked on the greenhouse and another part was more interested in the teepees. Personally, I worked mostly on the teepees. There were three being built and we finished one. I did some research on teepees and at one point I had to read a book in English because there wasn't enough information in French. It was one of my first contacts with "English literature" if I can put it that way ...

J.H.: When you arrived, you could get along in English?

Mario: I studied it in school like everyone else, but ...

J.H.: You couldn't really speak?

Mario: No. I never had the chance to practise ...

J.H.: You speak well now.

Mario: Yes, I can say that.

Wilcox, Saskatchewan

J.H.: After Larouche you went to an even smaller village — Wilcox, Saskatchewan.

Mario: I wasn't in Wilcox itself but in Milestone, a village nearby with a population of about 600. It's ten or eleven miles from Wilcox. But it's still quite isolated.

J.H.: At Milestone, did you feel disoriented?

Mario: Yes, that was a change, a real change ... I was finally seeing something of Canada and people with a different way of looking at things. Anglophones who even spoke with a different accent. I could already understand a little of the English the guys in my group spoke, but in Saskatchewan people have a special accent. It took me a little while to get used to it. And I couldn't speak English as well as I do now, but I was beginning to learn.

J.H.: What did your group do in Milestone?

Mario: We had to plan and carry out our own projects in Milestone, Whereas in Wilcox the projects were already there, organized by the sponsor, Notre Dame College. But our group was lucky enough to be able to decide what we wanted to do and then try to do it.

J.H.: What did you do, exactly?

Mario: We worked on building a café for old people. We redid the inside and outside of an old building. Lots of carpentry. And we gave courses in the schools, we got films from the NFB which we showed the students. At the high school, we were going to participate in French conversation sessions. We divided the class into small groups led by a participant — sometimes even a bilingual Anglophone participant. And we spoke French, only French, with the students. Until then they hadn't heard anyone but their teacher speak French: they'd never spoken with anyone whose mother tongue was French. They were very interested. It was new and different, and it worked. I worked in the public school, giving art lessons and music lessons. There was nothing in those areas in the school. At first the people in the village were a little recalcitrant toward the young "hippies" who were all living in the same house.

J.H.: Long hair ...

Mario: Yes, long hair, beards, "French," people from all over. When they saw that we didn't bite, that we weren't so bad, that we were interested in doing things with them, in helping them and working, they became more and more open. During the last week we were there we were invited to I don't know how many dinners, we were invited everywhere ...

J.H.: After three months the people were beginning to really like you?

Mario: Ah, yes! We had really good contacts with the community in Milestone. It was really very good in that respect. Before we left, the village put on a big farewell dinner. A lot of people came and told us how much they appreciated what we'd done.

J.H.: What did you notice in particular about the people in Saskatchewan?

Mario: Most likely because of the climate, which is rough, and because you have to work hard at certain times, people help one another a lot, they stick together. And everyone knows everything. In small villages you know what's going on everywhere. Gossip ...

J.H.: So in fact everyone knew what you were doing?

Mario: Yes, yes.

J.H.: If you'd made mistakes, they'd have known?

Mario: Yes, of course.

J.H.: You didn't make too many, I hope!

Mario: Oh no!

Grand River, Ontario

J.H.: After Saskatchewan your three groups of ten came to three different communities in Ontario.

Mario: Yes. I was at Belwood.

J.H.: Your work had to do with the environment?

Mario: We worked with the Grand River Conservation Authority. Grand River is the river that flows through the region. It's a government body responsible for protecting the environment, planning and controlling the Grand River. I made picnic tables, cut trees in the forest with a chainsaw, worked in the nursery preparing young trees that would be replanted elsewhere. And we collected wood for the sauna beside our house.

J.H.: In addition to the physical work, did you take part in the life of the community, as a volunteer?

Mario: We worked in a museum, in an old people's home, in a high school in town. And once a week we went to Radio-Waterloo to produce a program. Each one chose his own subject.

J.H.: What did you choose?

Mario: I'm very interested in folk music, in the Celtic music of Ireland, Scotland, Brittany and Quebec. I knew there were a lot of Scotch and Irish people in that part of the country so I decided to do research on Celtic music in the region I was living in. In the end I did a lot of research but I didn't produce the program as I hadn't found enough groups of people (aside from a pipe band and a few isolated individuals) who'd maintained a pure musical tradition. But I learned a lot.

J.H.: Did you do community work?

Mario: Yes, in a house for old people. I liked that a lot. I worked with one old man in particular, an old farmer from the area: we made wooden lecterns. That was good because it taught me something, a rhythm of life, an atmosphere that was different. In the past three months I've worked with children and now I was with men at the end of their lives.

J.H.: Did they appreciate your presence?

Mario: They liked having young people with them, who helped them, kept them company, talked with them. Some of them needed help, others not, it depended. Oh yes, I liked that old people's house. An enriching experience.

J.H.: And soon you'll be leaving Grand River, leaving Katimavik, the family will be breaking up ...

Mario: Yes. We think about that sometimes ... We sit in the living room, we're a little like a family ... After all, we've lived together twenty-four hours a day for ten months. That's almost a year. In two and a half weeks we'll be leaving. I think it's time. I said that a little earlier today: I've enjoyed Katimavik a lot but it's time for me to go on by myself for a while. It's fine to dream, to have ideas and think of all sorts of things, but the time comes when you have to put them into action.

J.H.: What will you do immediately after Katimavik?

Mario: I'm going to go home, take a good shower — because there's only a bathtub here and I'm sick of it. And sleep for twenty-four hours. At the end of June or early in July I'm going to work in a summer camp as a monitor, with children again, because I get along well with children ... Between now and then I'll spend a few quiet weeks at home ... watching ... taking my time ... getting back into my usual environment ... and think about what I'll do later.

25 *Cynthia Martin,*
Age 20,
Don Mills, Ontario

I was born in Toronto twenty-one years ago and lived there until I was eighteen. From when I was twelve on, I did volunteer work with the Red Cross and hospitals, etc, and when I was eighteen, I went to England for five months and lived there and worked, came back and went to college for civil technology for half of the year, left that to work for seven months.

J.H.: You go too quickly. What about your childhood?

Cynthia: Very happy. I'm from a "normal middle-class family." I have two sisters, one twenty-five, she's a mechanical drafter, one nine, and a brother-in-law. He and my sister own a great craft store.

J.H.: Before Katimavik, what was Canada to you? You did not know much about it except Toronto, which some people think is really Canada, but some don't!

Cynthia: I was never really impressed with the sort of life in Toronto, the sophisticated life, although I was involved with it. I had never been west of Toronto before; just as an example, Saskatchewan, I was really glad I went there. I'd always thought it was a barren place, really horrible and I didn't want to go there. And now that I've known it through Katimavik, I really love it. My province I knew, because I'd always take off for a weekend and go to a town that sounded good and I'd stay there for the weekend. But I never lived anywhere for any length of time.

J.H.: Had you ever met any French people before?

Cynthia: I had one good friend before who is French, but when I got to Duchesnay I could only say "bonjour" and "comment ça va?"

J.H.: What was your dream about the future? I'm still talking about before Katimavik, before something changed.

Cynthia: Before Katimavik I had a few options. I wasn't really happy and I didn't want that sort of life but I didn't know how else to change it. That's how I look at Katimavik: it's not just what I've done but the opportunities that it's given me. I can look further for things and I'm not restricted in any way.

J.H.: How did Katimavik come into your life? How did you hear of it?

Cynthia: I'd heard it on the radio and then I saw the ad in the *Canadian Magazine.* I filled it in, never thinking anything would come of it, and I was really pleased when I was accepted.

J.H.: What was it in the ad that you found interesting?

Cynthia: The emphasis on alternate technology, learning French, seeing people of another culture — not just French culture but people in British Columbia have their own special culture to me — seeing people and really living with them. I hate going somewhere and just passing through.

J.H.: Had you any idea what group life was about?

Cynthia: Well, I lived for one year in Toronto with five physically handicapped people and I had to live and work with them every other night and weekends, so we had to function as a group, doing simple things like meal preparation, and just in general being with each other. And I've worked with groups, volunteering, so I was always more of a leader type, non-participant.

J.H.: Was it a shock to find yourself with so many people at the training camp in Duchesnay?

Cynthia: I don't think it was so much a shock, it was more of a realization. We're all out here together, because we have the same general ideas. Every new person would come and people would go up and say hello and introduce themselves and it was really nice.

J.H.: But you like people, meeting new people?

Cynthia: Very much. I've always worked with people.

J.H.: So then it was an opportunity and not a shock?

Cynthia: No, I didn't find it that way at all. I enjoy talking to people and going out with them. In fact, some of them thought I was too outgoing!

J.H.: Who would say something like that was wrong?

Cynthia: Oh, I don't know, people will always find something wrong. There's always two sides.

Larouche, Quebec

J.H.: Let's forget all about training camp and jump right into Larouche. It was probably your first real stay in a French-Canadian village?

Cynthia: Yes, I've been to Quebec before many times, but that was just vacation. It doesn't count. It was good because we were in Quebec first off and we did have a house of thirty which made us all close, no matter how many problems we had at the time.

J.H.: I know the house is small and you were all squeezed in like sardines. Did that help or not?

Cynthia: I firmly believe that people can adjust to any situation they are put into. I always had my own room but it wasn't any problem for me to go into a bunk bed and sort of take over that little space and to allow for other people too. It's what you make it. If that sort of thing bothers you, then you shouldn't be there anyway.

J.H.: But it did bother some of you?

Cynthia: Yes, at times it bothered me also because there was no place, like once when a friend died I had nowhere to go and I felt really frustrated. Everyone did a lot of walking outside. But three months is not a very long time. The living conditions did not affect me that much but I think they were good because we were strong. We couldn't run away and hide so we had to solve things.

J.H.: What struck you about that community?

Cynthia: The first thing, I remember when we got there, was this big reception for us, and friendliness. I talked to the mayor and his wife a lot and they didn't know me but they made an effort. They would laugh at my French, but it wasn't laughing at me. I would have liked to have been closer to the town but we didn't work enough with the people in the community. They were really good people and I got along with them because it was at the end of three months and I was more confident with my French and was not afraid to make a mistake. I still write to them and I've got letters from them.

J.H.: The Tremblay family?

Cynthia: No, the Simard family, very gentle people. I enjoyed living on the farm and doing that sort of work. I think that's a good opportunity that we have to go out and billet and do something completely different. Quebec, I enjoyed, but it would have been better for myself at least, to have worked more with the people of the community — better for my friends, etc. It also focuses your energy on that rather than the group the whole time.

J.H.: In what way do you think it was different from what you knew?

Cynthia: Physically it's very much the same as Ontario, the mountains when you get up North — not mountains for a person in British Columbia — but the way of life seemed to be a little bit slower than what I was used to. I was always in a rush. I enjoyed just going for a walk, nobody being around, and quiet. Everybody seemed a little more relaxed.

J.H.: Did you learn something about Canada through the participants themselves?

Cynthia: Oh, yes. It was so much nicer not to have to look at a book and read about the place, but to talk to somebody about it. That was one thing I thought was really helpful. It was good too in a way because people ... well I'm not really proud of being from Toronto, but people would ask, "I've heard about this place in Toronto" and you'd have pride in telling something about it. It was like the people from Vancouver — I want to go there this fall, and it was so nice to hear about it from someone who's from there.

Wilcox, Saskatchewan

J.H.: So after three months the whole group moves to Wilcox. It was your first contact with the West.

Cynthia: Yes.

J.H.: What was your impression when you got there? At −40°F.

Cynthia: I'm not one for hot weather anyway, so I liked the cold. It wasn't a big shock. The flatness of it really amazed me. One thing that really surprised me was the sunsets and the sunrises, the beauty of the land. Everybody said it was so boring because it was so flat, but every part has a certain characteristic and I liked that. You could go anywhere and see for miles.

J.H.: Would you live there?

Cynthia: Yes, I think so. I have some good friends there. I really enjoy it. The people are so generous and really sincere. Many of these attitudes I've never been accustomed to before. The town of Milestone I really liked, about 700 people there. The work we did which I really enjoyed, was the café for the senior citizens. It's a drop-in centre where they can go during the day and rent it at night for special functions. It's for people over thirty so they have somewhere to go to. It's a small place, the size of a normal store. When we got in there it was an old restaurant. The people had to close the place because it had gone bankrupt and there were even things like salt and pepper shakers on the table and that, so we ripped out the whole restaurant and lowered the ceiling, ripped up the floor. We put up the frames and insulation, the dry wall, painting, light fixtures, oh everything. It was good and it taught us a lot about construction work. It's a lot better for you to do something rather than read about it all the time. But I really think we accomplished something and we did it well and people really enjoyed it and respected us for that. I have a lot more respect for people, older people, through the work I'm doing also. We worked at the playschool, cleaned the hockey rink, volunteering there. There was a restaurant close, so we volunteered serving coffee and little things, at the high school, teaching art and music. Generally we just got involved with the community and because we were living right in town, we got to go to all the things we liked, hockey games and simple things like that. People went to church and we organized some things for that. Not all the people were interested in everything, of course, but I think that was our best project.

J.H.: So you were pretty busy during your stay in Milestone?

Cynthia: Yes, quite. Every day we would have something — there was work from Monday to Friday and weekends and nights there would always be something going on. The friendliness got to the point where the mayor's wife invited us over for buns and cakes and jams, etc. I got a letter from them last week and they have invited me to their official opening of the café. Of course, I can't go. That was the sort of friendliness and now a lot of people write us how they wish we were there. It's very nice to see, it's very rewarding.

Grand River, Ontario

J.H.: Then after three months the group goes to Grand River.

Cynthia: I was in the Belwood-Fergus group. We worked for the Grand River Conservation Authority. Mondays we worked for the radio station, Tuesdays at the museum, Wednesdays at the home for old folks, Thursdays at the high school, and Friday some of us worked at the playschool. So we were busy the whole time and we never had an extra person away.

J.H.: Let's go back to Monday?

Cynthia: On Monday I went to the radio station. Two people were in charge there and I did things for them, filing records and doing manuals and tapes, general work that needed to be done. I had never been in a radio station before and now I know how it functions. It's really interesting the different things you can learn if you go in, and pick up. With everybody that we've met, if you ask them a question nobody will say no practically. I just worked at whatever had to be done there.

J.H.: What did you do Tuesdays?

Cynthia: Tuesdays I'd be at GRCA.

J.H.: I would say you were working hard?

Cynthia: Yes, there was always one person cooking and cleaning for one day, so some people would have two or three GRCA days a week and then one or two volunteer days.

J.H.: So in a typical week, on Tuesdays you would be working outdoors, doing what for example?

Cynthia: Cutting down trees, building picnic tables, building shelters for seedlings, sorting seeds, clipping the branches that were replanted for new trees. And the last part, we've been packing trees for shipment to individuals which defeated why we were there. We were taking the place of regular paid workers and the GRCA was benefitting from our non-salary labour.

J.H.: There are two sorts of things in Katimavik, the things you learn and the things you give. In some circumstances you may learn more than you give and in others, it may be the contrary.

Cynthia: True, but not in the situation I just explained. Then on Wednesdays I would try to go — a lot of times I wasn't allowed to go — to the home for old people. There were one hundred and seventy people, one man fifty-six but they were generally over sixty-five.

J.H.: Fifty-six, I don't think, is that old!

Cynthia: Not that I support his being there, but this one had lived in institutions all his life and never lived in the outside world. He was a bit mentally retarded and it would have been hard for him to adjust to the world. I enjoyed working with the old people. I'd go in the mornings. There were four women who were a bit distant from the others and would not come down to do crafts, so I would go with another woman and we would show them crafts.

J.H.: You do some crafts?

Cynthia: I know a bit and I can pick up on things easily and so it was just showing them, "yes this does go here and try that way," giving them a little help. In the afternoons there was a man who did macramé, I'd show him new knots. And I had a special woman I would go and visit and just talk to.

J.H.: Just to cheer her up?

Cynthia: This one woman's son put her in because he didn't want her around the house anymore and never came to visit her. A lot of them never have visitors. I really enjoyed just going and talking with them. The old people, they've got a lot of contentment. I don't know if they're just bored, so they don't want to speak anymore. They're very easy to be with and whenever you talk to them, they're more than willing to talk to you and help you. Thursdays I usually worked at GRCA again and, twice, I went to the high school there. One day I taught a Chinese cooking course at the school, just the basics.

J.H.: Chinese cooking? You have two Chinese-Canadians in the group. Couldn't they do that?

Cynthia: Well, I went out with a Chinese guy years ago and it started my interest and I really enjoy this type of food. In our Western world we put too much emphasis on sugar, in the East they have much more sophisticated eating habits. So when I went in I just taught how we've been brought up to put more emphasis on convenience than nutrition, showed them a few types of food in Chinese cooking. Fergus is not exactly the centre for Chinese food in Ontario so they'd never been accustomed to those things. I had always made a joke that I didn't want to get into the natural food bit because I thought it was just a fad and crazy, but now I have much more respect for nutrition and conserving the world's resources. I showed them other things like how to sprout beans and I cooked four dishes for the class and then they tasted them and then they could ask questions after. It was a lot of fun to be able to talk to young people and at the same time they would ask about Katimavik, and I would explain about that. I think it was good in two ways because they understood what I was doing and I could do so much and had a lot of scope. So once I did that, I was invited back another time and they presented me a meal in appreciation for what I'd done.

J.H.: A Chinese meal?

Cynthia: No, it was from Greece, a seven-course meal. I wasn't expecting it because I was there to do an evaluation, and help them do magazine reports, so it was really a nice surprise. Generally my week was two or three days at GRCA, one day radio, one day volunteer.

J.H.: Did you also spend one day doing domestic chores?

Cynthia: Yes and that could be Saturdays and Sundays too. Each week, one person would be responsible for cooking, cleaning, and everything to do with the house.

J.H.: You were a pretty good cook to start with?

Cynthia: Sometimes, I had worked in a café in England, and have been cooking since I was small.

J.H.: We made a cake together in Larouche, remember?

Cynthia: Yes, oh that was a horrible cake, my fault too.

J.H.: I thought it was a nice one.

Cynthia: I have a picture of Yvan, you, and I making it. Debbie and I had made a special "end of Larouche" dinner that day. Yes, I enjoy cooking. It's really nice to see the change in people from the start who were really afraid to start cooking. Then they got very extravagant and just threw in spices and that, it was really nice to see respect for food rather than just unwrapping something and throwing it in the oven. People take care now.

J.H.: Would you say that most of the participants are better cooks?

Cynthia: Oh yes, there's no question. Now we have a rule we started in Milestone that we would never buy bread, that the person who cooked that day would bake bread. So every day we have fresh baked bread — whole wheat, rye, anything.

J.H.: You said earlier that you thought natural food was a bit of a fad?

Cynthia: Yes, I used to joke about that with my friends, but now I have a lot more respect for the foods that we've eaten. I've cut down my intake of meat. I don't think I could ever give it up because of the Canadian climate, I think we do need meat and it's part of our surroundings. I don't rely now on convenience. I look for nutrition and in something new — is it going to be really good for you.

J.H.: Would you say that most participants are now concerned about natural food?

Cynthia: I think so, yes.

J.H.: Would it be for health reasons or for the wider aspect? Just to say that we have to stop wasting food, because we have to share food with the rest of the world. Has it something to do with that?

Cynthia: I think so, it's both now. There are a lot of us now who won't support McDonald's, and Kraft, Nestle, those sorts of corporations. What McDonald's represents, and the whole food industry, is really disgusting. It wasn't a big priority to people beforehand, but it will be a lasting thing. Everybody is involved and everybody realizes that's important now. If you can get somebody involved in something as simple as food, they can look at others, like nuclear involvement and the Third World. I think there should have been a lot more emphasis on that.

J.H.: I remember, at the beginning of your group, some of them were somewhat disappointed that one project would be in Quebec, the second in Ontario, the third in Saskatchewan, because the idea was to have three different parts of the country. Well they are different parts, but not as distant as you would have hoped. Which is difficult because we also have to respect the wishes of the people from British Columbia. It will be changed somewhat next year, but nevertheless you must have been among those who were not too happy to come to Ontario.

Cynthia: Very much so — the ad for Katimavik was misleading in that respect. I was very disappointed. Why have that many projects in Ontario, or why have them in southern Ontario because there are a lot of places in northern Ontario, like the town of Larouche, in northern Quebec, who need a lot of help and could have it.

J.H.: You are right about that and it will be changed next year — not completely because we have to respect the proportion of the population of each province. We cannot just say, well, we will not have any projects in Ontario.

Cynthia: No, but have it someplace where it's really needed. The area we're in now — Cambridge, Fergus, Luther — it's a very prosperous area, they don't need the help.

J.H.: You were not upset enough to leave, but did you ever think of leaving?

Cynthia: Yes, a couple of times I did. Once there were a few complaints about me being too forceful in the group, being a leader when I should be more of a participant. I just didn't want to be concerned if that was their idea anymore. I didn't think it was worth solving, because it was their own fault in not doing enough.

J.H.: In your group, the big group, you had some participants who were really typical of each one of the ten provinces. Did you learn something through them?

Cynthia: Yes, definitely. It's always nice to hear about something new that somebody else has done in their life, what their ideas are for the future and think — oh, there is somebody here who thinks like me. This morning, Kathy and I did a skit. We hated each other in Larouche for different reasons and now we are very close friends. It shows how things changed. Same with Peter. I never really talked with him, and once near the end of Larouche we just went for a walk and talked and found out just how much we were alike. When I find some information on nuclear energy, I give it to Peter. When he finds information on building a log cabin, which I'm getting interested in, he gives it to me and so we're contributing to each other, because we're thinking along the same lines. We respect each other's ideas very much. Somebody from Alberta, and somebody from a big city. It's nice to know the differences he can make in what I'm thinking.

J.H.: How do you qualify the kind of links that I, as an outsider, can see there is between each one of you with the whole group of participants?

Cynthia: We're all peers. We all were brought into it because of common goals, common ideas. We've all basically done the same work. It would be hard as an out-sider because I know we still get that sort of thing, "Oh, they're just a bunch of hippies from across the country." But it's good because we are really together and now it's not so far apart countrywise, Saskatchewan is not so far away for me anymore. I think we're all a lot closer.

J.H.: Would you consider yourselves more or less like brothers and sisters or special friends?

Cynthia: Oh, you'll always get problems with individual people but you let those things pass and if they don't, they don't. And besides that, you don't live twenty-four hours with your brother or sister, which we do. We're comfortable with each other. We know each other and when you live with someone that intensely, I equate it to a marriage. Even in a marriage you don't live twenty-four hours with a person. I know what people like to eat and don't like, their moods, and how they get into moods, and it makes you more sensitive and open. I know when I get home it will be hard to walk into my room and not have somebody there to sit down and talk to. We are intense now and everybody talks sometimes about getting away, but once you are away I think you begin to regret that you didn't take advantage of it when you were in it. "I would have liked to have talked to so and so about this sort of thing" and you never had the opportunity. There will always be a bond there.

J.H.: What if you go, for example, to British Columbia? I suppose you will want to see Dorle and Lap and Robert and Mark?

Cynthia: Yes. In fact I am going out West this fall and people I know will be there. It's just a comfortable thought, saying "I won't see you for a few months, do take care." They are very sincere in saying those words. There would be a bond.

J.H.: Well suppose I pick any name because I don't know your relationship with them at all, the names I can pick out like Mario, Serge, even if you don't see them for the next three years, but eventually you go to Quebec — would you feel that you are close to them as you are now?

Cynthia: I know I could call some of them and they would respond. I should hope it would be that way because I don't think we should drop those things just as easily as that.

J.H.: What do you plan to do with your life after Katimavik?

Cynthia: You sound like my parents!

J.H.: Oh, no I'm not asking it in that way!

Cynthia: I know, I'm just saying it, because lately they have been worried. I've been to college and I could return and do the same thing I was doing but I don't want to return there. I'd rather travel, work on the ships, learn the guitar, weaving, etc., more volunteer work — with the deaf, mentally retarded, old people. I would like to just go and live on a farm for a while and see. I would like to build a log cabin just orienting myself, but I think I have to be realistic and say I'm a city person, that probably couldn't happen for a few years.

J.H.: Build a log cabin?

Cynthia: Yes, I'd like to do that so much. I have a few books on it and I am reading them. I was reading an article the other day about this sixty-two-year-old woman who built her own house out in British Columbia, but of course I'd like to have help.

J.H.: Why do you want to build a log cabin?

Cynthia: Just for the experience, not having to rely on concrete, etc. to build a structure, planning it so that you are using your own resources. I have an aversion to being supported by Ontario Hydro. They can do whatever they want with their prices. We can do what we did long ago; we have the resources now and more information to get us back to alternate technology, solar heat. I think we should get back into that a little more.

J.H.: Why do you want to do that?

Cynthia: Because of concern for myself — I don't want to be over-indulgent — and concern for the others. I don't think that it's right that for example, we have hot running water all day long, while another country has never seen hot running water. I don't think it's like giving up part of life or anything. But why, why do we really need that? People have electric can-openers, electric knives, etc. I don't think it's giving anything up, it's just that what we've taken as rights are going to be privileges.

J.H.: I like to hear things like that, Cynthia.

Cynthia: Well, it's true, and if you'd seen me before Katimavik ... I was working in Toronto, I wasn't even concerned about that sort of thing, never thought about that at all. Now I am much more on the level with myself.

J.H.: Your log cabin, what will you do with it?

Cynthia: I would like to live there. I'm getting more into crafts, I am beginning to weave and I want to buy a spinning wheel. I would like to get into that, not as an artist, just to produce my own clothing and other people's clothing. Why should we not be concerned with these things?

J.H.: Yes, but it would have been hard to find someone your age who would react that way ten years ago?

Cynthia: No, I'm sure there were lots, but a lot of the time back then they didn't have the support. Now I have the support to do what I want in that sense, maybe they didn't have people then who would support them.

J.H.: So Katimavik was not such a bad idea after all?

Cynthia: If I didn't like it I wouldn't be here and that's what bothers me in a sense. People who complain about it so much — why are they here? — I have criticized too, but they seem to despise it.

J.H.: Well that's normal. If you love something you want it to be better, so why not complain and try to make it better? I don't disagree with people who disagree.

Cynthia: I see a difference between complaining and criticism. I think what I'm doing is criticizing, but I feel that I have a right. It's not really hurting anybody.

J.H.: You only want to improve?

Cynthia: Yes. I mean it's silly to assume everything is going to be there for you to do; you have to go and get it. I'm sure next year will be better and you'll know more, of course.

J.H.: You don't know how much better it will be. It will change dramatically but this year had to be, because there always has to be a first year, so you will have the privilege of saying, "Well, I was a pioneer in this thing. Now we are involved with 60 000 young people a year, changing this whole society, making a cultural revolution!" Would it really change this country deeply if Katimavik was available to more and more young people each year?

Cynthia: Yes, I think it would if more emphasis was put on Third World, alternate technology, etc., it would be so good for the young as you don't get that taught anywhere else. However, publicity and the negative reports will come out of it — which always come out anyway.

J.H.: By the way, about the negative reports. I have a file of all the clippings for the last ten months. There are about four negative articles and hundreds of positive articles.

Cynthia: Now I think if it was a very large scale program it would be good. Also, I heard a very interesting theory when we were in Saskatoon. These people that run a centre there emphasize concern with the Third World and that sort of thing. They were saying one of the theories is that Katimavik is going to introduce a level of sub-standard living so we will be able to adjust when the depression comes or when the war comes. It was a really interesting theory. This is why we can adjust to any situation — we've had it on a silver platter too long. We can take it and there's really no doubt that we have to work for things and make things better. If the aim of Katimavik was true and consistent people would have a lot more faith and want to give more of themselves. I'd like to work with Katimavik in a few years again if this happens.

26 Lap Wong, Age 19, Burnaby, British Columbia

I was born in Hong Kong and I was raised in Hong Kong too. My parents do business there. I remember as a small boy I always stayed with my mother because my father went to other places to do business. I stayed in Hong Kong until I was eighteen years old.

J.H.: How old are you now?

Lap: I am twenty.

J.H.: Then your family decided to immigrate to Canada?

Lap: Because they say there is better opportunity for young people, so we decided to move. We live in Burnaby, near Vancouver.

J.H.: What was your impression when you moved from the Orient, from Hong Kong and then Taiwan, to Vancouver? What did it feel like?

Lap: It was different because in Hong Kong there are so many people and it is always crowded. When I moved to Canada I cannot get used to it, because it's so big and not so many things around and seldom see the people on the streets. But now I have gotten used to it.

J.H.: You were bored because it was too quiet?

Lap: Yes, that's true. And also everything is much slower than in Hong Kong.

J.H.: What did you do upon arriving in British Columbia? Did you go to school right away?

Lap: Yes, I went to school. I wanted to apply for the college before I finished my high school in Hong Kong and I took a half year off because we were waiting for an answer from immigration, so I decided not to go back to school. I worked for people and learned different things. Then I moved to Canada.

J.H.: Your high school, did you do it in Chinese?

Lap: No, bilingual, Chinese and English. You must pass English and Chinese if you want to be promoted to another grade.

J.H.: So you were bilingual then?

Lap: Not really, I learned a lot of English but we did not have much chance to speak, just like English people learn French. They don't speak French, they lose it.

J.H.: When you arrived in British Columbia and went back to school, was it difficult for you because of the language?

Lap: No, not really. When I study, I do not find it difficult, but when I try to express myself, it is difficult and people do not understand what I try to say. When I read a book, many words do not make sense to me.

J.H.: How long had you been going to school in Vancouver before you heard about Katimavik?

Lap: Only half of the semester of high school. I planned to go back to college but I cannot, it's too late for the college, so I decided to go back to high school to get used to English. After this I read in a magazine about Katimavik and I thought it would be good for me to learn more about Canada.

J.H.: You knew very little then?

Lap: Yes, because before I came to Canada I always thought Vancouver was pretty close to Toronto, but now oh, it's too big for me!

J.H.: When you applied for Katimavik, you were accepted as a participant and then you received a telegram saying that you were expected at a place called Duchesnay, Quebec. What was your impression when you got there?

Lap: When I received a telegram saying that I was accepted, my family didn't believe that. Why, it's not that easy, and you had to have interview, and they would ask, "Is that true, is that really true?" Then we received the tickets and my brother then had to say, "Then it's true." It really was not a joke. When I arrived at Duchesnay I just stopped. The people around me all speak French and I never heard French before. I know French, but I never heard that so I think I will have a very hard time to learn.

J.H.: On top of the fact that you still had a little bit of difficulty speaking English, you must have asked yourself, "What am I doing here?"

Lap: I remember at the beginning of the program, I speak English then but not as good as now. I was so scared when I spoke English.

J.H.: You improved your English through the program. Did you pick up some French too?

Lap: I picked up a lot of French in Larouche and I am sure that if I had stayed in Larouche for six months I don't think I would have any problem speaking.

J.H.: You would learn French quickly. I have heard you speak and you are not bad.

Lap: It is too bad that in the last two projects we don't have enough opportunity, except with participants. We were too lazy to motivate speaking French in the house.

Larouche, Quebec

J.H.: But in Larouche you picked up some French?

Lap: Yes, because you needed to speak French to communicate with other people. Also French language interested me a lot.

J.H.: What are your best memories of Larouche?

Lap: I liked it because it was all new for us and I had more energy because I really wanted to learn something and do something. We had a lot of problems but everything has worked out okay.

J.H.: You arrived in this small house where there were thirty of you; you'd said that in Vancouver you felt lonesome with nobody around on the street, so it must have been like Hong Kong all over again. How did you feel? Did you get along all right?

297

Lap: I got along with people very well and it was a great experience too for me. In order to get along with people who have different cultures, I need to sacrifice a lot of my culture.

J.H.: Living in that house, all squeezed in like sardines?

Lap: Yes, but only for three months. At the beginning I didn't mind living in that house, but later people complained and we had many problems and I started to change my idea and I began to think it was too small for us. Once people get too close together, bad things happen easily.

J.H.: And you went to a farm. Which family were you with?

Lap: The Simards. They are dairy farmers.

J.H.: Did you like them?

Lap: Yes, I still write to them and they were very nice to me too. They keep writing to me at every project.

J.H.: What did you learn from the Simard family? From their way of living?

Lap: They are very nice people but very straight and they are very quiet, friendly and they work and we work for them and they showed us how to do things. We were just like a family. They teach French to me and things like that and we would go out together. I really enjoyed it.

J.H.: Did you ever have any experience before with farming?

Lap: Yes, when I was around eight years old, I spent one summer with a Chinese farmer. I remember they were agricultural farmers and everything was done by hand and cows. The farms in Larouche were mechanized even though it was only a small farm.

J.H.: What did you learn especially about farming?

Lap: Gardening. Actually I didn't learn much about their farm because it was autumn and there was not much things to do. What we learned was how to milk a cow every morning, work in the garden digging up some potatoes, etc.

J.H.: It was an experience, but you wouldn't like to live all your life on a farm?

Lap: No, I don't think so, because I have grown up in a big city.

J.H.: What else did you learn in Larouche?

Lap: I learned how to build a greenhouse, and prepare food for thirty people!

J.H.: Did you do something in the town itself?

Lap: We worked in the library. Just collecting books and marking down the books when people need them. We went to a party in the town, not many actually, just a few.

J.H.: You seemed to know quite a few people. The mayor and his wife were very friendly with you.

Lap: Yes, that's true. They knew me pretty well, maybe because I'm Chinese, and they never see a Chinese before.

J.H.: Yes, but there was another one with you, Robert?

Lap: Oh yes, Robert.

J.H.: He's been in Canada longer, but he's of Chinese origin also.

Lap: Yes, he's a Canadian-born Chinese and he's quiet. At the beginning I was always jumping around, always trying to learn a new language, that's why I keep on talking. Some people tell me something and I talk with some people and maybe that's why they like me.

J.H.: Maybe they like you because you are a likeable person. Did it help you to understand Quebec?

Lap: I learned the reason why they wanted status-ship, and I learned the different culture between the English and the French and their way of thinking, how they react to their own province. I like French culture because it gives me a sense of belonging.

Wilcox, Saskatchewan

J.H.: So then you went to Wilcox. That was quite a different kind of place. How did the countryside strike you?

Lap: No mountains, very cold and storms, wheat farming everywhere.

J.H.: Did you like that?

Lap: It was an experience. I wouldn't live there, but it was an experience for me.

J.H.: How do you like the people there?

Lap: I liked the people, in our project in Milestone. They are very nice and they accepted Katimavik very quickly

299

and they respect us and always helped us. It was a very good project.

J.H.: Did you help them at all?

Lap: We worked and because it was totally new for us, we started to rebuild a project by ourselves and went to talk with the people and met people. We built a coffee shop for the old people in the town and we worked in the high school.

J.H.: What were you doing at the high school?

Lap: You could do anything. If you wanted to teach macramé, you can teach it during the recess time. I taught Chinese cooking, and helped the school whenever they needed us.

J.H.: Are you a good cook?

Lap: Not really, but I knew enough.

J.H.: What did you teach them, for example, what dish?

Lap: Meat balls, won ton soup, fried rice and things like that. And I sang with them.

J.H.: Chinese songs?

Lap: No, English folk songs.

J.H.: You liked the contact with the school?

Lap: Yes, it was fun and at least you had a chance to meet more different people.

J.H.: As a whole were you happy with your project there?

Lap: Not really. I liked the project and I like the town very much but we had many problems in the group life, many things happened. During the first month we didn't have a group leader and we got along quite well because all the people knew we had to do something for ourselves. Then suddenly we found out that we were going to have a group leader and we all got upset and we couldn't get used to our group leader. Then we had some problems with the participants, personal conflicts, power games, and things like that.

J.H.: It was all finally fixed?

Lap: No, really everybody started to watch out and kept in mind what was going wrong. Ontario was the place where our group had explosions between participants.

Grand River, Ontario

J.H.: So then you moved from Milestone, Saskatchewan, to the Grand River project. There were three locations there; where were you?

Lap: In Belwood. I liked the place very much because we lived right in the park and we had more space and we could walk around and it is very beautiful. But personal problems were getting worst and worst, some people lost their sense because of the power game.

J.H.: What were you doing there?

Lap: We worked for the Grand River Conservation Authority and we did some community work too. I really like the volunteer work because we were in a nursery school and worked with small children. We worked in a museum and it is very different, these two things. We worked in an old folks home. I liked it because the people were nice and we could learn many things from the old people.

J.H.: Now, what work did you do with the Grand River Conservation Authority?

Lap: We made picnic tables, pruning trees and cutting wood. I am not very interested in working just in the woods.

J.H.: Did you learn something through it?

Lap: I learned how to be patient.

J.H.: You did some carpentry?

Lap: Yes, but I learned more in Larouche than here with GRCA.

J.H.: What you did, wasn't it useful to anybody?

Lap: Yes, it is useful to the public. We built picnic tables for the people and we planted trees, but I still like to work with the community more.

J.H.: What did you find out about the people there? Were they very different from the people in Milestone or Larouche?

Lap: Yes, a little bit different with the people in Milestone, Saskatchewan. The people here have small reality. They are nice but they are not as friendly as in Milestone. They won't invite you for supper and they won't come up to your house and visit you. In Milestone you do have that kind of thing happening. Here they just talk to you and are nice to you.

J.H.: They are nice, but they don't go so far?

Lap: Yes, that's right. Maybe it's because we live far away from the town.

J.H.: Yes, that's another problem. So, we are getting nearer the end of the program now. Do you feel you have changed in some way?

Lap: A lot.

J.H.: Could you tell me in what way?

Lap: I see more negative things than positive things. That's the main change. I complain a lot more than at the beginning!

J.H.: Oh, that's not very good. What does that mean?

Lap: I am concerned more about one thing. It's like when we do something, before I would just do it and not care about what would happen, but now I think that maybe it's bad or maybe it's good. Also we need to care about other people. Caring about other people or respect other people is not a bad thing, but for me through these ten months, I found out that generally, Canadians have a closed mind and they need a lot of respect from other people, if not they will complain.

J.H.: You are more critical?

Lap: Yes, that's it. Also more confused in my mind.

J.H.: Is that the only change that you feel?

Lap: No, more knowing of the world, like how to deal with different people.

J.H.: You learned how to get along with people more easily?

Lap: In a sense, yes. But in our group, at the end of the program, we still left with unsolved personal problems.

J.H.: Did anything else change with you? Did other people notice the change?

Lap: Not as lively as at the beginning. Now I am getting tired and I'm always quiet and speak less.

J.H.: I noticed that in the last few weeks. Maybe it's because I forgot how noisy you were at the beginning!

Lap: I don't know yet if there is anything else. I just think that I may have changed in this way. I know that after Katimavik I am going back home and stay with my friends and then I will know where I've changed. They will tell me or I will feel how to deal with my friends. I am sure I changed a lot but I don't know exactly where I changed.

J.H.: Your view of Canada, did that change?

Lap: Yes, changed a little bit. There are a lot of people that are very well-educated but they cannot satisfy what they want. They cannot find a job that they would find interesting. The people have different kinds of cultures and different ways of thinking of things. Also, Canadians are hard to get along with, because they see things differently.

J.H.: What about the group? Some participants told me that the group was like a family to them. Do you feel that too?

Lap: Not really. I don't feel like that particularly about that. But I do feel that we get along when Gordon got kicked out. We got really upset because he really meant something and when we go in the house and feel that there's something missing — that's the kind of feeling I had there.

J.H.: That's one out of twenty-four.

Lap: Yes, but then Yvan was quitting.

J.H.: That was tough too. Do it means that there are some links among you all. Do you think these links will last long?

J.H.: You, yourself, will you keep in touch with them?

Lap: Sure, I will try. I will write and I will go and visit. Canada is much more smaller for me because I've been to many places and I know how to get to different places. Yvan lives in Montreal so I can go to visit him any time I want.

J.H.: Yes, you have friends there now. And in Newfoundland, you have Gordon and Joyce, etc. So you feel that Canada is not as big as it was. Well that's good. Now what will you do right after Katimavik?

Lap: At the beginning I plan to go right home because my family needs me and my brother want to travel this summer. I promised them that I would go back. Now I have changed my plan because I applied for the French immersion in Quebec and they accepted me in Trois Rivières.

J.H.: So you will be in French immersion in Quebec?

Lap: Yes, for one and a half months — from July to August, so I am not going back home until August.

J.H.: Your family will be a bit disturbed by that?

Lap: Yes, but I wrote them and told them. I think it is good for me because I like to learn more French and learn it right away. At least I have some basic ideas and if I just leave it I may forget it.

J.H.: Yes, that's a good idea and you will meet new people there. After this French immersion course, what will you do?

Lap: I am going back to school in September.

J.H.: What do you plan to do in the future?

Lap: Go to university. I have decided to study business and administration.

J.H.: Like your father?

Lap: Yes. I realize and I see so many people who study very hard and they graduate from university but they still cannot find a job that they want. I think, if I study business things, and because I got a background, maybe I can find a job more easily.

27 Roy Gilpin,
Age 19,
Kitchener, Ontario

Well, I was born in Toronto and I only lived there for three years until my father got a job in Kitchener and that is where I have been living ever since.

J.H.: Did you travel at all before Katimavik?

Roy: Oh! You bet! I have gone to the northern United States and to the Maritimes. My mother is from Nova Scotia, from Sydney. So we have been there a number of times, visiting my grandparents, different relatives and friends of my mother. I knew a bit about the West, but certainly not firsthand. I have read books and other friends have told me about it. I have been in Quebec but very, very quickly, very circumspectly. "Sort of in-and-out." The best thing I remember about Quebec was that my dad luckily could speak some French, so that we were never completely "out of whack" with everything, and that every time we went in to Quebec, it rained. That's about it.

J.H.: You didn't speak any French at that time?

Roy: I spoke about as much as any person who is not concentrating very hard on high school French would speak French.

J.H.: Which I think is very little.

Roy: Very little.

J.H.: So you were at school when you heard about Katimavik?

Roy: Yes.

J.H.: What kind of plans did you have for the future?

Roy: I hadn't completed grade 12 and I didn't have any idea what I was going to do. I certainly didn't want to go right into the work force and I didn't feel like bumming around the country. So, I just thought I would try something different and entered Katimavik.

J.H.: How did you hear about it?

Roy: The first thing was my mother finding something in the newspaper about it. She brought this to my attention because she was quite worried that I wasn't going to do anything useful in my life. This seemed like something that would be good for me, good for them, good for the country.

J.H.: But what struck you about what you read in the paper?

Roy: Well, it seemed that it was a little of what I was looking for, hard work. I would be seeing some new people and some different parts of the country, and even learn to speak French. I was kind of apprehensive about that. I didn't know whether I would be able to do that, that really didn't even enter into my mind, funny enough, until I entered the first training camp.

Larouche, Quebec

J.H.: Yes, with one-third of the people being Francophone and ...

Roy: Yes. The culture factor was just incredible. I had lived for nineteen years of my life, almost twenty years of my life, beside another province. It was almost like another country as far as our cultures and languages were concerned. I sat in the group: there was Yves and Daniel, and Serge, and two group agents. They all sat down and started speaking French. I could not really comprehend anything of what they were saying at all. I could get a feeling, that it was sad, that it was serious, or that it was some sort of joke, but that was about it.

J.H.: You were lucky, then, that your first project was in the Francophone province?

Roy: Yes. I think I am really very fortunate that it was. I am the sort of person who procrastinates unless I am pushed in a group. The thing is when I was in the group, I had to learn French. That was all there was to it. We were always pushed and some of us were very upset. I was upset, I know, very tired, and very, very, very teed off that I had to learn French, but it was real funny to be pushed that way because I really started to feel the problems that the Francophones were having with us and in their province. And we were going into Quebec City for one day and tried to buy things in French. All the staff were so helpful and so nice. I tried and I guess it seemed kind of silly, and pretty poor French, but the salespeople were laughing, so that made me happy. The sort of idea I kept getting was, we are not worried that you are speaking it poorly, you are trying and that's the first thing. When I made a mistake, I felt embarrassed but most of the Francophones are not nearly as embarrassed trying to speak English as the English trying to speak French. I guess we have a very strong feeling about our language, a very protective feeling. It's too bad, I think. I am looking forward to going back hopefully and stay in Quebec for a while.

J.H.: What about Larouche?

Roy: Larouche? Larouche was very interesting for me. I think I am one of the only participants who enjoyed being with all those people ...

J.H.: Crowded as you were?

Roy: Yes. It never bothered me that much, really. I think that the only thing that bothered me was that other people were bothered ... I enjoyed that house, I didn't think it was that bad. I thought it was really fun, a lot of times. If you were feeling kind of depressed or low, there was usually someone who didn't feel that low and they'd bring you up a little bit; or if you were really high, someone could regulate you and bring you down a bit so you weren't bothering everyone else. And every once in a while, everybody would be upset together and of course misery loves company and it is a bit easier to bear in that way, I think.

J.H.: What did you learn in Larouche?

Roy: I learned some patience, I learned French and I learned a lot about Roy Gilpin. My dad had died just before I came to Larouche and I felt very special for a while but I started to lose that feeling of specialness and I started to work and to understand why I needed to work, why I needed to do things. It is a funny feeling, you get when ... I don't know whether it happens to a girl with her mother but I think when a boy's father or a young man's father dies, he tends to feel a lot of things that have come from his father to himself. I started to feel certain things were similar to what my father had been and some things that he was very much against and I started to sort through those things and I think Larouche was very helpful in that. It gave me the time. With those thirty people, I had time to not be interacting with everybody all the time and yet I was not cut off from them. If I was out clearing some trails for the *ski de fond* or if I was on the farm doing something by myself I could ... it was just the time when I could think.

J.H.: Were you on a farm for some time?

Roy: Yes. I was staying at a farm, the Tremblays, for three weeks. And that again was an experience in patience and trying to understand things that I had to do, my responsibilities and ...

J.H.: What were your responsibilities?

Roy: Working on a farm and trying to learn French, trying to become a part of the family. The other people there on the farm felt that they were very much integrated, but I never felt integrated on the farm, unfortunately. Whether that was my fault, partly my fault I must say, partly the fault of the Tremblays', perhaps we weren't just, you know, the right ones to get along with one another. That happens. I don't regret that fact. That again is another part of learning. They were a very interesting family to be with, they were very large ... I am from a small family so it is a very new feeling to be coming to a new family, such huge proportions. They were a very close family but, I don't know, I felt I was in the way sometimes and that I didn't really know what my job was on the farm. I knew certain things that they were doing, that they needed our help on. I didn't reject that. That was all, I liked to help. I enjoy doing that.

J.H.: Like what? Milking cows?

Roy: Yes, milking cows and making sure that they were cleaned before the milking and then carrying the milk back to the cooler, things like that. Diane Tremblay who was really our sponsor on that farm was rebuilding one of the garages, so we were helping her with that, putting in fiberglass, then putting gyprock on the top. She had a small, small chalet that she had built for herself and so we were chopping wood and clearing things out and just doing small things.

J.H.: I am told that she is quite a person?

Roy: She was quite interesting, I think I learned some things from Diane as a matter of fact. She was a single woman, I think she was thirty-five, I am not too sure, I wasn't too interested in that but she had been an "arts plastiques" teacher at the CEGEP, I believe in Alma, and she had stopped working there. It was not fulfilling enough, she had other things that she enjoyed doing more on the farm. And most of the males were away from the farm. Diane was very independent and very, very, open about wanting to do things by herself and I felt I cramped her style. That was one of the reasons why I felt a little bad. We were ... I felt like I was sort of muscling in on certain things, but of course she accepted us. But I learned things from her, yes. I wasn't as dumb as I thought. I kind of made mistakes sometimes and she tried to help me with them, whether it was a language mix-up, or just with the cows. So it was alright.

J.H.: Through Larouche, did you learn something more about Quebec?

Roy: I learned an awful lot just about the problems, I think, of Quebec. The idea of a farmer who had certain quotas to meet, and if he went over them, he had to get rid of his milk and if he went under them, he would have to somehow try to make up that quota. And the idea that not everyone was sympathetic with the P.Q. government, that a lot of the people are still very federalist. They have a large farm that they have to keep running, they have to keep going to the bank and have a working relationship with this bank and it's pretty hard if your insurance company is thinking about leaving you or your bank system is slowly going apart at the seams because they don't know where the money is shifting and moving from and there is a lot of movement of economics and, you are only a farmer, you don't understand this sort of thing or if you do, you have a very deep understanding of it and you know, it's hard for you, it's upsetting and you are trying to run a large family besides and feed eight or nine boys. I wasn't actually supposed to do it, I don't think, but I went in to town on a school bus a couple times with Jérome Tremblay, the youngest boy, and those rides were quite an experience. I learned an awful lot from those, just going to town with him and seeing different things. I went in to the CEGEP for a while in Jonquière, and just sat down and read some books and tried to see what that was like, I don't know, I guess I am still just so fresh from school that there are things that I relate to and understand a little bit better. I learned the similarities too between the cultures: the children still have to go to school, the adults still have to go to work and there are still pizza places on certain corners and there are still little stores that you can buy your pop from, and little hang-outs. There were a lot of similarities.

Wilcox, Saskatchewan

Roy: We had an evaluation in Montreal and then after that we went on to the West to Wilcox. Now one of the other participants, Claire and I went home. I needed some moral support. It was very depressing to go home, my mother was still very, very upset and it was Christmas time, it was also near my birthday, and Christmas time, of course, for the family is a very important thing. My dad having died three months before, it was still very, very sad for my mother. We left from Toronto for Regina and then from there to Wilcox. We went by bus and it was a very long

long ride. When we got to Regina, things were happening already in Wilcox and looking very bad, with one house having sewage problems and another house was having problems with a group agent and, everything was just happening all at once. I was in one of the two houses in Wilcox, and Claire was in a house in Milestone so we were quite separate. We had come to be very close while we were travelling alone and while we were at my home, so we were very, very sad to be parted but then two things happened very quickly. One of the group agents got in a fair amount of difficulties with his group and he decided along with Russell the coordinator there, that it would be better if he left, and quite soon after that one of the participants in that group, Peter, switched to this group, way back in Larouche, when Michael had to switch because of problems in the group he was in. So Peter felt that he was not accomplishing anything and it was just not a group for him. So he asked me if I was still interested in changing, and some people were leery of this, because Claire, of course, was in that group and they were afraid that we'd break apart the group or something. We would just be together too much. So I switched into that group, kind of glad. I felt not too bad, there were more people that I was comfortable with and the main thing was, I felt I could be of more help in that group than in my own. So I was just happy to change and I changed. And there was a certain animosity about Claire and me being together. It wasn't all the group, it was only a few people. We tried our best, I think, to be sensible, to be responsible within the group, do our jobs, and to be with one another when it was reasonable to do so. I think we did our best. I feel that we actually did not co-habitate, we were together but we worked separately, much of the time.

J.H.: In what kind of work were you involved in Milestone?

Roy: The physical labour was mainly done in the senior citizens' drop-in centre. The senior citizens' group had bought this café and what we did was destroy it entirely on the inside and then rebuild it. We built walls, put in more insulation, gyprocked and painted over that, we put in new ceilings, suspended ceilings and we cleaned out a lot of junk and put up concrete supports, down in the basement, because the wall was buckled in, we did some work on the back roof and did some shingling ...

J.H.: Had you done any carpentry before?

Roy: No, I had no idea about that at all, so I learned an awful lot from the men I worked with. They were very, very intelligent men. They were craftsmen. Then something that I did by myself: they had wanted some garbage cans built, so I decided to try to do up some plans. I did one of an elevator, sort of a small elevator model and they seemed pretty happy with it so I was kind of glad. That was the time of the flowering of my physical labour, I went to work and I did an awful lot of work. I worked there almost every day. I tried not to push everybody to do work, but I got tired and upset sometimes because everybody wasn't working as much as I was. I also worked a lot with the children's pre-school.

J.H.: What did you do there?

Roy: That was a lot of fun. A lot of time it was just going there, having ideas to help out the two mothers and the school teacher who were working with the school children, keeping the little ones busy, playing games and trying to teach them little things; reading them stories. We took them on a tour of the fire department. They kept the fire equipment in a garage and the back part of that was the pre-school, playschool. There were about fourteen kids every Tuesday and Thursday and two and a half hours every afternoon, so one day we took them on a tour of that and they liked that an awful lot. I got to play with kids; I love little children, bigger children I have to learn how to work with a little bit better first, but I really like little kids, they're a lot of fun.

J.H.: What did you learn about the population there? Did you like the people?

Roy: I liked the people an awful lot. I've always known that people were different, I think we all do, but I think it takes something in each of us to jag that knowledge, so

312

that it goes from being a known thing to a learned thing. These older people in Milestone weren't hard to live with. They were different from the other people in town; they had grown up during the depression when it was necessary to save your money. They were very spend-thrifty and that was hard for me; they were different from the older people that I associated with. They were a little different because they had stayed in the same place all their lives. Some other people had been overseas, during the war, other people had travelled a bit, but these people had never moved from that area. The largest part of the populace of Milestone had lived in Milestone or that area all their lives and that was something very, very new to me. These people had a very limited view and it was very hard to discuss things with them. They didn't understand things away from that area. They were very open, but in the same way very closed about many things. They did not understand the problems in Quebec, they had never been there, so they were very one-sided and it taught me a lot of patience. I had to help them instead of being upset with them, so that taught me to be just a little bit more human.

J.H.: As a whole would you say that Milestone was a good experience?

Roy: Yes, oh, it was great. The people on the whole enjoyed our being there. Some of them resented it but that I thought would happen anyway. From Cheryl Black, the minister who was quite helpful to some of us, she wasn't helpful to all of us, to Mr. Lible who ran the store in town and was also "the man," to Dave Wilson, the insurance agent and town secretary, to anybody. Some were farmers in town and the people whom you billeted with, they were all very helpful. They were all people I learned something from.

Grand River, Ontario

J.H.: Then the whole group moved to the last project which was in Grand River, Ontario. There were three houses there; which one was yours?

Roy: Mine was in Belwood, just north of Fergus near the Shan Dam. That was like home for me. It was sort of funny because everybody else was upset; a lot of the Ontario people thought it would be very upsetting to be home. I didn't think that for one minute, I thought it would be great, that I could help everybody out if they wanted to do some things in different places. The way I took it to be, Katimavik was supposed to be an experience, it was supposed to be hard work, and it was supposed to be something I'd be living in. I didn't care where it would be because I would be learning something everywhere that I went. If I didn't learn anything, it was my own darn fault, not the fault of being in Ontario or Quebec, or not being in Vancouver, say. I found it very interesting to be working with CKMS, the University of Waterloo Radio Station.

J.H.: What did you do there, yourself?

Roy: My feature was on juvenile delinquents. Claire and I are working on it together, so I've been doing a lot of interviews with different authorities, sort of experts, you would say, on the subject. I've had some interviews with the judge, with a staff sergeant who's in charge of the Youth Bureau. A woman whose child was a delinquent and who went through some of the processes.

J.H.: Did you enjoy it?

Roy: Oh yes, very much. I'm still working on it, I'm not done yet. It's opened a lot of doors. That's what Katimavik has been for me in a lot of ways, it's opened up a lot of doors. I'm going back out West after this is all over, during harvest, to work on a farm. A lot of people have already said that if I want to come out, they're sure I can find work around Wilcox. The other part of the work was with the GRCA and working in a high school in Fergus and in a pre-school in Fergus.

J.H.: What did you do for the GRCA?

Roy: Mainly physical labour, from cutting down trees with a chainsaw to pulling trees out of the mud. That was our last thing, pulling trees out of the mud in the rain. It was terrible but it was very fulfilling, working with the ground

314

again for a while. I enjoyed the work, it was interesting but I did not feel it was in keeping with the ideas of Katimavik, unfortunately. I felt that we were taking jobs from other people.

J.H.: I'm pretty sure you were right.

Roy: Yes, so now Katimavik knows. Like that's what happens in the first year.

J.H.: And you worked in a high school for a while?

Roy: Yes, I worked in a high school. It was funny, I have done alternate technology on my own before Katimavik, so I have always been interested in solar energy and things like that. So I got to go into some classrooms, Environmental Learning, or something. They were lucky enough to have two greenhouses at this high school, and so they had flowers growing and plants growing and they were learning about agriculture. Some of the kids were farm kids and some of the kids were city kids. It was pretty open and so I just went in and talked to them and showed them a film about people who had tried to work with alternate technologies and to live a little more with their environment. With most of the kids that was pretty new to them and I didn't expect much, but some of them were really quick to pick it up, so that's great. They made me feel good because the kids there really do care about doing something for somebody other than themselves. I worked with the drama teacher and that was kind of fun too. I worked with one girl who had just come into the class. She was kind of quiet and reticent and she needed someone to help her doing this scene; she had to do an evaluation after and she said it was one of the most fulfilling experiences she had, that it was very, very educational to work with someone as good as I was. It's funny, I've done a little theatre work but not very much and it was really a lot of fun.

J.H.: You have the magic ...

Roy: Yes, I'm a magician. So it was fun to have somebody say I did something well.

J.H.: Now, near the end of the last project, do you feel that you have changed a little bit?

Roy: I changed a tremendous amount.

J.H.: For the better or ... ?

Roy: Yes, I'd like to think so. I've been told that I have changed for the better by people who count as far as I see things.

J.H.: You mean people in the group?

Roy: People in the group, yes. People outside the group too — some friends, some people in the community I came from, that I respect. They could feel a little more vitality and energy. I've quieted down I think, a fair amount; I'm not quite as silly or childish sometimes. I've always been told that my humour is a good thing, that it makes people feel liked, that it is not a bitter sort of humour that makes people feel bad. I think I've learned to do that a little better, yet more maturely and I've learned when to shut up too. I've learned that I have to work sometimes without saying anything, and that I have to be patient with other people and try to understand more than just my point of view. I've learned a lot of things that it takes to be a man and I'm happy about that.

J.H.: What about the group: how do you feel about the group?

Roy: Unfortunately, I'm not much of a group person I guess and other people found that out. I tried, and I failed sometimes and other times I did pretty well. I feel very close to a lot of people in my group. Unfortunately, we've had some problems in our group, problems that I'm sure you're very well aware of, so I don't want to go over them in depth. I don't dislike anyone in my group, I'm sad that some people aren't quite as open or aren't quite as able to bend or resolve conflicts. I'm very sad that I haven't been able to meet everyone as well as I'd like to. It's only now that I'm beginning to know some people, and of course I can't expect that in ten months I'd become a brother for Lap, for example. I can't, we were perhaps never meant to be that close so "que sera sera," that is the way it's going to be. I can't change the world.

J.H.: But even if you cannot be very close to Lap, do you

feel that because you have lived through so many things together ...

Roy: Yes, Lap will always be a part of me. Whenever I think of dancing, whenever I think of many, many little things, and many big things. I think I've grown to understand how little understanding I've shown to him and sometimes how much I gave to him. So I think, it was an experience for both of us that neither of us will forget, I hope. Each person in that group has become a part of me. Mr. Hébert has become a part of me ...

J.H.: Thank you, Roy ...

Roy: ... and everyone's become a part of me, I'll never forget anyone. I'm not the sort of person who forgets anyone. Unfortunately I'm not the sort of person who likes being taken down either in a photograph or on a tape. I just hope that if people care enough to remember me, they'll put away a little space for me and, again, I have to be a little more adult and say "No, no people aren't that way." Each person remembers a person a different way. I'm lucky I have a memory that will remember people for all time and I'll never forget anyone.

J.H.: Has your view of Canada changed at all? Not only through the three projects but also through thirty young people who included, say, a girl from Newfoundland or a boy from Saskatoon? Did it help you get a better view of Canada?

Roy: Oh yes. All I had to do was open my eyes and see that there are many differences between each of us. Again, as I was saying about just going to Jonquière and seeing the same things there, I see the same things in each place, so that's very reassuring. We are the same and yet there are differences that have to be noticed too.

J.H.: What are you going to do the day after Katimavik?

Roy: The day after Katimavik I believe I am going to be heading East for Montreal. I have been invited to the anniversary of Claire's grandparents. It's going to be a real big shebang and we are going to have a good time. She's going to introduce me to all her relatives. I'm very frightened, but I think it will be okay. After that I think

317

I'm going a little further East and then back home to spend about three weeks just cleaning up the house. My mother unfortunately hasn't had the get-up-and-go to do things. She's a strong woman but this has taken her back a tremendous amount. I, unfortunately or fortunately, feel a great responsibility there. I feel that my mother or my sister are dropping a great load on me in a way and I don't feel it's fair. I know I have responsibilities so that's all there is to that, but I still have the feeling that I want to do a little more and I don't want to forget travelling and doing different things that quickly. So I will go home eventually, probably after I'm done out East. I intend to take one month, probably July, just go out East and do different things. I love the East and Claire really loves the ocean, so we felt it would be really nice to be together. Then after that when I work I probably won't be seeing her for three or four months. She's going to Vancouver, she thinks, with one of the other participants and stay with Dorle. They're going to be together for a while and then, when I'm done in Milestone, I'm going to visit her. We were thinking of probably going south for a little while and then we'd go our own ways for a while, live our own lives for six, seven, or eight months and then hope to come together again next summer, decide what we would like to do. We're very serious about one another and I always felt that all the way through Katimavik we've had a very special relationship. We've been told by different people in fact Michel Larouche, our first co-ordinator said right at the beginning that we had a very intelligent and a very adult relationship. There aren't too many who harbour any ill feelings toward us. We've always done our work, we've tried our best not to become separate from the group which we both thought co-habitation meant. We tried very hard, sometimes to the pain of each other, but it was worth it.

J.H.: In the long run, what do you plan to do with your life?

Roy: I don't know, I'm thinking of different things. Through this project with juvenile delinquents, I've been thinking of going into that sort of field. I've been helped by

Katimavik and I'd like to show some of that to people. Warm friendships I've always thought were just things that were never meant to be kept away and given to somebody else. I guess that is why I end up short at one end, but I don't mind, I always end up getting them some way or other. I'm a very strong Christian, I live it as much as I can. I fall down a lot and I know the Big Fellow upstairs knows but I hope he understands that I try at least and that I can take it a little bit further. I guess I just like to live and be a good human being. I don't know, I haven't thought a lot about an exact occupation. I think I'd like to come back into Katimavik, but I need to do more growing on my own first. I'm not going to jump right back, but I'd like to come back because I think I have things that are valuable to offer.

J.H.: As a group leader, you mean?

Roy: Yes, as a group leader. I'd like to try, I'm going to see though.[1] Katimavik has also given me the chance to respect whether I can do something or whether I can't. So, if I can't be a good leader, I won't do it. If I do come back then I shall try my darned level best to do it, that's all there is to that. Just trying to be me, I guess. I'd like to work with my hands, I'm thinking of going into perhaps masonry or something, heavy work but in a fulfilling sort of way that will last for a while. I've always felt that there's been one goal in my life all the time, and if I could leave one thing for one person, then that's all I want to do. If I can make one person grow, or one person rich by being on earth then that's all I want, that's been a good life.

J.H.: That's great for last words. Thank you, Roy.

---

1 Roy is now a group leader in Katimavik, Year II. And a very good one, I've heard ...

Epilogue – A Plea

And there it is! Everything has been said, felt, experienced. I could be quiet now, but no: I want too much to utter one last cry, in the hope that over the tumult of their dreadful everyday lives, I'll be heard by the men who matter, the ones who decide, those who "can" ...

Being a politician, exercising power, is undoubtedly an exalting profession.

Being a senior civil servant who can put policies to work, suggest millions for one program or another, the essential or the incidental, is probably just as exalting.

Being Peter Newman or Roger Lemelin, Allan Fotheringham or Michel Roy, Jack Webster or Charles Lynch, constantly influencing public opinion, defending some important cause or bemoaning the state of the world – that too is very important.

To all these men, to all these women (alas, more rare!) who govern us, administer us or influence our society, I submit a dream which they have the power to transform into reality. A very simple dream that can be summed up as follows: while there's still time – in other words, right away – bring about a profound change in the way people look at things – and now come the big moves! – by setting in motion a *cultural revolution* through the young people of this too fortunate country, which is dying of boredom.

Jean Monnet, the "father of Europe," who fought until his last breath to transform the old continent with all its nationalisms, all its forms of racism and, consequently, all its wars, into a humane and fraternal society, teaches us that there's no time to waste, that we must as quickly as possible "change the course of events. To do that, we must change the minds of men." But he doesn't suggest speeches, committees and all the other ways of killing time to which we're so partial in the democratic countries and elsewhere: "Words are not enough. Only immediate action focused on an essential point can change the present static state. Profound, real, immediate and dramatic action is required, one that will change things and turn into reality those hopes which people are on the point of abandoning."[1]

This sort of change in intellectual attitude, this "cultural revolution" won't be accomplished by the old people. Not even by adults, who are always divided between the large number who wish to change nothing and the small number who want to destroy everything. Only the young people are truly available for such grand designs, for only young people are still free, still generous, still pure. What I've seen in nearly three years at Katimavik (and even longer at Canada World Youth) has given me all the evidence I need: yes, *the young people are ready*. Their dissatisfaction with the selfish, wasteful society we have made for them, their anguish as they contemplate the bleak, disastrous future offered to them, their scepticism before the pitiful solutions that are discussed in public, might lead them to despair or — even worse — to resignation. And yet and yet — in spite of everything, young people today want to change the world, they want to save the world! And that's what it's all about; and now for the first time in human history it's a deadly serious matter: either we change the world or there'll be no more world.

---

1 Jean Monnet, *Mémoires*, Fayard 1976

I've just torn myself away from a remarkable book and I'm still worked up over it: *De la biologie à la culture,* by Jacques Ruffié.[2] It traces biological development from the origins of life to that of the human race, its slow evolution up to the present crisis which, for the first time, is endangering humanity itself. In his own way Jacques Ruffié also concludes that we must stop beating around the bush: we must change the world!

> The requirements are visible: more justice, co-operation, awareness; a certain renunciation of our individual and patriotic selfishness that still correspond to animal modes of behaviour; the adoption, without hesitation or regret, of altruistic behaviour, specifically human. Frontiers of class, like national frontiers, belong to the past. The attempt at integration must be carried out within nations as well as among them, on the global level. And all that must lead us to change not only our way of living, but, even more important, our way of thinking. The program? To revise the relationship among individuals, among nations, to define a new hierarchy of values. The true revolution in these modern times has yet to be carried out; and it is first of all a cultural revolution.

The expression keeps coming back: "cultural revolution." It's no longer enough to fiddle with structures, institutions, constitutions, borders: we must change the way people think, change their hearts, stir up a new art of living, create a harmonious, more humane society. Prepare the next generations — and the ones after them, if there are to be any — to build a society that will not only be as self-sufficient as possible in terms of food and energy resources, but that will consume far less in order to share the earth's limited resources with the one-third of mankind that *at this moment* is dying of hunger, and the other third

2. Flammarion, 1976.

that *at this moment* lacks the necessities of life. Everyone knows that the poor population of this earth is growing at a terrifying rate, while individual poverty is getting worse, whereas the few rich countries, including ours, continue to grow richer and to consume more — while reproducing less and less! And we don't need the Club of Rome to understand the disaster that's looming ahead.

Only a few years ago, anyone who suggested such things to politicians, economists or other serious types would have passed for a damned nuisance or, at best, a dreamer. Ecology was still a strange word reserved for specialists who were hardly listened to. Self-sufficiency, modest consumption, planning economic growth in terms of environmental capacity, research into appropriate technologies and more rational diets, the notion of a world becoming a global village in which every man is responsible for his brother — all these ideas, essential though they are for the survival of mankind, didn't seem too important, just good enough for stirring up bearded youngsters who probably smoked marijuana too, and who, it was hoped, wouldn't go too far from San Francisco or Vancouver. The prospect of an early return to "joyous austerity," to use the expression of Pierre Dansereau,[1] didn't sweep people off their feet.

Then bang! the oil crisis. At first, people refused to believe in it. There was a mistake ... it's a trick ... likely something to justify raising the prices! But since yesterday our powerful American neighbours, the greatest consumers of oil in the world *after* the Canadians, have had to line up at gas pumps. (Henry Ford must be rolling over in his grave!) And after oil, another of the earth's resources will be exhausted, then another and another.

The fifty-year-old dentist who earns $80,000. a year, the honest law professor at Université de Montréal or

---

1 Pierre Dansereau, *La Terre des Hommes et le paysage intérieur,* Leméac, Éditions Ici Radio-Canada, 1973.

Simon Fraser University, the big farmer in Alberta — all these fine people don't have to worry about tomorrow. Most likely they'll all be well-off when they die, and even if they were to give all their belongings to the starving masses in the Sahel or in Bangladesh, it wouldn't change very much. But what *can* change everything is the tiny flame of anguish burning at the bottoms of the hearts of their sons and daughters. At the bottom of Cynthia's heart and Peter's, of Lise's and Roy's, of Kathy's and Mark's and all those young people to whom we can offer only one inheritance: the right and the responsibility to build a new society, in solidarity with the rest of the world.

Only ten or fifteen years ago no one would have dared propose such a Utopia. Before the oil crisis... "You're out of your mind," the $80,000. dentist or the businessman in the black Cadillac would have told us. "My sons and daughters will get the best education in the world, they'll become dentists, go into big business. And what the devil would they do in your wretched Katimavik? Learn how to build log cabins? Plant trees? Grow tomatoes in a greenhouse? Heat water with solar energy? Clean up garbage? Work with handicapped children and mope about the miseries of the lazy louts in the Third World? You're out of your mind!"

Today, these wealthy gentlemen have lost a little of their fine confidence in the invincibility of the consumer society. A little doubt is gnawing at their bellies. Already, they're more attentive to the concerns of their son who's left the School of Dentistry to reorient himself in agriculture, or their daughter who isn't going to be a fashion designer now, but a social worker on an Indian reservation. All sorts of mutations are slowly being produced in people's consciences. And it's most important not to be frightened by them! Listen again to the words of Jacques Ruffié:

The mutation that's in progress is so vast that it will be necessary to build, in the face of our old, maladjusted culture, the counter-culture of the future. Why fear it? It is through periodic questioning that mankind has passed through all the important stages of its existence: Neolithic farmers and shepherds represented a counter-culture with respect to the hunters and gatherers who came before them; Christianity was a counter-culture in the face of the Roman empire, the Renaissance in the face of the Middle Ages, the Revolution in the face of feudalism ... The counter-culture now being built will, of course, represent a far deeper, faster break than the preceding ones; we have only a few decades to redress the balance and set out on a new adventure. In a word, it comes down to affirming that when human societies have suppressed what separates them (class, nations), they can be included in a new and perfectly integrated grouping, one that would lead not to a superman, but to a superhumanity.

It's still a question of a "cultural revolution." And it's still the young people we must think about for producing it; the "old people" can, at the very most, give them the means. As Franklin Roosevelt said: "We can't always build the future for our youth, but we can build our youth for the future." Now it's quite possible that the best, most effective and least costly of these means is called Katimavik. It responds marvellously well to the noblest aspirations of today's young people, and to their most confused expectations.

So what's he complaining about, you might ask. Katimavik exists, costing the state millions — there's no question of cutting it off ... Just what is he complaining about?

I'm not really complaining. On the contrary, I'm very proud that Canada was the first country in the world (there will soon be imitators) to offer such a program to its young people. What bothers me is that you don't change the way an entire people thinks by touching only 1000 or 1500 young people a year. It's not enough. At that rate it would take more time than we have left before it's too late.

What is needed is not 1500 Katimavik participants per year but rather 15 000, 50 000, even 100 000 if we were to be bold enough to follow through to the limit of our resources, to the limit of our faith in the young people of this country.

And if we were to go that far, in a few years the new society, humane and joyous, that we so urgently need, would be a reality, Canada would be a country profoundly different from all the others — and from what it is today. It would be a land of love and peace and, in spite of itself, the conscience of the rich countries which, gradually, would agree to be less rich so that other countries could have more. And the North-South dialogue in which we are timid participants might cease to be a dialogue of the deaf.

"How much would it cost?" my dentist asks, a little less sure that the idea is *completely* hare-brained. In the course of the two world wars, when Canada's borders weren't threatened and all mankind wasn't in danger of extinction, modest Canada signed up steadfastly. No one asked "How much will it cost?" In money or in human life ... But because my dentist insists I'll answer him: the 1978-79 Katimavik program, which involved 1 485 young Canadians,[1] cost the State exactly $6,570. per head. Compare that with the cost of any job-creating program, with the cost of unemployment insurance benefits, with the cost of a year in secondary school or university. And the figure doesn't even take into account the economic fallout that occurs when ten, twenty or thirty young volunteers live in some sixty small or medium-sized Canadian communities for nine months, or the considerable work accomplished by these young people in the communities, often poor ones, work that wouldn't have been done without them, or the skills they acquire in the most varied areas, talents they discover ... and I could go on for a long

---

1 This figure includes support staff which is also made up of young Canadians.

time, there are so many marginal benefits that flow from Katimavik. At $6,570. per person per year, it's the bargain of the century!

To reduce the costs even more, it would just be necessary to persuade the Ministers of Education of the ten provinces to consider a year at Katimavik as equivalent to the last year of secondary school, or even guarantee credits at a higher level. And what Minister could deny that Katimavik is a truly extraordinary school? That young people learn infinitely more there than on the school-benches they loathe so much, often with reason? In what school do students become bilingual in only a few months? In what school do you learn about three different regions of the country, one of them French-speaking? In what school are you truly sensitized to the crucial problems concerning the environment and international development? In what school can you become familiar with techniques as diverse as agriculture, reforestation, breeding Eskimo dogs, building, cooking, wilderness survival, water purification, cultivation in solar greenhouses, etc? In what school can the students still live at a human level, in a group of their peers, learning sharing and generosity, building firm friendships with young people from every corner of the country, finding out about themselves, developing personally at an accelerated rhythm, finding the answers to a thousand questions they'd never even asked before and, after nine months, knowing at last what it is that they want to do with the rest of their lives?

Tell me – at $6,570. isn't that the biggest bargain of the century?

Is it even thinkable, I ask you, that under the pretext of saving money or being cautious, we might refuse our young people and our country as a whole the means to rediscover a feeling of hope?

That's the question I'm asking bluntly of those who have the power to decide, the power to facilitate these things, the power to persuade public opinion.

Politicians, senior civil servants, journalists: you have the floor! And better yet, you have the power to give wings to the hopes of our young people. Before you speak, before you exercise your power, read again what Michael from Brockville, Ontario, is telling us, and Daniel from Drummondville, Quebec, and Dorle from Burnaby, British Columbia.

Oh, I realize you all have fine and noble professions. But do you know the finest profession in the world? The first words in this book were borrowed from Saint-Exupéry. Let me borrow the last ones from him too:

"The finest profession for a man is to bring men together."

Appendix

Katimavik Board of Directors

Honorary Chairman

Right Honourable Roland Michener
Toronto, Ontario
Companion of the Order of Canada
— President, Canadian Institute of Internal Affairs
— Chancellor, Queen's University
— Governor General of Canada (1967-1974)
— Canadian High Commissioner to India and Ambassador to Nepal (1964-1967)
— Speaker of the House of Commons (1957-1962)

Executive Committee

Co-Chairman
Donald Deacon
Toronto, Ontario
— Chairman, F.H. Deacon, Hodgson Inc.
— Director, Candev Financial Services
— Deputy Provincial Commissioner of the Boy Scouts of Canada
— M.P.P. for York Centre (1967-1975)
— Councillor and Deputy Reeve for the Township of Markham (1955-1957)

Co-Chairman

Jacques Hébert
Montreal, Quebec
Officer of the Order of Canada

— Founding President, Canada World Youth
— Member of the Canadian Radio-Television and Telecommunications Commission
— Member of the Board of the North-South Institute
— Founding Member and Past President of the Civil Liberties Union

---

Vice-President

Judge Raynell Andreychuk
Saskatoon, Saskatchewan

— Judge of the Saskatchewan Provincial Court
— Chancellor of the University of Regina
— International Vice-President, World Alliance of YMCAs
— Chairman, International Human Rights Commission
— Chairman, Board of Directors, Canada World Youth
— Chairman, Federal Government Advisory Council of Voluntary Action (1974-1978)
— Alderman for the City of Moose Jaw (1969-1971)

Vice-President

Larry Huddart
Victoria, B.C.

— Vice President, Boy Scouts of Canada, Greater Victoria Region
— Professor, Lester B. Pearson College of the Pacific (1974-1977)

Vice-President

Guy Lefebvre
Hull, Quebec
— Director General,
  Evaluation and Audit,
  Secretary of State

Secretary General of the
Canadian Radio-Television
and Telecommunications
Commission (1967-1977)

Board Members

Pierre Dansereau
Companion of the Order of
Canada
Professor Emeritus
University of Quebec
Montreal, Quebec

Billy Diamond
Grand Chief, Grand Coun-
cil of Crees (Quebec)
Val D'Or, Quebec

William Dodge
Officer of the Order of
Canada
Past Secretary-Treasurer
Canadian Labour Congress
Ottawa, Ontario

Julie Donahue
Dietician
Summerside, Prince
Edward Island

Victor Emery
V.E. Management Ltd.
Montreal, Quebec

Guy Fortier
Ottawa, Ontario

Consultant, Federal
Treasury Board
Director, Planning
Branch, Federal
Treasury Board (1977-
1978)

Anne Fouillard
Past Co-ordinator
Canada World Youth,
Atlantic Region
Halifax, Nova Scotia

Norman Godfrey
Yorkwood
Investments Ltd.
Don Mills, Ontario

Normand Hébert
Former Katimavik
Participant
St-Pierre, Manitoba

George Lee
Associate Director,
Extension Service
Memorial University
of Newfoundland
St. John's, Newfoundland

Claude Longpré
Longpré, Marchand

& Associates
Montreal, Quebec

Marcel Masse
Vice-President,
Lavalin Services
Montreal, Quebec

Jack Matthews
Director,
Lester B. Pearson College
Victoria, British Columbia

Coleen McCormack
Former Katimavik
Participant
Sidney, Nova Scotia

Marion McNair
Fredericton, New
Brunswick

Howard Nixon
College of Physical
Education
Saskatchewan University
Saskatoon, Saskatchewan

Joanne O'Connell
Former Professor
University of Alberta
Calgary, Alberta

Keith Spicer
Officer of the Order
of Canada
Journalist;
Former Commissioner
of Official Languages
Vancouver,
British Columbia

2270 Avenue Pierre Dupuy   (514) 861-9901
Montreal, Quebec
H3C 3R4
Executive Director
Paul Phaneuf
Deputy Executive Director
Jacques Burelle
Director of Administration
Gilles St. Arnaud
Director of Program
Marcel Hue

Regional Offices

British Columbia and Yukon   (604) 736-8991
  Regional Office
1587 West 8th Avenue
Suite 201
Vancouver, B.C.
V6J 1N1

Regional Director
Gordon Therriault

Prairies and Northwest Territories   (306) 652-5100
  Regional Office
245 3rd Avenue South
Suite 605
Saskatoon, Saskatchewan
S7K 1M4

Regional Director
Gordon Benton

Ontario Regional Office (613) 238-4525
323 Chapel Street
Ottawa, Ontario
K1N 7Z2

Regional Director
Lillian Ross

Quebec Regional Office (514) 861-9901
2270 Avenue Pierre Dupuy
Montreal, Quebec
H3C 3R4

Regional Director
Claude Raîche

Atlantic Regional Office (902) 422-1311
1541 Barrington, Suite 218
Halifax, N.S.
B3J 1Z5

Regional Director
Tom Garland

Printed by
PAYETTE & SIMMS INC.
300 Arran, Saint-Lambert, P.Q.